# RESURRECTING GRACE

# Resurrecting Grace

REMEMBERING CATHOLIC CHILDHOODS

⚭

edited by Marilyn Sewell

BEACON PRESS

BOSTON

*Beacon Press books are published under the auspices*
*of the Unitarian Universalist Association of Congregations.*

© 2001 by Marilyn Sewell

05 04 03 02  8 7 6 5 4 3 2 1

This book is printed on acid-free paper that meets the uncoated paper
ANSI/NISO specifications for permanence as revised in 1992.

*Text design by Lucinda Hitchcock*
*Composition by Wilsted & Taylor Publishing Services*

LIBRARY OF CONGRESS CATALOGING-IN-PUBLICATION DATA

Resurrecting grace : remembering Catholic childhoods / edited by Marilyn Sewell.
p. cm.
ISBN 0-8070-1240-8 (cloth)
ISBN 0-8070-1241-6 (pbk.)
1. Authors, American—20th century—Biography. 2. Catholics—United
States—Biography. 3. Children—United States—Biography. 4. Catholic
authors—Biography. I. Sewell, Marilyn.
PS129 .R47 2001
282'.092'273—dc21
[B]

*for Mother*

CONTENTS

## III. *Redeeming Grace*

I WAS TOLD EARLY ON IN MY DEVELOPMENT AS A WRITER TO WRITE ABOUT WHAT I know. But I discovered that if a writer does only that, the result will not go beyond mere reporting. The juice is in what you don't know – in the mystery that draws you down deeper. As you struggle with what you *thought* you knew, you evolve into a new creature with new understandings. Catholicism is a subject matter that affords that challenge and that opportunity in spades.

When I initially conceived the idea for this book, I thought the personal essays I collected would be – well, chiefly satirical. All of us who grew up Catholic know of the excesses of thought and practice that we had to cope with: the solemnity and dignity of ritual that dazzled; the fear of punishment that terrified; the complex rules that, try as we would, we ultimately just couldn't keep. Finally we were pushed to the point that we had to laugh or simply fall into despair.

I sent out a call for contributions to this book, and sure enough, the biting humor, the sarcasm that I expected, characterized many of the pieces. But as I read and read and read, I found this writing to be strangely thin. The laughter was a cover for the pain, and the pain obscured the beauty. I put these pieces aside, and as I began to dig deeper in my research, I soon found pieces that resonated with the ironies and incongruities of this ancient faith. I found writers who had been willing to let the entirety of their experience wash over them, allowing them to discover the gifts they had been given, gifts that had become an incontrovertible part of their spiritual development.

Cheap shots just won't do for the Catholic Church. For every Inquisition, there is a Lourdes. For every scheming Pope, a saint. For every seller of indulgences, one who spilled blood for others in a true expression of the sacrificial love of Jesus. The writers included in this volume are those who have been willing to work through the confounding complexities of their childhood faith. For the most part the humor is not bitter, but is more likely rueful. The writers struggle with acceptance, move to assimilation, and finally from the perspective of distance, make peace with the past. The act of writing, I would wager, has made these men and women more fully accepting of their own humanity and that of their subjects. They have written to learn what it is they did not know, and they have grown deeper roots in the process.

In Patricia Hampl's "Virgin Time," she says, "And now, educated out of it all, well climbed into the professions, the Catholics find each other at cocktail parties and get going. The nun stories, the first confession traumas — and a tone of rage and dismay that seems to bewilder even the tellers of these tales." And yet at the end of this graceful and telling piece, she crosses paths with a "plain and pale" parish woman, a single woman, whom she vaguely knows, walking home from Mass. One hand is in the woman's cardigan pocket, touching the beads of her rosary as she prays. Hampl reflects: "When finally we were close enough to make eye contact, she looked up, straight into my face, and smiled. . . . She shed light."

Brian Doyle's essay "Altar Boy" is full of wry humor and yet deeply moving. Toward the end of the piece, we find him standing over his little daughter, who is very ill: "I make a prayer in the dark. I believe so strongly, so viscerally, in a wisdom and vast joy under the tangled weave of the world, under the tattered blanket of our evil and tragedy and illness and brokenness and sadness and loss, that I cannot speak it, cannot articulate it, but can only hold on to ritual and religion like a drowning man to a sturdy ship."

I myself began writing an essay that placed me apart and above, with an unmistakable tone of self-righteousness. But as I collected memoirs from other writers, I began to get a sense of what separated the proverbial wheat from the chaff, and I wondered how to approach my own essay in a way I could respect. I threw out the original piece and started over. I stared at the computer screen for a while and then began to write about my mother. Every time my fingers touched the keys, I went to Mother. Well, she was the Catholic in the family. And a more devoted one I've never known.

As I recount in my essay, when I was nine years old, I was taken abruptly from my mother by my father, for his own good reasons. That day was the day I began my long journey away from her and from the Church. Writing my piece for this anthology forced me back there, to that loss, forced me to encounter my mother again, and for that I am deeply grateful.

As one of my writer friends, Gurney Norman, used to say, "Find the right metaphor, and it will change your life." That is the promise of writing, and the sure gift. The writers in this volume have had the courage to dive beneath the surface, to ferret out the contradictions, to acknowledge the blessings, and finally to stand in a faith that is their own. The reader, I believe, will find in these pieces a beauty that is born of integrity. In the presence of such integrity, we become more nearly whole ourselves.

# I

*The Gift of Faith*

 .

# Heaven, 1957

SOLEMN HIGH MASS AT THE EASTER VIGIL. I'M NINE AND I'M STANDING AT THE VERY edge of the choir loft of St. Peter's Church in Steubenville, the oldest parish in town, staunchly Irish Catholic since its beginning before the Civil War. And this is pre-Vatican II Catholicism, and before me, up on a stand so high that if she fell backward, she would plunge sixty feet to the floor of the Church below (but even to think that she could fall was simply impossible – God does not allow such things) – high up before me, then, Sister Malachy directs the men's, women's, and childrens' choir of one hundred voices, and I am chanting, solo, the Litany of Saints, and the whole choir is responding:

*Sancta Lucia, orate pro nobis*
*Sanctus Michael, orate pro nobis.*

And the air is filled with incense and song and light, and I am trembling with fear and pride, with my parents and my Pap Pap and my grandma and all my cousins and aunties and uncles down below, and the cassock and surplice I am wearing are heavy and starched and and smell strange and white and holy like the hands of the nuns who washed and ironed them in the convent just across the playground by the church and Mrs. Gilligan, the organist, is in a kind of ecstatic state, her eyes rolling back in her head as she hits the great Alleluia chords, and all the men in the choir with their deep voices – men who drive beer trucks, men who work in the mill, men who fix cars – they too are in cassocks and surplices washed by the sisters, and maybe they too, as boys, had the same sisters teaching them the lives of the saints in school, but now tonight their polished shaven faces are flushed and gleaming with sweat – my God, I think, they're all angels – we're all, for the hour and a half of Mass – we're all angels, and heaven is right here, in the light and smoke and song of the choir loft, Sister Malachy levitating, almost bodilessly rising before us as if on the swells of the song, and she is coaxing out of us the great Hebrew Hosannas, the beautiful Greek Kyries, and all this – the Greek and Latin, the incense and organ tones that get you deep in your chest, even lower, that resound in your groin, and make you want to melt into it, give in and be taken up by it, to circle the dim shadows of the dome overhead, the stained glass glinting from the candles below, but the dark night pressing all against them from the outside, and the incense gathering to a nimbus up there, and the strange dream I had of kneeling there, on the tiny ledge around the bottom of the dome, all alone, on a red velvet kneeler, and that is somehow heaven, not pleasant, exactly, but holy, and high up there, and alone, and Sister Malachy now floats three feet above the platform, and all the choir men's eyes are closed, and they are lifting her up into the air on their voices, grooms accompanying the bride she is as she meets her husband who is God and we will get to see him, we will be there when the great burst of light appears with the Alleluia and Amen and Monsignor Grigsby below will explode into a thousand candles, orate pro nobis, and Sister Malachy and Sister Mary Anthony and Sister Mary Hubert orate pro nobis, will turn into white birds, and the music will be clouds to walk on, orate pro nobis, and it will be heaven, right here, the mills all gone, the dirty streets all gone, the mill dust rubbed off the stones of the church revealing gold, and more gold, and it is heaven, orate pro nobis, heaven, Sister Malachy, heaven, Mrs. Gilligan, orate, o kyrie kyrie kyrie eleison.

PAT MORA

# *from* House of Houses

I LOOK OUT AT THE COVERED PORCH THAT BORDERS THE GARDEN, THAT SHADES US when we sit in the wide, rawhide and wood chairs, *equipales.* On warm days, sparrows wade in the fountain whose quiet splash, *ps-slp-plop, ps-slp-plop,* lures us all into these adobe walls. In Nigeria, Morocco, Spain, Syria, fellow humans also find comfort from such mud-rounded protection. Rumors of my unending questions alter the pitch and rhythms of speech within these walls I know. All know: I'm after stories, brewed in the bone. It's the older voices and bodies who have the patience to talk and remember.

Watching white branches sway in the transformed garden, I recite John Greenleaf Whittier's "Snowbound" to myself, think of Sister Godfrey, her perfect posture and wild gray eyebrows, the acrid-smelling sheets of purple mimeographed lines she'd have us recite weekly in eighth grade. Where did they hide their doubts, those confident women in black folds? Maybe where they hid their round watches, in tiny, secret pockets near their hearts.

This is a "world that we can call our own," this family space through which generations move, each bringing its gifts, handing down languages and stories, recipes for living, gathering around the kitchen table to serve one another; in the walled garden, engaging in the slow conversation of families sitting to pass the time. Voices mingle with the voice of the fountain, parrot, broom, wind, *voces del jardin.*

The walled garden, a design indigenous to Mexico and also Iranian, then Islamic, brought to the Americas by the Spanish, is a tradition Moorish and Mexican. A garden can be enchanted, bewitched, bewitching. To enjoy the lush beauty throughout the year, Persians in the sixth century even created garden carpets patterned after the courtyard foliage and blooms. And gardens flourished on this continent. When the Spaniards entered Mexico in 1519, they found *chinampas*, which *los españoles* mistook for floating gardens, plots covered with dahlias, amaranth, chiles, corn, willows. Moctezuma, who had established an aqueduct to bring spring water from Chapultepec to the island city of Tenochtitlán, is credited with the construction of splendid, verdant spaces tended by experienced horticulturalists.

In the desert, a garden demands as love does everywhere, care, intentionality. Ignore the soil, food, light, and water needs of caladiums or cannas, and they will soon shrivel from neglect, vanish from this space both private and communal; a space of labor and frustration, also of meditation, solace, hope, and sensory delights.

Plants, humans' first medicines, through ritual and religion intertwine with our lives, become sources of food, shelter, warmth, weapons, clothing, dyes, cosmetics, wine. The world's flora nourish, inspire, intoxicate. Rich sources of mystery, magic, and mythology; they flavor our dishes, beautify our rooms, soothe our aches, scent our beds, decorate our bodies and altars, perfume our paths and poems; these green lifeforms that rise from the dark tangle of underground life, like our subconscious, fertile and full of promise.

In the evening, the family scatters throughout the house. Some work or pray in their rooms, some visit at the kitchen table. Lobo reads on the living room sofa, Mamande says her novena in her chair, and at the piano Mother plays Schubert and the adagio movement of Beethoven's "Pathetique," the notes of the treble sinking into us like falling stars. My father comes in, stands at the foot of the piano, conducts, eyes closed. After I water the houseplants, the ficus, bougainvillea, miniature orange, and snake plant, I sit on the sofa, read in the *Popul Vuh*, Quiché Maya book of creation, about the conversation between sky and sea gods, words that created this world, ". . . the earth rose because of them, it was simply their words that brought it forth."

Aunt Carmen, Mother's sister-in-law, hands me the new gardening catalogues, and I thumb through them, study ideas for the small wildflower garden behind the house, and for the small rock garden we started last year, a good excuse to buy assorted ice-plant and portulaca to tuck among the river-rolled stones that fit snugly in my palms, all the hard smoothness, embedded water sounds.

I show the catalogues to Uncle Lalo, Mother's brother and our favorite uncle, who says, "Reminds me. Tomorrow I've got to start cleaning, sharpening, and oiling my tools. New gardening year. Who knows what mischief your Aunt Carmen will have me up to out there."

I read of vespertine flowers, night bloomers like four o'clocks, opening like mouths in evening prayer. My devout relatives will like such bloomers near the grotto they built to San Francisco.

*"Planta flores con nombres religiosos como Varitas de San José,"* says Mamá Cleta, my great-great grandmother exhorting me to plant flowers with religious names. She slid into my life this year, silent and transforming, like light shines through stained glass windows. She hopes for plants with the names of saints, hers a religious rather than scientific taxonomy. I know the hollyhocks she mentioned, the blooming staff associated with Saint Joseph, the name in English originally meaning holy mallow reflecting the belief that they had come to Europe directly from the Holy Land, but how many plants do I know that have religious connotations in their Spanish names? I make a note to look for *Manto de la Virgen*,

Virgin's Bower, *Flor de San Juan,* Evening Primrose in English, and *Flor de Santa Rita,* Indian Paintbrush. *"Como siembras, segarás,"* says Mamá Cleta, the gardener's wisdom, the link between sowing and harvest.

I also jot a note to buy crimson and white thyme this year for planting along the flagstone paths to scent the air when we walk through the garden with this small, erect relative, her gray hair always in a soft bun at the top of her head, her hands snapping off dead blooms, grooming the garden that holds the whispers of her long dresses. Even without the luxury of their scent, she and I enjoy the catalogue pages about roses, the flower of flowers, symbol of the beloved as well as the Virgin Mary. We read in a book on Persian gardens, about a hundred-petaled rose and the custom of sprinkling guests with rose water, of consuming the essence of the mesmerizing flower in rose preserves and sherbets. Mamá Cleta, never embarrassed by her synesthesia, sighs, *"¿La oyes?* Do you hear organ music when you look long at the yellow rose?"

The next morning, Aunt Chole shuffles into the kitchen wearing a purple velour jogging suit, two pairs of socks, sturdy shoes. *"Buenos días, buenos días.* Is that you, *reina?* What are you doing?"

I've been sitting at the table staring in wonder at the soundless movement of snow in the courtyard, at the bare honey locust branches, listening to the quiet of a new year. Such a hush, even when the wind blows through the trees sending snow flying from their limbs, the world seems dormant, pensive.

"Reading Lobo's missal, *Misal Diario San José,*" I take some liberties with the truth since I'd actually only opened my aunt's missal, sat and watched light slide on the gold edges of the pages like music on violin strings. Pictures and holy cards flutter out, prayers Lobo wanted to repeat, faces to be prayed for, pictures of my children when they were little. Out falls a holy card of the Good Shepherd, pale, sweet, brown-haired Jesus stroking a white lamb. The cold, black words on the back of the card given out at Lobo's rosary the night before her burial,

*Jesús ten piedad del alma de Ygnacia R. Delgado, November 16, 1983*

Someone tucked the card in her thick prayer book after her death. She spills out to me from her missal, a photo dated November, 1966. She's standing by a bridge railing, brown skirt, black sweater, black scarf; with her sister, Dolores, Aunt Lola, who's frowning, probably giving firm directions to the son taking the photo.

"Read me the missal, *mi amor*," Aunt Chole says trying to suppress a cough. "You know I can't see to read." I ask her if she'd like tea with honey, urge her to eat more, my bent, fragile aunt.

"Did you put birdseed outside for *los pajaritos, corazón mío?* It's so cold outside, and my little birds will be waiting. *Ay, querida,* how I used to love to go out early in the morning to feed them."

My youngest daughter, Cissy, comes in wishing the snow would melt so that she could return to her jogging. "So what do you think of my idea of propping the Christmas tree in that corner as a bird feeder instead of just throwing it away? Pretty clever, huh? I'll put seeds and stuff on it.

"Aunt Chole," she says raising her voice, "I put food for the birds on a tree, *para los pajaritos.*"

"*Ay, que mi querida tan chula,*" her aunt says in a high, sweet octave. Cissy feeds the parrot more seeds, in the living room curls up with cat and book.

I savor each simple gesture in this kitchen, filling the tea kettle, lighting the stove, click of the cup in the saucer. They've all been here, are here, the family of women, nursing one another with teas — *de canela, hierbabuena, gordolobo.* Straight and erect in their good health or bent with age and arthritis, sacramental acts for another woman, or a husband, father, or child, steeping an old cure that began underground. "It is strange to be so many women," as Adrienne Rich says.

I watch Aunt Chole momentarily lost in the act of sipping the hot, sweet liquid, the comfort of memories, of repeated acts that stream us back to our small selves, the child bundled in the bodies of family, watch her freely since she can't see me watching.

"Smell this, Aunt Chole. It's a vanilla candle. I'm going to light it and put it here on the table while we talk." I love the privateness of this time with her. She rises in the dark, on Mexican time, she says.

"Vanilla?" she frowns. "*¿Vela de vainilla?*"

"Aromatherapy."

"*¿Qué?*" She looks confused.

"It's a new idea, Tía, or maybe an old idea using new technology."

"*¿Qué? ¿Vela de tecnología?*"

"Remember how you'd use rose petals and cinnamon sticks or cloves to make rooms smell good? Now they sell scented candles and oils and organic sprays, environmental fragrancing, herb and flower essences. They say the smells can relax you or give you energy," watching her face, I say the last words slowly, "or even make you romantic." Sure enough, her little laugh rises. "*Ee-ee,* romantic! Don't start asking me about that man today." She sips her tea.

"Are you eating, Tía?"

"*Querida,* you know how colds are. I'm not hungry these days, but I'm drinking that Assure." She sips. "Read me from the missal. I can't see, *mi reina.* You have to help me."

"It says the priest would wear white today, like the snow outside." I stare out again at the adobe walls of this refuge from the heat and cold of the desert and its denizens. Of course, walls, like doors and locks, can be confining, but a home can be liberating if I have the physical and emotional strength to enter and exit at will.

In spite of the family tensions, like the tensions within myself or the structural tensions of any house, I retreat to this space to hear myself, and to hear those often silent when they left these walls, reticent to reveal themselves.

I read the liturgical calendar in Lobo's missal, the cycles of Advent, Christmas, Epiphany, Ordinary Time, Lent, Easter, Pentecost, the annual repetition of the events in Christ's life or in ecclesiastical language, "the re-enactment of the mysteries of salvation"; the religious repetitions – litanies and rosaries, rhythmic as the seasons. I read to Aunt Chole about the Feast of the Holy Name.

"The missal says, 'Let every knee bend at the sound of His name.'" She begins to coo about her *"Diosito,"* how much He helps her.

*"Ya, ya, ya,"* teases my father, entering the dark kitchen in his pajamas as always looking for something to eat. *"Uds. platicando y yo muerto de hambre.* And why are you sitting in the dark? *¡Ándenle, ándenle. A trabajar!"*

*"¡Ándenle, ándenle. A trabajar!"* the *guacamaya* echoes, urging us to get to work, another phrase the bird hears often.

We hear the *sw, sw, sw* of Lobo's broom, and sip in silence, listen to the song of the winter wind, its deep song, its *canto hondo.*

# *from* All Souls

"HEY MIKE, YOU GOT FIFTY CENTS SO I CAN GO TO THE IRISH MAFIA STORE?" I HEARD Seamus's voice from inside the dumpster I was about to toss the trash into. He popped his head up and laughed. Stevie was in there too, along with his best friend, Tommy Viens. They said they were playing cops and robbers and were hiding out from the bad guys. "And who are the . . . ? Never mind," I said. We'd all talked about how the little kids had been able to "bounce back" from the tragedy they'd lived through. Seamus was nine and Stevie eight, and here they were, having the time of their lives, making their own fun in the same courtyards and dumpsters where I'd followed Kevin around as a kid. I gave Seamus and Stevie three dollars, one for Tommy, but I told them they couldn't go to the Irish Mafia store, or to the Clam Shack, and then I knocked off a few other stores that I knew had connections to what *I* had started to identify as "the bad guys." My list didn't leave them many places to go, and in the end they just tramped off to Whitey's headquarters anyway.

We didn't feel the same about our neighborhood now that the kids were dead. Ma said she wanted nothing more than to get the hell out. But there was nowhere to go. Ma was getting $250 a month from welfare, less than a month's rent in apartments outside the projects. She was going to hairdressing school, hoping to get a job; but the people in the neighborhood who had jobs, usually at factories and plants that bordered the neighborhood, were losing them.

This was while downtown cafes and wine bistros continued to pack in the crowds of yuppies who were taking over traditional working-class neighborhoods like Charlestown and the North End. With the rents outside the projects going up, we knew Southie was next.

Ma worked hard just to keep herself busy after the kids were buried. She said she had no time to sit around feeling sorry for herself, thinking about them. She said they were in a better place, better off than the rest of us. Ma went to hairdressing school every morning, and spent the afternoons cutting hair at the local homeless shelter, even though she always found head lice walking on her scissors afterward. Ma loved being around the homeless. She said it kept her going, listening to all their stories and sending them off "looking like a million bucks." She said when she got through with them they looked like Johnny Cash, Conway Twitty, or one of her other favorite country stars. But when Ma started to hang out with the young gay men from hairdressing school, and going to gay clubs, she updated, and sent the homeless off looking more like Cindy Lauper. Then she started volunteering nights at AIDS wards, giving complete makeovers – hair, makeup, nails – and playing her accordion between stories that kept everyone in stitches – stories about her husbands, her boyfriends, and courtroom scenes with Nellie. Ma said she wanted to help the dying patients prepare to "cross over to the other side," and she figured some makeup and a few laughs were as good as the rosary any day.

Ma was going mad with the makeovers, though. One time my Aunt Sally cried looking into the mirror after Ma got through with her head. She'd been given what Ma was calling "the windswept look," and the helmet of orange hair plastered to Sally's forehead and chubby cheeks looked like a cyclone frozen over. Ma told her she looked like Liza Minelli, and Sally said she wanted nothing to do with Liza Minelli. Ma had plucked off Sally's bushy eyebrows with the tweezers, and her chin whiskers too, which was really why

Sally was crying. "Oh, shut up!" Ma snapped at her younger sister. "Dan'll be thanking me now that I got rid of your beard."

That night we heard a gunshot on Patterson Way and Sally made me walk her to the train station, saying anything was better than spending one more minute with Ma, and her cutting and plucking.

Ma was just doing whatever she could to keep her mind off what she was feeling. But the hearses kept rolling down Dorchester Street, where in better days we'd watched the St. Paddy's Day parade and the antibusing motorcades. And every time it was another Southie mother's turn to see her child off at Jackie O'Brien's, it brought Ma right back to reality. She started going to all the wakes, even if she didn't know the family, and in about a year she counted that she'd been to thirty-two, all dead from suicide, drugs, or crime. Ma started hanging out with other women whose sons or daughters had died, and she started cutting some of their hair too – until they learned to make sure they went to the hairdresser's on a regular basis so Ma wouldn't have them walking down Broadway in one of those new-fangled cosmopolitan hairdos she was bringing to Southie from the gay clubs.

Then Ma got into the holy water, after Grandpa took her on a trip to Fatima where the Blessed Mother had appeared to the three children. Holy water and haircuts. Ma was on a mission. To give whatever she was able to give. She was always pulling something out of her pocketbook, whether a piece of toast for the guys on the wino wall, or a rock for someone who needed strength. Besides the scissors and jug of holy water, Ma's pocketbook was full of rocks that she had brought back from Fatima. "Oh . . . thanks. What's this for?" I asked Ma, trying to sound grateful as she handed me a three-pound rock. She told me that when Grandpa and the other pilgrims to Fatima had crawled on their knees to the next holy site, she'd run back to the well where the Blessed Mother had appeared and chiseled out a few stones. "Get down on your knees for Our Lady, you damn fool," Grandpa told her when she returned. "Like hell I would," Ma told me. "You should have seen the face on my father, like he was wearing the crown of thorns himself." Ma was inspired by her own relationship with the Blessed Mother, saying she needed the rocks for some of the mothers burying their kids in Southie. Most people actually treasured their rocks, and some told me that they kept them in their pocketbooks always, to remind them of Helen and all her strength.

I was worried about Ma in those days, with her running out to gay clubs and blessing the mothers of Old Colony with holy water, but everyone else saw her as an inspiration, just to have gotten up in the morning and put her spike heels on the right feet. The mothers who'd lost one kid didn't know how she could do it, having lost four. And Ma was even smiling again, as much as she could make herself do. She said she had no other choice, except suicide, and she couldn't do that. . . .

Ma got me to go back to school. She said I was sleeping my life away, and I was. She started making calls, setting up appointments for me to get my GED, and then to take the SATs. She knew how to work the financial aid applications to get the most money for school, even with the cutbacks in education grants. I didn't know the point of it all, but it felt good to score high on the SATs despite having dropped out of high school. And before long, I was getting up early mornings for the two-mile walk from our apartment to the University of Massachusetts. Being busy like Ma helped me to forget about the kids being dead, sometimes.

Now Ma had only Seamus and Stevie to worry about. She didn't want them bused across town, and she couldn't afford to keep Stevie as well as Seamus at St. Augustine's. Ma called the Boston School

Department and tried to find out where Stevie would be assigned for first grade. It all depended on your address. "If I lived at 8 Patterson Way, would my son be able to go to the Perkins School across the street?" Ma said the woman on the phone understood what she was getting at. She said she was from Roxbury and wanted to send her own kid to school near home. The woman told Ma that if she did live at 8 Patterson Way, her son would be bused, but that if she happened to live at 9 Patterson Way, he could go to the Perkins. Ma hung up the phone and called back, saying she lived at 9 Patterson Way, even though there was no such address. Later that morning, Ma whispered to the mailman that she'd be getting mail sent to 9 Patterson, and to tell the other guys at the post office just to get it to her and to not ask any questions. The mailman was happy to help. "Hey, I gotta try that for my kid," he said.

"Just keep going, and hold your head high!" Ma told her new friend Theresa Dooley as they walked past the gossipers who'd left their stoops in the project to stroll down Broadway. Ma barged her way into Theresa's life after she heard that her fifteen-year-old son had hung himself in his bedroom. "Two kids! That's like a double murder, and these dirty bastard politicians keep saying there are no problems in Southie?" Ma knew that Tony Dooley's suicide had everything to do with the murder of his big brother Tommy — who he'd idolized — in front of Kelly's Cork and Bull. Ma went over to the Old Harbor Project on the feast day of the Mother of Sorrows and asked neighbors where Mrs. Dooley lived. She walked into her house, telling her to get dressed and to come for a walk up Broadway. Ma knew that people liked to whisper when the two of them walked by. Some would stare into their eyes looking for the grief. But Ma said she wouldn't satisfy them. "If they want to talk, they should talk about what the hell is happening in this neighborhood before it's their turn next!" One woman actually told Ma she didn't want to get too close to her or Theresa, that the bad luck might rub off on her. Within a month the same woman nonetheless ended up burying her own son, dead from an overdose. That's when she found out that in Southie it had little to do with luck.

# The Doll

WE USED TO HAVE THIS *VIRGEN DE GUADALUPE* NIGHT-LIGHT. EVERY TIME YOU CON-nected her to an outlet, she would turn and bless all sides of the room.

We bought her on one of my dad's surprise drunken trips to Tijuana. He would come home from the racetrack at about midnight, wake us up, get us dressed, and we would all hop into the station wagon. My mom drove and my dad lowered the seat in the back and he slept with us. My grandmother, *la Abuela*, lived in one of the *colonias*. She hated our three a.m. visits. But you see, *blood is thicker than water, family is greater than friends, and Our Lady watches over all of us.*

When I was ten, I gave the *Virgen* night-light to my *tía* Ofelia. My *tía* Ofelia lived across the street with my *tía* Tita, who lived with my *tío* Tony, who lived next door to my *tía* Romie. Back in those days, everybody was either a *tía* or a *tío*. They lived in a big beautiful two-story house with a balcony overlooking the street below. We were crowded in by downtown skyscrapers, packs of roving *cholos*, the newly built Convention Center on Pico, and portable tamale stands. But our families always managed to live together, because we all knew: *Blood is thicker than water, family is greater than friends, and Our Lady watches over all of us.*

My *tía* lived on the second floor, and on the first lived the Eighteenth Street Gang. There was Smiley, Sleepy, and La Sadgirl, and a bunch of other homeboys who hung out in the front yard playing

Bloodstones' "Natural High." They split, like *cucarachas* exposed to light, at the sight of a cop car slowly cruising through our Pico-Union neighborhood, like tourists on Hollywood Boulevard.

My *tía*, she hated *cholos* and she would spit the seeds of grapes she ate out the window, just to annoy them. She was like all of my relatives back then – a grape picker from Delano, California. She claimed to have dated César Chávez, and to know everyone in Mc Farland, Tulare, and Visalia, the farmworker capitals of *el mundo*. I couldn't call her a liar, because she had *breast cancer*. My mom told us this in a voice reserved for nights when we didn't want to wake up my dad after one of his drunken soccer celebrations. Doctors at County General took away her tits in hopes of driving away *la Bruja Maldita*, who was slowly eating at her insides. When she was feeling okay, my *tía* would tell me stories about the farmworker movement and picking cherries one summer.

The day I brought her the rotating Our Lady doll, I knew she was in pain. I knew I probably should have waited, but I asked her quite innocently if I could see her chest. She slapped me hard on the face, calling me a *malcriado*. While she sobbed, her hand searched for medication. I felt so bad that day. Even I could feel *la Bruja Maldita* eating at my heart. I never got the nerve to go back up there again.

Weeks went by and my *tía* continued to rock in her chair. When the weeks turned to months, she slowly started to forget us. People would walk by and offer up a *"Buenas tardes, Señora,"* but you could tell she was having trouble remembering faces. My grandmother sent a crate of grapes to help her remember, but nothing worked. My mom and my *tía* Romie said that my *tía* Ofelia was becoming a baby, *otra vez*. La Bruja Maldita ate at her bones and slowly she started to melt like the G. I. Joes that my brother and I set fire to with burning tamale leaves. Her cheeks caved in like the plaster *calaveras* that you could buy at the border on *el día de los muertos*. And one day, on my way home from school, I looked up and she was gone.

Phones rang, food poured in, little envelopes with twenty-dollar bills. Hysterical screams from aunts on a Mexico-to-L.A. party line. Dramatic uncles openly wept and the tears of my relatives were covered with huge veils that they wore to our parish, Immaculate Conception. My grandmother, *la Abuela,* got into the drama when, at the burial, she jumped onto the coffin, screaming.

A few weeks later, the Crips drove by and shouted, *"Chump Motherfuckers. Greasy-assed Messicans. Go back to Teehuana!"* And they firebombed the Eighteenth Street Gang on the bottom floor. A great ball of fire and light filled the downtown sky, and for just a moment there, it was better than fireworks at Dodger Stadium. But it lasted for just a moment. Then seriousness took over. Followed by weeks of tears and sorrows and that same story about my *tía*'s escape from the second story. Crazy relatives would start crying every time you turned on the burner on the stove.

Smiley, Sleepy, and La Sadgirl died, but we couldn't go to the funeral because my dad said they were *perros desgraciados.* Instead, we rummaged through charred remains looking for usable clothes and my *tía*'s collection of Vicki Carr records.

My brother found what was left of the Our Lady doll and he used her head for BB gun practice. My mom cried because the memory of my *tía* Ofelia would now be an empty lot where bums would piss and tires would grow. Every day she watered a little flower she had planted in memory of my *tía* Ofelia, until the Community Redevelopment Agency built the Pico-Union Projects over her memory.

When I was eighteen, I met this guy with a rotating Our Lady doll. He bought it in Mexico, so, of course, I fell in love.

His skin was white, he ate broccoli, and he spoke like actors in a TV series. He was every *Partridge Family/Brady Bunch* episode rolled into one. He taught me many things — how to kiss like the French, lick an earlobe, and dance in the dark. Onoo, my grandmother, *la abuela*, sent us lovers a crate of grapes. We took off our clothes, smashed the grapes all over our bodies, and licked them off each other.

When he left, *la Bruja Maldita*'s hand replaced his in my heart. And she pounded on it. She laughed like Mexican mothers laugh while hanging *la ropa* at a clothesline. My sorrow was so strong, but I kept it hidden with smiles that were like the veils my aunts wore at Immaculate Conception church. But my sorrow bled through, like stigmata, like rushing waters, and my relatives would say, *Ay mijo,* don't you understand? *Blood is thicker than water, family is greater than friends, and that old Virgin, Our Lady, she just watches over all of us. . . .*

# Getting Here from There

I DON'T KNOW HOW SUCCESSFUL I CAN BE IN CONVEYING THE EXTENT TO WHICH MY family life was shaped by Catholicism. My parents' whole marriage was based on it; it was literally the only thing they had in common. My father was an intellectual Jew, who had had a very wild life. And simply to give you the outlines of it will give you a sense of its wildness. He was born in Lorain, Ohio. He also lied a lot, so it's extremely hard to trace what's the truth. I think this is the truth; at least I'm not consciously passing on lies. But it could also perhaps *not* be the truth. So I possibly have a great-grandfather who was a rabbi, but my father also said that his mother was a concert pianist, and who knows? He told me, for example, that his father ran a saloon; in fact, he ran a dry goods store.

In any case, my father went to Harvard in 1917. At that time there was a rigid quota system for Jews, and I think it must have caused him tremendous pain. Because what I think is that at Harvard he determined to "pass" at any cost. And my father, who was endlessly inventive, figured out that the best way for a Jew to pass was to be right-wing. My father became righter-wing than anybody, with a couple of interesting pit stops. For example, he went to Paris and England for a while in the 1920s. And one persona that he created for some reason was to pass himself off as a Middle West Presbyterian. He looked a lot like me — I don't know why anybody believed him. Maybe they thought all Americans look alike. He wrote a series of articles in English journals, passing himself off as a Midwest Protestant who understands that Europe is really a superior culture to his own.

His other pit stop was also in the late twenties. He published a girlie magazine called *Hot Dog*. I remember being twelve, and my father had died when I was seven, and I came upon this magazine while looking through his pictures. By today's standards it was exceedingly mild. But I was an exceedingly prudish twelve-year-old, and I took a look at this thing and I saw that my father had been the editor, and I was appalled and I ripped it to shreds and threw it away. So I have no record of it. But I'm pretty sure I didn't make it up.

In any case, my father became a Francoist in the thirties. You rarely meet somebody who can say that sentence — everybody else's father was in the Lincoln Brigade. Not mine. And in the course of several later adventures he met my mother. They met through a priest. My mother is the daughter of very simple Irish and Italian Catholics. I think she embodied for my father a kind of peasant Catholicism that he romanticized. But both of them could say with truthfulness that their faith was the most important thing in the world to them.

From an early age I had to take the measure of myself against their devotedness, and I always found myself wanting. Throughout my childhood I prayed to be spared martyrdom. But then I always felt guilty for the prayer. I was no little Teresa of Avila setting out in the desert hoping to convert the Moors; the priests in China having bamboo shoved under their fingernails and Cardinal Mindszenty imprisoned in his upper room terrified me. I didn't want that for my fate, but I was told that it was the highest fate. So as a child I had always to be consciously choosing an inferior fate. It was a real burden.

But I do remember that, although I didn't want to be a martyr, I did want to be a nun. I remember being taken by my parents to the Convent of Mary Reparatrix on Twenty-ninth Street in New York. It's a semicloistered convent – the nuns weren't allowed out, but people could talk to them. And I remember going into the chapel with my parents and a very old nun. I saw a young nun kneeling in a pool of light. I saw her from the back only. The habits of the Sisters of Mary Reparatrix were sky blue. I've never seen a color like that in a nun's habit, and I'm quite sure I didn't invent it. But if I had wanted to invent it, it would have been perfect, because it was a color dreamed up for movie stars. It was the color of Sleeping Beauty's ball gown, and that was what I wanted for myself. I wanted to be beautifully kneeling in light, my young, straight back clothed in the magic garment of the anointed. I knew that was what I wanted, but I knew I didn't want to drink filthy water or walk barefoot in the snow. A few times, though, I did try some local freelance missionary work.

Once, for instance, I had just finished reading the life of Saint Dominic Savio, who was a Neapolitan orphan. I was six or seven. Saint Dominic walked into a playground and heard his rough playmates – nobody uses the phrase "rough playmates" anymore – using blasphemous language. And he didn't skip a beat. He held up a crucifix, and he said to those boys, "Say it in front of Him." And the boys fell silent. Inspired, I tried the same thing in my neighborhood. I walked into the crowd of boys with my crucifix aloft, and I said, "Say it in front of Him." And they were glad to.

The comedy of Catholic life. It comes, of course, like all other comedy, from the gap between the ideal and the real. In my case the ideal was so high and the real was so real that the collision was bound to be risible. I tried walking with thorns in my shoes for penance, but then I found out that it hurt. So I walked around on the heels of my shoes and put the thorns in the toes, so I could have them in my shoes but not feel them. My heroisms were always compromised and always unsuccessful. I tried to talk the man in our gas station into taking the nude calendar off his wall. He told me never to come into the office again. I tried to make the candy store man, whom I genuinely liked, stop selling dirty magazines. He stopped giving me free egg creams, and our friendship ended. But he went right on selling dirty magazines.

I always tried. The serious part of the ideals that shaped my early life was that they did teach me that life was serious. I think all children believe that. I think parents cheat children by refusing to understand that everything is serious to them and that it is the modulations of the adult world that cause them such confused grief. At a very early age I was taught that happiness was not important; what was important was to save my soul. I was not supposed to be only a good girl or even a lady, although I was supposed to begin there. I was not supposed to even strive to be popular, successful, beloved, or valued by the world. I was supposed to be a saint. The cautionary and inspirational tales of my youth were the lives of the saints.

The lives of the saints. I recently took down a saints' lives book that was mine as a child. I sometimes read it to my children today. To my children, these people – Saint Barnabas who juggled, Saint Nicholas who found children pickled in the basement of an inn and brought them back to life – are fairy-tale characters. They're characters like Ali Baba or Rapunzel. My daughter likes the picture of the boy Saint Hugh kicking the devil downstairs. She asks me if the devil is real. And I tell her, "No, no, he's not real; he's like the banshee or the Loch Ness monster." And as I tell her that, I realize that for me the devil *was* real. And he was feared. My mother cured me of early narcissism by telling me that if I kept looking in the mirror the devil would pop out behind me and that when I was looking at my face it would turn into the face of the devil. I stopped immediately. I was thinking about eternal life, and so was she, and we couldn't afford to take the risk.

There's a sentence in the incomparable story "In Dreams Begin Responsibilities," by Delmore Schwartz, in which the boy says, "Everything you do matters too much." Did everything matter too much for me? I'm not sure. But at least it mattered. What you learned with a background like mine was that everything mattered terribly and that you could never do enough.

I remember a friend of mine, a Jew, telling me years later that he felt sorry for Christians because if you took seriously the words of Christ "Greater love hath no man than this, that a man lay down his life for his friends," then as long as you were alive you hadn't done enough. But this is not such a bad thing for an artist. For the life of the working artist is a perpetual reminder that everything you do matters. Nothing is enough.

Speaking of the lives of the saints makes me try to differentiate among the kinds of narratives that a pious Catholic child encountered. There were the Old Testament narratives, which always seemed to me forbidding and harsh and frightening – exciting as war movies were exciting and dangerous, but of no comfort. Abraham and Isaac, Moses left in the bulrushes, Joseph thrown down the well by his brothers, the boy David all alone with a slingshot: you had the vision of children for whom the adult world offered no protection. There were the failing parents and the implacable voice of God. I always felt as if the narratives of the Old Testament were accompanied by a kind of rumble. The colors were dark and vibrant. I was drawn to them, but I wanted to get away. To Jesus and the children.

I remember a jigsaw puzzle I had of Jesus and the children: the warm, inviting lap, the face of infinite acceptance. And there were the other images – the prodigal son forgiven, the daughter of Cyrus raised, the blind man given his sight, the lame man his nimbleness, the good thief ushered into paradise. But there was also a disturbing underside of New Testament violence. It was disturbing in a way that Old Testament violence was not, because in the old narratives the violence all seemed of a piece with the rest of the vision of the world, whereas in the Gospels it was always a surprise and something of a cheat. It was the terrible massacre of the innocents, the beheading of John the Baptist, the sufferings and death of Christ himself—somehow the triumph always paid for by some ancillary, unwilled or only partially willed carnage. Easter paid for by Lent. How fully I lived my childhood Holy Weeks, the most solemn time of the year, religiously then as now my favorite! The black vestments, the stripped altar, the shocked silence of the congregation, and then the midnight fire and the morning promise of Easter. In my memory Easter was always warm; you could always wear your spring coat and your straw hat, although in my adulthood more than half the Easters have been covered in snow.

The third kind of narrative, the lives of the saints, were magical in ways that the Bible of both Testaments was too austere to permit. Saint Francis talked to birds and wolves. Saint Elizabeth of Hungary, a queen, carried bread to the poor and the plague-ridden, although her husband the king had forbidden it. She hid the bread in her apron to keep it from the eyes of her husband and the palace guards. Her husband the king found out; he confronted her with his soldiers at the castle gate, demanding that she show him what was inside her apron. She opened her apron, and where there had been bread there were roses. He fell on his knees before his wife.

It occurs to me that one good fortune in being brought up a Catholic and a woman was that you did have images of heroic women. And that's not so frequently the case in other religious traditions. In the tradition of Catholicism you have a poem spoken by the Virgin Mary that points out her place in the divine order. And she speaks with pride. She says, "My soul doth magnify the Lord and my spirit hath rejoiced in God, my savior. Because He has regarded the loneliness of His handmaid, and behold from henceforth all generations shall call me blessed, for He that is mighty hath done great things to me and holy is His name." That's an example of a woman's speech and a woman acknowledging her importance in the hierarchy, which at least in some subliminal way a girl got to hold on to.

In the lives of the saints you had a lot of examples of women who defined themselves not in terms of men but in terms of each other. You had the founders of orders. You had women who defied the Pope, defied the bishops, to go off and do things that women were not supposed to do. You had "doctors of the church" – women saints who were given that title. Did I know at age five what that meant – "doctor of the church?" Not exactly. But there was something there. You had an image of an alternative female world that often had to trick the male world in the same way that Saint Elizabeth had to trick her husband the king. A lot of women have survived through trickery. It was not entirely a bad life, but I hope it's one we can soon forget. Still, it wasn't a bad arrow to have in your quiver.

JOSEPH MAIOLO

# The Girl and the Serpent

MY MATERNAL GRANDMOTHER WAS BORN AND RAISED MARIA ANGELICA PAONESSA, one of a large family of children in the destitute village of Gimigliano perched high in the Sila Mountains of southern Italy's Calabria. Anyone not fully impoverished before going there, must surely have become so; any vaunting of a past life would have been met with howls of derision by those who competed with one another for the droppings of donkeys, fertilizer for their otherwise scrawny tomatoes. Only the Madonna, a few favorite saints, and an occasional Pope were ever paid homage in a village with a single water spout and no central anything, let alone heat.

One day, when Angelica was twelve and out gathering wood, she tied a fagot of sticks and put it on her head and started the two-mile walk home with her sisters. Boys, carrying what logs they could find, had stopped ahead of the girls and hidden in ambush. They had waited long weeks for the patches of snow lying here and there, and now they made their snowballs and hid behind trees. Angelica heard the boys laughing, her sisters' pretended screams, and she turned, a smile on her face, into . . . a red, searing pain beginning in her right eye.

She awoke to the same red pain, but now she was lying on the cold stones in the *piazza*, her mother holding her and bathing her eye with cold water. In the narrow streets off the *piazza* several men were shouting, boys yelling and crying.

29

Anyone needing a doctor badly enough had to be taken to Catanzaro, several miles away. But there was no money, and so Angelica's mother, after consulting with the village elder, an old woman who knew best about sickness and death and all manner of mystical states such as *malocchio* (the evil eye), convinced herself and her husband, and Angelica too, that the eye would heal.

But it had begun to die the very moment the rock inside the snowball had damaged those minute connectors deep in the cornea. Angelica prayed and waited for the eye to heal; she believed that it would. But when it began to turn white, she knew that only a miracle could restore it. The miracle did not come, and the eye had to be removed. This confirmed for some in the village, who called the boy who threw the snowball *il diavolo* (the devil), that what had been visited upon the girl from the haughty Paonessas, who claimed lineage from a Greek village, was in fact the real thing — the very evil eye itself.

There was but one mirror in the two small rooms the family of ten called home. After the initial shock, shortly after the operation, of seeing what had been done to her, for a year Angelica would not look at her face before concealing the sunken eye socket with her hand. Gradually, though, she began to feel out the concavity, to trace with hesitant fingers her left eye and compare the two, until she adjusted somewhat to the loss of half of her direct sight. But she could not adjust to having no side-sight on her right and feared for years that someone was sneaking up on her.

A year after the boy threw the snowball, Angelica went off into the mountains with other girls, gathering wood. When they were returning with bundles of sticks on their heads, she stopped to rest. The others usually waited for her because of her eye, but they told her that day that they would go on and meet her at the shrine where they always stopped for a drink of water. So she rested for a while, and hesitated for a longer time, and when she reached the shrine there was no one there.

The girls were anxious to get home before dark that day. It was a feast day to the village saint, and there was going to be singing and dancing in the *piazza*. Which was the very reason why Angelica had delayed.

At the shrine she took the load of wood off her head and set it aside. She knelt at the pool in front of the shrine and bent over and scooped the cool water with her hands. As she drank from her cupped hands, her long hair fell over her face and touched the water. She closed her eyes briefly, savoring the cool, sacred place, and bathed her right eyelid, even then hoping for the miraculous intercession of her beloved Madonna. Tradition held that after drinking she cross herself, look across the short distance of the pool into the grotto where the wooden statue of Mary and the infant Jesus had been harbored for wayfarers for over a century, and say the Magnificat.

"My soul doth magnify the Lord," she whispered in her dialect. ". . . From henceforth all generations shall call me blessed."

She felt that she was being watched before she raised her head, and as she looked below the earthen apse where the spring poured, she heard above the trickle the slight sound of hissing. She sensed a movement above, only a flicker, from out of the bottom of the grotto; then she looked up slightly. It took a moment for her to realize that what she saw was the head of a serpent. It was looking at her. Its tongue came out, wavering. She was fixed by its strange eyes and held her own gaze upon it as she asked for help, aloud, as if the Lady she called upon were there before her:

*"Aiuta mi, Madonna mia."*

The snake came out of the shrine, revealing its great length and thickness, and went off into the woods.

. . .

On the day Angelica was to leave the village and her family, forever, to go to America, where she was to marry a man twenty years older she had never seen even a picture of, everyone in Gimigliano came to the *piazza* to see her off. As in America and elsewhere, there are at least two things indicative of class even in southern Italy: rail passage, lodging, all of that. In Gimigliano, there are two Gimiglianos. While the village is divided at about the midpoint of the hill, Gimigliano *Superiore* is not just higher in altitude; it is somehow understood that the villagers who live higher up are better than those in Gimigliano *Inferiore*. To hear some of the talk, one would think that Brahmins inhabited the upper reaches.

That morning, as Angelica left the village for the last time — not to continue on into the mountains in search of the ever-disappearing wood or to gather chestnuts from random-growing trees that would be blighted in a few years — but to go down the hill, through the band of separating terrain, and into Gimigliano *Inferiore*, all the souls who had defined the universe for her came to the wall above, waving their backhanded farewells and their handkerchiefs and screaming their dramatic syllables — "*Ciao*, Angelica! *Arrivederci!*" — as if they knew they would never see her again, yes, but also because they longed to be the teenage girl, even without an eye, on her way to a new life across the world to become an *Americana*.

Thirty-five-years later, Angelica Voni was living in a rowhouse on the main street of an Appalachian town — Norton, Virginia — whose livelihood was dependent upon the mining of coal. She'd raised six children alone, having chased her gambling husband off after the last one was born. She'd taken in washing, had run her own cafe below the rowhouse, and was now settled into her mid-fifties, when the war, my parents' war, all war was over, and my mother, brother, sister, and I went to live with her.

In five years we too had settled into the rowhouse, listening to her tales about life in the Old Country and the characters she'd brought with her, scores of others from her village, referring to them as naturally as if they walked our streets and sat at our table. I especially liked the story about her coming upon a serpent in the woods when she was a girl. We spent many nights gathered with her around the stove, listening, asking questions, afraid to go to bed when the stories were over.

And then it is an Easter morning. The sun is up; those of us in the house are up; the Lord is up. One aunt has come from her house on the hill, another from where she lives with her husband behind the barbershop below, both in fine dresses showing womanly shapes. Their black and wavy hair, their straight white teeth, their red lips and rouged cheeks – they are a beautiful pair. They wear light crocheted shawls, and hats to be kept on at Mass. Their presence is a great part of the joyful air of the Resurrection that surrounds us all this morning.

All except Mother, who seldom attends Mass, because of waitress work or housework or something else. The Liberty Cafe is closed today; everything in town is closed. Housework can wait.

"Mari," my grandmother says to my mother, "why noncha coom-a with us?"

We are going to walk the five blocks up Main Street and a couple more. Mother's face could contain a smile and a frown at the same time, and there they are, like opposite masks. She is, I realize only now, communicating the "something else."

Then we are strolling. The women's high heels peck out measures of music during our Easter parade. One aunt holds my sister's five-year-old hand; the other aunt and her mother are arm-in-arm. Every now and then the women change around, and my brother and I are free to wander from woman to woman. My sister's curls bounce like springs as she breaks into a skip in her patent leather shoes.

Since my brother and I served Mass on Palm Sunday, we are free to sit in a pew, and we take the one in front of our women. We, and the other families, have assembled in our Sunday clothes, and the opening hymn is in full timbre for us Catholics, our aunts' voices behind us rising easily to the high notes.

At the Communion rail, as I close my eyes and put out my tongue to receive, I become sufficiently penitent without effort. I bow my head, and the old miracle comes back as it always does at this moment: I have received the Body of Christ. All my sins are wiped away.

The spaghetti or cabbage rolls or stuffed green peppers simmer in a pot large enough to absorb an uncle's frequent samplings. Other uncles and uncles-by-marriage have come to wedge in with us at the round table. Chairs are found in the back hall and somehow fitted in for the noisy bunch of us.

My grandmother never sits down but moves between the top arc of the table and the stove and sink, her eye ever vigilant. She has become accustomed to eating small portions at irregular times. She cannot understand why anyone (herself excepted) would not simply load up with food. She replenishes the serving bowls; and, clamping a hot loaf to her chest, she cuts the bread with one of her famous butcher knives. I always think she is going to cut herself, but she never does. Taking the slice into the same hand as the knife, she places it onto someone's plate, the blade dangerously close to an ear, and I think of Peter, only days before having wielded his knife against the soldier in the garden. Then she might dip through the cloth curtain into the back hall and come up with peppers, cheese, pepperoni, olives. *"Mangia, mangia* (Eat, eat)!" she exclaims. Then someone will say in Italian, "You all eat, because I don't want any," and others will mutter repetitions of the old saying she used during bad times. I sit in the corner where the round table creates a perfectly defined seat, with a full view of it all.

After dinner (which is what we called the noon meal) my brother and I go to the back, where our grandmother is hiding hard-boiled eggs for our sister, and where every Easter for four years she had hidden them for us. Already the snowball tree is blooming, brightly concealing the coal shed and what has spilled out of it. Grandmother Voni has shored up the bank with rocks brought by anyone that she knew in advance was going to High Knob; likewise, she has replaced much of the red clay with the mountains' rich black dirt and exotic ferns. It is mid-spring, and already she has coaxed from this unlikely hillspot a chaos of color.

My brother and I join our sister in the egg hunt and find one peeking through the dirt, one deep within the point of emanation of fern branches, and one held as within an egg cup by one of the snowball blossoms whose branch has grown at right angles to present the flower like an oblation to the small Statue of Saint Francis near the coal bin. We inspect the tiny green marbles on the grapevine that will turn into dark purple grapes with thick skins and a dozen seeds in each. It is as if for forty days there has been a lull, and today *la Primavera* – the first truth, Spring – has been revealed with an abiding sun. Standing on the bank, I look over the long tarred roof to the opposite side of town, and up to Flag Rock. The mountains seem like deep green flames, coolly licking up to the bright blue bowl that contains us all.

I go to my brother's and my small room, made from half of the old kitchen, with an open-top partition, and remove my Easter coat and white shirt. I have been waiting all week to put on my new long-sleeved brown pullover shirt with a salmon-colored elastic waistband, collar, and panel in the middle. My britches are tan gabardine, made over from a pair of Uncle Chester's, with pleats and cuffs a bit wide. I move my belt buckle around to the side, take up my short bamboo cane, roll up a comic book to carry, and go to stroll by myself up Park Avenue. Only I am careful not to wield the cane too flamboyantly.

And good thing, because here comes the brilliant, red-headed scoffer who lives with his sister and must go "over to Marion" from time to time, our way of saying the mental hospital there. He spits on the street. "Where you going so gussied up, you little tramp?"

"It's Easter. I got things to do."

"Been to church?" he asks gruffly, as if, if I have, I could be guilty of something.

But it is only mock drama. We have been bantering for a year; we will continue until he or I leave (I cannot remember which). It will be many years before I find out what I will take to be the cause of his condition. When he was a young man, walking through the streets of Pittsburgh with his brother, he witnessed, and was powerless to prevent, his brother's violent death, but could only watch as his body was run over by several cars.

The marquee at the show, which I set myself from the twelve-foot stepladder last night, proclaims the year-long wait for *Easter Parade*, to begin tomorrow. Beyond the dead show is empty street, all the way to the end of things. I stroll another couple of blocks, and when I see some of my classmates driving by with their parents I turn around and go back. I can only hope they have not seen me admiring my thick-soled Buster Browns with a ridge on top of the front. The night before, I shined them, and I washed and stretched my pinkish shoelaces between two weights. I like seeing them straight and squared-up in the eyelets.

My grandmother and several others are standing in front of the rowhouse. One aunt has the black-box camera, and I can see they have been taking pictures. "*Here* he comes," she says, with mock impatience in her voice. "Joey, doll, stand over there with Mama, and let me" – she rolls her eyes and shakes the camera – "see if this little ol' thaing cain't capture some of that gorgissimo face of yours."

"*Eh, piccirello, veni qua* (come here)," my grandmother says to me, lifting her arm for my place beside her.

The store has been partitioned lengthwise, so that two long half-spaces could be rented. I go to stand with her in front of the The Star Barber Shop on the right and squint as I turn to face the camera.

My grandmother's dress is black taffeta, imprinted with a gray, flowered design. She is tall for a woman; with high heels she is a full neck and head above me. As my aunt directs the scene, my grandmother and I move closer together, her large hand, its ring finger weighted with shine, draped down from my shoulder. I must have put my hand up on her back, because now as I look at the picture – a petal from all the flowers of that spring day – I cannot see my hand around her waist. There is something – a chain? it couldn't be a rosary! – partially visible around my neck. Just below the watch pocket on the britches a dark object dangles or is caught.

It is as if I am standing beside a strong tree, a lowering branch having taken me in close, so that I have become, myself, a part of its rootedness. As I look out again now from that pose, through those squinting eyes, I see the sun high over Flag Rock and I can hear, if I listen well, the banter from my aunts and uncles and, now, even from Mother, who has put on her Sunday best and come down to join us. It must be that this second picture of her and her sisters was snapped that day. They are young, dark and comely, dressed as if for beaux; yet Mother's heart is already broken for life, and one aunt's is soon to be. The other aunt and her husband will last and last. They are there yet, in their house on the hill.

My grandmother's face has the soft smile – except her teeth are showing slightly – that will be there, in the casket, in twenty years. I am not of course aware of that in the picture; I am certain, now, that she was fully aware. That is why she is smiling. It is her forever smile, what she will leave us even after she is gone. She is a figure of Old World stature done up with thick, modern hair and the baubles of coquetry; and so the smile might be partly that. She looks directly into the camera with it, as if to say, *Noncha be so serioso.*

For years, the girl who faced down a serpent would divine meaning from my dreams, tell my fortune with a deck of cards, cure my warts magically, make cautionary tales out of broken mirrors and umbrellas opened indoors, teach me the power of a candle lighted in prayer and hope, and admonish me never to throw away a piece of bread, if I had to at all, unless I kissed it first.

Just before the picture was snapped, I remember, she squeezed me. It was slight, but enough to let me know that I still counted as much with her on this special day as ever. That is why, I suppose, I am in the picture a stalk eager for sun, and why, when Easter comes around each year, I feel deep in my bones the need, and the promise, of resurrection.

ESMERALDA SANTIAGO

# *from* When I Was Puerto Rican

SUNDAY MORNING BEFORE BREAKFAST ABUELA HANDED ME MY PIQUÉ DRESS, WASHED and ironed.

"We're going to Mass," she said, pulling out a small white *mantilla*, which I was to wear during the service.

"Can we have breakfast first, Abuela. I'm hungry."

"No. We have to fast before church. Don't ask why. It's too complicated to explain."

I dressed and combed my hair, and she helped me pin the *mantilla* to the top of my head.

"All the way there and back," she said, "you should have nothing but good thoughts, because we're going to the house of God."

I'd never been to church and had never stopped to classify my thoughts into good ones and bad ones. But when she said that, I knew what she meant and also knew bad thoughts would be the only things on my mind all the way there and back.

I tried to look as holy as possible, but the white *mantilla* tickled my neck and the sides of my face. I wished I didn't have to wear it, and that was a bad thought, since all the women and girls walking in front of us wore theirs without any complaints.

I love my mother, my father, all my sisters and brothers, my *abuela* and *abuelo*, all my cousins, the governor of Puerto Rico, Doña Lola, my teacher. A boy went by too fast and bumped into me, so I bumped him back, and that was bad, because Jesus said we should turn the other cheek, which seemed stupid, and there went another bad thought.

I counted all the squares on the sidewalk up to the steps of the church, then I counted the steps, twenty-seven. No bad thoughts.

The church was cool, dark, and sweet smelling. Abuela dipped her fingers into a bowl at the entrance and crossed herself. I dipped my fingers, and there was nothing but water. I tasted it, and she gave me a horrified look and crossed herself. She took my hand and walked me down the aisle lined with pews. When we came to the front, she half knelt, looking up to the altar, and crossed herself again before sliding in to take her seat. I did the same thing.

We were early. Music came from somewhere behind us. When I turned around to see, Abuela leaned down and whispered, "Face forward. You should never look behind you in church." I was about to ask why, but Abuela put her fingers to her lips and shushed me as everyone stood up. I couldn't see anything except the back of the man in front of me. He wore a wrinkled brown suit that stretched into folds around his waist because he was so fat. That must have been a bad thought.

The church's windows were of colored glass, each window a scene with Jesus and his cross. The two I could see without turning my head were beautiful, even though Jesus looked like He was in a lot of pain. The priest said something, and everyone knelt. The altar had an enormous Jesus on his cross at the center, the disciples at his feet. Tall candles burned in steps from the rear of the altar to the front, where the priest, dressed in purple and yellow robes, moved his hands up and down and recited poetry that everyone in the church repeated after him. Two boys wearing white lace tunics helped him, and I was jealous, because their job seemed very important. Envy, I knew, was a bad thought.

I counted the times people stood up, knelt down, stood up. That didn't seem right. I shouldn't be in church counting things. I should feel holy, blessed. But I got an itch in the space between my little toe and the sole of my foot. I scraped my shoe against the kneeling bench on the floor. The itch got worse. We knelt again, so I leaned back and took the shoe off to scratch my foot. But I had to get up, because the person next to me wanted to get through. And other people in the same pew got up and squeezed past me, kicking my shoe toward the aisle in the process. Abuela leaned down. "I'm going to take communion. You wait right here."

As soon as she was gone, I slid over to the end of the pew and looked up the aisle. No shoe. I felt for it with my foot all along under the pew but couldn't find it. It was wrong to look back in church, so it seemed that it would be worse to look down. But I didn't want Abuela to come back and find me with one shoe missing.

The people who went up to the altar knelt in front of the priest so he could put something into their mouths. As soon as Abuela knelt, I dove under the pew and looked for my shoe. It was under the pew behind us so I crawled under ours, over the kneeling bench, and stretched to get the shoe. I crawled up just as Abuela came down the aisle. I knelt piously, my hands in prayer, and stared in front of me, trying to look like I was having nothing but the very best thoughts. Abuela went into the pew in front of me, looked over, seemed confused, got out, then knelt next to me. "How foolish. I thought we were one pew up," she whispered.

When everyone had come back, I realized the man with the wrinkled brown suit was two pews up, and I looked up at Jesus on his cross and prayed, "Please, Jesus, don't let her find out I moved during the service." Which I knew was a bad thought. . . .

"Papi, what's a sin?" I was collecting grass for the camels of the Three Magi, who were coming that night with presents for all the children. The only grass to be had in the *barrio* grew in the alley, along the edges of fences that kept chickens and scrawny dogs separated from one another.

"A sin is when you do something that makes God angry."

"Like what?"

"Well, let's see. There's the first commandment, 'Honor thy father and mother.'"

"What's a commandment?"

"It's actually commandments. God wrote ten of them so people would know what to do."

"What do the others say?"

"Thou shalt not take the Lord's name in vain."

"What does that mean?"

"It means you shouldn't mention God except in prayers."

"You can't say *'Ay Dios Mío'?*"

"Not technically."

"But everyone says it."

"Very religious people don't."

"We're not religious, right?"

"We don't go to church, but we believe in God."

"Is it a sin not to go to church?"

"If you're a Catholic."

"Are we Catholic?"

"Yes. But not very good ones."

I finished collecting grass for the camels, while Papi told me more about the commandments. We never got through all ten, because I kept interrupting him for explanations of what murder was, and what adultery meant.

Papi was to lead the novenas for Don Berto. After dinner he washed and put on a clean white shirt, pulled a rosary and a Bible from his dresser, and started out the door.

"Do you want to come?" he asked me.

"*¡Sí!* I would! *¡Sí!*"

"Only if you bring a long-sleeve shirt," Mami said. "I don't want you sick from the night air."

We walked on the pebbled road as the sun set behind the mountains. Toads hopped out of our way, their dark brown bodies bottom heavy. The air smelled green, the scents of peppermint, rosemary, and verbena wafting up from the ground like fog.

"Papi, what's a soul?"

"The soul is that part of us that never dies."

"What do you mean?"

"When people die, it's just the body that dies. The soul goes up to the sky."

"I know. Mami told me that already."

He laughed. "Okay, so what more do you want to know?"

"What does the soul do?"

"It goes to live with Papa Dios in Paradise."

"When people are alive . . . what does the soul do?"

He stopped and stared at the tip of his work shoes. "Let's see, what does it do?" He massaged his forehead as if that would make the answer come out quicker. "Well, it is the soul of a person that writes poetry."

"How?"

He pinched his lower lip with his thumb and index finger, and pulled it back and forth in small tugs. He dropped his hand and took mine in his then began walking again.

"The soul lives inside a person when he's alive. It's the part of a person that feels. A poet's soul feels more than regular people's souls. And that's what makes him write poetry."

Clouds had formed above the mountains in streaks, like clumps of dough that had been stretched too thin.

"What does the soul look like?"

He let out a breath. "Well, it looks like the person."

"So my soul looks like me and your soul looks like you?"

"Right!" He sounded relieved.

"And it lives inside our bodies?"

"Yes, that's right."

"Does it ever come out?"

"When we die. . . ."

"But when we're alive . . . does it ever come out?"

"No, I don't think so." The doubt in his voice let me know that I knew something he didn't, because my soul travelled all the time, and it appeared that his never did. Now I knew what happened to me when I walked beside myself. It was my soul wandering.

The sun dipped behind the mountains, leaving flecks of orange, pink, and turquoise. In the foreground, the landscape had become flat, without shadow, distanceless.

"Papi, what happens to the body when it's buried?"

"It decomposes," he said. "It becomes dust."

We were joined by a group of mourners on their way to the Marín house. They wished us all a good evening, and the rest of the way we walked in dreadful silence.

Papi settled into his place in front of the house, next to an altar with a picture of Don Berto holding his machete. I wondered if his soul had already gone to live with Papa Dios, or if he was floating around watching to see if his daughters and sons were paying him the proper respect now that his body was rotting under the ground. I tried to send my soul up, to meet him halfway between heaven and earth, but I couldn't get out, held by the fear that if he saw my soul he might try to take it with him.

# *from* Altar Boy

*I will go up to the altar of God*
*The giver of youth and happiness.* — PSALM 43

### Introit

I MISSED ONE MASS AS AN ALTAR BOY – THE TUESDAY DAWN PATROL, 6:00 A.M., FATHER
Dennis Whelan presiding. He was a good-natured fellow, a cigar
smoker, although he was a little young for it, that kind of guy, but he
was furious when I trudged back to the sacristy after sitting through
the second half of Mass in the very last pew.

Where were you?

I was late, Father.

You miss another and you're out of the corps.

I'm very sorry, Father.

It's no joke to be all alone out there.

Yes, Father.

I knew why he was peeved: I was the key to his famous twenty-
two-minute Mass. He pulled off this miracle week after week, without ever looking at his watch. His Mass drew the faithful by the doz-
ens, especially businessmen trying to catch the weekday 6:30 train
into New York City. One time Whelan had the six o'clock on St. Pat-
rick's Day, and we had nearly fifty people in the church — still a record for our parish, I bet.

Working with Whelan was a pleasure; he was a real artist, someone who would have made his mark in any field. He had all the tools — good hands, nimble feet, a sense of drama, a healthy ego, the unnerving itch to be loved that all great performers have. He did not rush his movements, mumble, or edit his work. He was *efficient*, yes — he'd send his right hand out for the chalice as his left was carving a blessing in the air, that sort of thing — but every motion was cleanly executed and held in the air for the proper instant, and he had astounding footwork for such a slab of meat. He was one or two inches over six feet tall, two hundred and fifty pounds maybe, big belly sliding around in his shirt, but he was deft on the altar and could turn on a dime in the thick red carpet. He cut a memorable double pivot around the corners of the altar table on his way to his spot, and he cut that sucker as cleanly as a professional skater before a Russian judge.

My job was simple: I was the wizard's boy, and the whole essence of being a great altar boy was to be where you needed to be without seeming to get there. Great altar boys flowed to their spots, osmosed from place to place. They just appeared suddenly at the priest's elbow and then slid away like Cheshire cats. There were other arts — quick work with the hands, proper bell ringing, a firm hand with matches and candles, the ability to project a sort of blue-collar holiness on the stage, that sort of thing — but the flowing around like a five-foot-tall column of water was the main thing, and it was damned hard to learn. Rookies spent their whole first year, and often two, lurching around the altar like zombies, a tick behind Father's moves, which led to, horror of horrors, an irritated Father gesturing distractedly for what he needed. Extra gestures from the wizard were the greatest sins, and we recoiled in horror when we saw them when we were at Mass with our families and out of uniform. At such moments, when the clod on the altar forgot to ring the bells, or brought the wrong cruet, or knelt there like a stone when he should have been liquiding around the altar in a flutter of surplice sleeves, I closed my eyes in shame and in memory, for my rookie year was a litany of errors too long to list, and my graduation from rookie to veteran was a source of great pride to me.

### Gloria

Whelan was all business out there from the moment he strode purposefully through the little doorway from the sacristy. He had to duck a bit to get under the lintel easily, but even this dip was done smoothly and powerfully, as if he had trained for it. This quick duck-and-rise move made it appear that he was leaping onto the stage, and he always startled the rail birds getting in a last ask before the lights went up; by the time Whelan was front and center, the old birds were back in their pews doing the rosary ramble.

Whelan ran his Mass like clockwork, and God help the boy who was still sleepy, because the man knew our marks like they were chalked on the floor, and he expected us to be quick with the equipment of the Mass – glassware, towels, smoke. Cruets were to be filled to the neck, incense respectfully removed from the boat and properly lit in the thurible, hand towel clean and folded over the left arm, Mass book open to the right page, bells rung sharply at exactly the instant he paused for the sharp ringing of the bells. He also liked his wine cut with water in advance, half and half. Most priests liked to mix it themselves during Mass. Some drank mostly water, with only a touch of wine for color and legitimacy; some drank the wine straight, with barely a drop of water. Few priests drank a full load of wine; even the heavy hitters found cheap burgundy distasteful at dawn. We did, too, although there were more than a few boys who drank wine in the musty stockroom, and every altar boy at some point gobbled a handful of Communion wafers to see how they tasted fresh from the box. They tasted like typing paper. After I discovered that the hosts came wholesale from a convent in New Jersey, the consecrated Host never tasted quite as savory again.

### Oremus

I joined the altar boys because my older brother was in the corps and because my parents expected it. Also, you could get out of class for funerals. Funerals didn't pay anything but weddings did, usually a buck, although there were rumors of five-dollar weddings, and it was said of one boy that he had once received a twenty-dollar bill from a bride's father who was drunk. Baptisms didn't pay – a quarter, maybe, if you were doing twins. The way to make money was to do funerals and to work the banks of candles on either side of the altar. The big ones were on the left and the little ones were on the right – "big ones for the horses and little ones for the dogs," as Mr. Torrens, the altar master, said with an enigmatic smile. He was a horseplayer, I think.

People would come up to the candles before and after Mass, and if you were there in uniform, they'd hand you the money, even though the steel box was right in front of them. Large candles were a dollar and small ones were a quarter.

Light a big one for my grandmother, they'd say, crumpling a bill into your hand.

Here's a quarter for my boy at sea.

Here's a quarter for a marriage.

A quarter for the Pope's health.

Two smalls, for my intentions.

A dollar for the dead.

The code among us was that coins placed in your hand were yours; bills went into the box. The theory was that we were just standing there and the women (they were mostly women) were handing us money out of the goodness of their hearts. This was the first tickle of sin for some of us, and while the practice enriched some boys, it was by no means universal, partly because our cassocks had no pockets and partly because Mr. Torrens learned about it from a first-year boy and after that kept a sharp eye on us from the sacristy door. A boy named Frank Rizzo (not the Philadelphia mayor) was asked to leave the corps because of this, and it caused great embarrassment to his family. He became a bully in adolescence and probably still is.

### The Poem of the Twenty-two Rites and Thirteen Masses

When I was an altar boy, there were twenty-two rites for the Mass, and we were expected to know them even though we were to be witnesses and assistants at only one, the Roman rite, by far the world and Olympic champion in Western civilization. There were actually two other Western rites and a startling total of nineteen Eastern Catholic rites. All twenty-two rites remain in my mind not unlike a poem, and so I chant the Poem of the Twenty-two Rites, which I dedicate to Father Dennis Whelan, wherever he may be: Abyssinian, Albanian, Ambrosian, Armenian, Bulgarian, Chaldean, Coptic, Georgian, Greek, Hungarian, Italo-Albanian, Malabar, Malankar, Maronite, Melkite, Mozarabic, Roman, Romanian, Russian, Ruthenian, Serbian, and Syrian. I even remember that the Ambrosian rite was used only in Milan, and the Mozarabic rite only in Toledo and Salamanca in Spain. And then there are the thirteen Masses within the Roman rite: the Missa Cantata, or Sung Mass (or "High Mass"), sung by a priest and a choir, the Gregorian Masses (a series celebrated for thirty consecutive days, for the release of a soul in purgatory), the Low (the "usual Mass," like the ones I assisted Father Whelan with), the Pontifical (said by a bishop), the Solemn (sung by a priest with acolytes, choir, deacon, and subdeacon), the Votive (priest's choice of intentions), Missa Pro Populo (said by pastors by Church law eighty-eight times a year), Mass of a

Saint, Mass of Exposition, Mass of Reposition, Mass of the Cate-
chumens (the first half of Mass, before the big moment), Mass of
the Faithful (second half), and Mass of the Presanctified (part of
the Good Friday Mass during the Passion of Christ).

To remember all this, is that prayer or foolishness?

### Mass of the Faithful

After Father Whelan was on his mark, facing the congregation from
behind the altar, Mass was under way. The pieces of it snicked into
place like oiled parts of an engine. Opening prayers, prayer for the
intention of the day, Gospel, Eucharist, serving of Eucharist along
the rail, left to right and back again, cleanup and closing prayers,
back to the front of the altar for the brisk procession back into the
sacristy. Or, in the order of the Latin prayers we learned and then
unlearned, *aufer a nobis, oramus te, Kyrie* (Greek, left over from the
first and second centuries A.D., before the Mass went Latin), *Gloria,
Alleluia, Credo, Dominus Vobiscum, Oremus, Sanctus, Te igitur, Com-
municantes, Hanc igitur, Quam oblationem, unde et memores, Supra
quae, Supplices, per quem, per ipsum, Pater Noster, Libera nos, Agnus
Dei, Domine, Ite missa est, placeat,* and then a rush for the door, or, in
the case of the priest and the altar boy, a dignified retreat to the
sacristy.

As Whelan ducked back under the sacristy lintel, he was a
different man, and even before he was across the room you could
see the steel go out of his body. At the counter, he took off his alb
and hung up his rope belt on the inside of his closet door. Then he
peeled his surplice off over his head like a boy yanking off a
sweater, and then he sat down on his stool and lit a cigar. By then
my surplice and cassock were hanging in my locker and I was sitting in one of the two chairs by the door. It was considered bad form
to leave the sacristy before Father left. Some boys waited impa-

tiently by the door, but I rather liked Whelan and enjoyed the postmortem:

Good job out there, son.

Thank you, Father.

Could do the bells a little sharper.

Yes, Father.

Then still them with your off hand.

Yes, Father.

Are we on next week?

Monday for me, Father.

Ah, that'll be Father Driscoll.

Driscoll was another brisk guy, although not quite so smooth as Whelan. He was a good deal younger, and he lingered over the prayers a bit. It was said that he had a hair shirt and the stigmata, and we watched his hands closely when he carved the prayers during Mass. You couldn't really tell about the stigmata; there were marks there, but he could have cut himself working in the priests' garden, which was the domain of a short Italian Jesuit who made pickles and such. Driscoll's small hands were always moist, and he had the unusual habit of shaking hands with his altar boys after a Mass; he did this as part of his disrobing ritual, and he would actually come into our little locker room to shake hands if we'd forgotten about it. He always seemed out of place there, and he didn't stay any longer than the handshake.

Once a visiting Franciscan who didn't know the custom wandered into our locker room after a Sunday Mass and sat down companionably. There were four of us boys there at the time, two just finished and two suiting up, and I remember the uncomfortable silences after the priest's friendly questions; we weren't used to a priest in our room, and he was an oddity anyway, with his hooded brown robe and bare feet in enormous sandals. He had gnarled feet like the roots of oak trees. The veins on his feet looked like cables and his toenails were as big as quarters. He finally realized the score and left, after shaking our hands. His hands were a lot bigger and drier than Father Driscoll's. He didn't have the stigmata.

Years later I realized with a start that Christ probably looked a good deal like the Franciscan, with his dusty feet and pocked face, and I had ignored the guy, wished him gone no less than shaky Peter had wished Jesus gone from his past before the cock crowed; Peter standing there in the icy darkness, the fire at his feet sparking up into the dangerous night, sharp voices coming at him like needles, and he shifts uneasily from foot to foot and damns his friend as easily, as thoughtlessly, as you might crush a beetle; then a shooting pain of light in the sky, dawn crawls over the hills, and right in his ear, as loud and shrill as a scream, comes the shriek of a rooster and the horrible knowledge that he has betrayed the man he loves. . . .

Consecration

Actual belief in the miracle was mixed among the boys, although all of us watched the priests' hands with awe at the instant the Host was changed into the living, breathing Body of Christ. We did not expect actually to see change steal over the Host itself, as we had been told ad infinitum by the nuns that the miracle was beyond human ken, but we did half expect to see a priest's hands burst spontaneously into flame as he handled the distilled essence of the Mind that invented the universe. There was some discussion about what we should do if a hand fire broke out. There were two general camps: the first insisted that the water cruet should be flung at the fire, and the second advised a sprint away from the awful miracle and toward the janitor, who spoke only shards of English but who knew how to deal with shards of glass, fire, locked doors, broken bicycle chains, vomit, heart attacks, dog bites, broken teeth, broken noses, blood, and sobbing first graders who wet their pants because they were too shy to raise their hands and ask Sister if they could go to the bathroom.

I could never turn my eyes away from that key moment, though. It was and is the single most mysterious and bizarre belief of my faith, and it was in many ways the thing that set us apart from all other Christian denominations. In later years I would sit in Congregationalist and Episcopalian and Lutheran services and observe the Communions of those faiths, the passing of torn bread among the faithful and the circulating cups of wine, and while these acts seemed friendlier to me, more communal than the shivering magic of the transubstantiation, they seemed insubstantial, too, muted, more like a casual brunch than a heartbreaking Last Supper. I always wanted to like the Communions of other faiths, but they seemed pale to me. I suppose being dipped in miracles every day inoculates you against the mundane; or at least it shoots your sense of perspective all to hell. I still expect miracles, and I have seen some: my wife, my daughter coming out of my wife, my twin sons coming out of my wife one after another like a circus act, the bolt of light that shot around the room when my uncle died.

### Requiem

Recently I went to Mass in the Cathedral of the Madeleine in Salt Lake City. This edifice, a monument to the staying power of Catholicism in the heart of Mormon country, is the church where my late father-in-law was an altar boy in the 1920s. He was also a student there, as the cathedral once housed a grade school in its nether regions (four Congregation of the Holy Cross nuns taught eight grades). But it was the altar itself that I was interested in. During Mass I deliberately detoured past the immense stone altar and proscenium, thinking of the man who once knelt there, garbed in acolyte's robes, draped in youth, not yet the affable patriarch who would sire six children and build a business and hammer a home out of the Oregon woods and die there suddenly among his pastures and gardens, his breath sliding to a halt as his lungs filled with fluid, his wife holding him in her arms as he slumped helplessly to one side of the bed, the look on his face more confusion than pain, his death a great surprise to him on a lovely April morning, the scents of horses and blackberry trickling in the window.

I don't know what I expected to see there, amid the pomp and circumstance of Mass in this garish old castle. I suppose I was looking for the marks of his knees, or the hovering nugget of his soul. He died before I met him, before I could thank him for his daughter and show him my daughter and sons. I have looked for him in the woods and in the wood of the house he made. I have been closest to him near a small pond that he labored to clear from the woods, but the forest in Oregon is a tenacious thing, and it took the pond back after the man died.

### Adolesensuous

Certainly, being an altar boy was training for the priesthood, in the way that baseball's Little Leagues are training grounds for the big leagues. We were encouraged to go on outings with the younger priests, who took us to carnivals and baseball games (always the Mets, never the Yankees) and bowling alleys. The eighth-graders made a pilgrimage to the seminary at Garrison, New York, every year; the year I went the school had just opened a vast and gleaming sports center, and a quiver of athletic lust went through me like winter wind when the doors to this Xanadu swung open and revealed an oceanic swimming pool and a glittering gymnasium with polished hardwood floors and *glass backboards*. We nearly fainted with desire. The young priest showing off this gem had the wit to remain silent as we gaped at Neverland, and my friends and I spent the rest of the day envisioning ourselves sprinting and spinning and scoring thousands of points on that perfect floor, the stands throbbing with local girls tantalized not only by our patent skill but by the thought that we were tadpole priests – how much more enticing to lure a prospective saint down into the willow trees by the river, and there slip a tongue in his mouth and get his hand on your breast and see if the Catholic Church in the vaguely sanctified person of this gangly zit of a boy was indeed convinced that asceticism was a road to holiness.

Combine this athletic Xanadu with the sweeping view of the Hudson valley below, and the lush playing fields terracing off into the distance, and the sense that a boy living at a high school fully two hours from home was an independent and mature creature, and you had a potent draw for boys on the lip of puberty; but then we were served mystery meat for lunch, in a dank military-style cafeteria, and shown through the cold moist barracks, where narrow metal cots stretched away for miles, where a thousand boys had pulled the pud in a thousand slate-gray stalls, and they lost us. All the way home Father Driscoll chirped the virtues of the seminary, but we were silent, each boy afraid to be the first to burst the poor man's bubble. He might, after all, bear the stigmata; plus we felt sorry for him. He had once been sentenced to a narrow cot and horseburgers and dismal mornings in a dank gray stall where cockroaches did the fandango through scummy puddles.

We went home to our bright houses with joy.

### Catechumens

On mornings when I had the six o'clock Mass, I would awake in the woolly dark and leave my brothers snoring like bears and pedal through the empty streets with my fists clenched in my jacket pockets and my collar turned up against the whip of dawn. The church was silent and dark. The only light in it was the tabernacle lamp, and the only sign of human life the stray Styrofoam coffee cups filled with cigarette butts in the back entry of the church, the spoor of the Nocturnal Adoration Society, which met once a month to conduct a vigil before the Blessed Sacrament, which reposed inside a monstrance on the altar; teams of men would arrive every hour and replace the team in the church, each team yawning as it passed the other, each exchanging muted greetings, a handshake here and there in the dark air, the men checking their watches and settling down on their knees like old horses waiting for dawn.

There were seven lay societies: the Altar Society (for women), the Blessed Virgin Sodality (for young women), the Holy Name Society (for men), the Legion of Mary, the Mothers' Club, the Nocturnal Adoration Society, and the Rosary Society (for women). While my ambition was someday to join my father in the Nocturnal Adoration Society, my admiration was highest for the Altar Society, whose members worked like bees to keep the church and its accoutrements sparkling. "It was they who undertook the laundering of altar linens, communion cloths and surplices, the polishing of the brass candelabra and altar vases, as well as the disposal of withered flowers, ferns, and pot plants," the Irish writer Mary Lavin recounts in her story "A Voice from the Dead." They were an efficient lot, friendly but brisk, and the good Lord himself could not help a boy who got in their way when they were stripping the altar linens; more than once I was shouldered against the cold wall of the sacristy by a brisk Altar Society woman with an armful of God's laundry, on her way purposefully, moving through the waters of the day like a battleship, toward her dank basement laundry room and the magic Maytag thundering away down there like the monstrous engine in a tramp steamer.

### Incense

Almost always I was at the church before Father Whelan. I would hear his steps in the courtyard and smell his cigar. He smoked villainous cigars, execrable things that smelled like peat moss and burned fitfully if at all. He was always at them, lighting, relighting, puffing determinedly, moaning with despair at the shoddy plug that hung like a zeppelin between his lips. He got them from the tobacconist in the village, a seedy man with a harelip who gave the priests a break, 20 percent off, probably in exchange for future considerations. I knew the price because I once bought a box for Whelan after Mass; he'd been caught short, and after thrashing his pockets like a man with bees in his pants, he sat me down in the sacristy.

I need a favor, son.

Yes, Father.

It's unorthodox.

Yes, Father.

I need cigars.

Cigars?

Cigars. A box of them.

Yes, Father.

You'll have to go up to the village. You have a bike.

Yes, Father.

Get a box of panatelas. Here's a fiver.

Yes, Father.

Don't smoke any.

No, Father.

Keep the change.

Yes, Father.

None of these coronas, now.

Yes, Father.

What?

I mean no, Father.

### Memento

I remember the dark scent of the church at dawn, the dense purple light, the smells of incense and cigars and dust. I remember the dry shuffling of shoes as communicants shambled toward the Host. I remember the twisted faces of saints in the windows, Veronica's pale hand outstretched with a cloth for the face of Christ, the bulging Popeye forearm of Simon as he supported the collapsing Savior. I remember the groaning organ and the reverberating yowl of an infant being baptized in the nave. I remember the stiff black cloth under which you hid all desire and personality as you prepared to assist at a miracle that you did not and could never understand but which you watched for ravenously, like a hawk after meat. For a time we were expected to wear ties under our cassocks, but eventually this stricture was lifted and we were allowed to wear just shirts. No jeans, no sneakers, no sandals – this last despite the gnarled tree-like feet of the Franciscans on the altar once a month. You buttoned your cassock from the bottom up, to be sure of symmetry, and then you slipped on the starched white surplice. A simple uniform, black and white, unornamented, memorable.

### Credo

I have come, in my middle years, to a passionate belief in a Coherence – a pervasive divineness that I only dimly comprehend and cannot at all articulate. It is a feeling, a sense. I feel it most near my elfin daughter, my newborn sons. Last night I stood over the huddled body of my daughter, asleep in her crib, her hair flowing around her like dark water. She had fallen asleep only minutes before, sobbing herself to sleep after soiling herself and her bedding and her bear. She is very sick and cannot control her bowels, and she is humiliated and frightened by this; she fell asleep in my wife's arms, her sobs muffled in the folds of my wife's deep, soft flannel shirt. I stand above her now in the dark. She is curled like a question mark in the corner of her crib. My body curls itself into an ancient gesture of prayer and humility and I place my hands together and begin to weep — for love of this child, in fear of illness, in despair at my helplessness. I make a prayer in the dark. I believe so strongly, so viscerally, in a wisdom and vast joy under the tangled weave of the world, under the tattered blanket of our evil and tragedy and illness and brokenness and sadness and loss, that I cannot speak it, cannot articulate it, but can only hold on to ritual and religion like a drowning man to a sturdy ship.

### Benedicamus Domino

"And so the Mass comes to an end, in a whirl of purifications and postscripts that do not seek to impress themselves deeply on the mind; one has not enough capacity left for receiving impressions," wrote Ronald Knox. " 'And every man went to his own house,' as it says frequently in the Old Testament and once in the New, and that is what we do; we must be alone."

Many a time I was alone when it was all over, when the rail birds had gone from the rail, when the businessmen were walking briskly to their trains. When the audience was gone the janitor would whip through the church, slamming the kneelers back up and slipping missals and songbooks back into their racks behind each pew. Then he would bow before the altar and slip out a side door toward the school. I would wait for the click of the side door closing and then wander out of the sacristy and sit down in a pew and think and listen and wait for something to happen. The building groaned and creaked, the candles fluttered and sizzled, bees and flies bounced off the windows. In the windows were the saints, red and blue and green and pink, their faces and bodies and fluttering hands outlined in lead. After a few minutes I would walk down the aisle, past the empty pews and kneelers and missals and Stations of the Cross, and push through the massive oak door and into the broad fat light of the new day, dazzled.

THOMAS MERTON

# *from* The Seven Storey Mountain

*As this piece of the narrative begins, young Thomas Merton has just moved with his family to Italy, where he begins discovering the great churches of Rome.*

I NEVER KNEW WHAT RELICS AND WHAT WONDERFUL AND HOLY THINGS WERE HIDDEN in the churches whose doors and aisles and arches had become the refuge of my mind. Christ's cradle and the pillar of the Flagellation and the True Cross and St. Peter's chains, and the tombs of the great martyrs, the tomb of the child St. Agnes and the martyr St. Cecilia and of Pope St. Clement and of the great deacon St. Lawrence who was burned on a gridiron. . . . These things did not speak to me, or at least I did not know they spoke to me. But the churches that enshrined them did, and so did the art on their walls.

And now for the first time in my life I began to find out something of Who this Person was that men called Christ. It was obscure, but it was a true knowledge of Him, in some sense, truer than I knew and truer than I would admit. But it was in Rome that my conception of Christ was formed. It was there I first saw Him, Whom I now serve as my God and my King, and Who owns and rules my life.

It is the Christ of the Apocalypse, the Christ of the Martyrs, the Christ of the Fathers. It is the Christ of St. John, and of St. Paul, and of St. Augustine and St. Jerome and all the Fathers – and of the Desert Fathers. It is Christ God, Christ King, *"for in Him dwelleth the fulness of the Godhead corporeally, and you are filled in Him, Who is the Head of all principality and power . . . For in Him were all things created in heaven and on earth, visible and invisible, whether thrones or dominations or principalities or powers, all things were created by Him and in Him. And He is before all, and by Him all things consist . . . because in Him it hath well pleased the Father that all fulness should dwell . . . Who is the image of the invisible God, the first-born of every creature . . ." "The first-begotten of the dead, and the prince of the kings of the earth, Who hath loved us, and washed us from our sins in His own Blood, and hath made us a kingdom and priests to God His Father."*

The saints of those forgotten days had left upon the walls of their churches words which by the peculiar grace of God I was able in some measure to apprehend, although I could not decode them all. But above all, the realest and most immediate source of this grace was Christ Himself, present in those churches, in all His power, and in His Humanity, in His Human Flesh and His material, physical, corporeal Presence. How often I was left entirely alone in these churches with the tremendous God, and knew nothing of it — except I had to know something of it, as I say, obscurely. And it was He Who was teaching me Who He was, more directly than I was capable of realising.

These mosaics told me more than I had ever known of the doctrine of a God of infinite power, wisdom and love Who had yet become Man, and revealed in His Manhood the infinity of power, wisdom and love that was His Godhead. Of course I could not grasp and believe these things explicitly. But since they were implicit in every line of the pictures I contemplated with such admiration and love, surely I grasped them implicitly — I had to, in so far as the mind of the artist reached my own mind, and spoke to it his conception and his thought. And so I could not help but catch something of the ancient craftsman's love of Christ, the Redeemer and Judge of the World.

It was more or less natural that I should want to discover something of the meaning of the mosaics I saw — of the Lamb standing as though slain, and of the four-and-twenty elders casting down their crowns. And I had bought a Vulgate text, and was reading the New Testament. I had forgotten all about the poems of D. H. Lawrence except for the fact that he had four poems about the Four Evangelists, based on the traditional symbols from Ezechiel and the Apocalypse of the four mystical creatures. One evening, when I was reading these poems, I became so disgusted with their falseness and futility that I threw down the book and began to ask myself why I was wasting my time with a man of such unimportance as this. For it was evident that he had more or less completely failed to grasp the true meaning of the New Testament, which he had perverted in the interests of a personal and home-made religion of his own which was not only fanciful, but full of unearthly seeds, all ready to break forth into hideous plants like those that were germinating in Germany's unweeded garden, in the dank weather of Nazism.

So for once I put my favorite aside. And I read more and more of the Gospels, and my love for the old churches and their mosaics grew from day to day. Soon I was no longer visiting them merely for the art. There was something else that attracted me: a kind of interior peace. I loved to be in these holy places. I had a kind of deep and strong conviction that I belonged there: that my rational nature was filled with profound desires and needs that could only find satisfaction in churches of God. I remember that one of my favorite shrines was that of St. Peter in Chains, and I did not love it for any work of art that was there, since the big attraction, the big "number," the big "feature" in that place is Michelangelo's Moses. But I had always been extremely bored by that horned and pop-eyed frown and by the crack in the knee. I'm glad the thing couldn't speak, for it would probably have given out some very heavy statements.

Perhaps what was attracting me to that Church was the Apostle himself to whom it is dedicated. And I do not doubt that he was praying earnestly to get me out of my own chains: chains far heavier and more terrible than ever were his.

Where else did I like to go? St. Pudenziana, St. Praxed's, above all St. Mary Major and the Lateran, although as soon as the atmosphere got heavy with baroque melodrama I would get frightened, and the peace and the obscure, tenuous sense of devotion I had acquired would leave me.

So far, however, there had been no deep movement of my will, nothing that amounted to a conversion, nothing to shake the iron tyranny of moral corruption that held my whole nature in fetters. But that also was to come. It came in a strange way, suddenly, a way that I will not attempt to explain.

I was in my room. It was night. The light was on. Suddenly it seemed to me that Father, who had now been dead more than a year, was there with me. The sense of his presence was as vivid and as real and as startling as if he had touched my arm or spoken to me. The whole thing passed in a flash, but in that flash, instantly, I was overwhelmed with a sudden and profound insight into the misery and corruption of my own soul, and I was pierced deeply with a light that made me realize something of the condition I was in, and I was filled with horror at what I saw, and my whole being rose up in revolt against what was within me, and my soul desired escape and liberation and freedom from all this with an intensity and an urgency unlike anything I had ever known before. And now I think for the first time in my whole life I really began to pray – praying not with my lips and with my intellect and my imagination, but praying out of the very roots of my life and of my being, and praying to the God I had never known, to reach down towards me out of His darkness and to help me to get free of the thousand terrible things that held my will in their slavery.

There were a lot of tears connected with this, and they did me good, and all the while, although I had lost that first vivid, agonizing sense of the presence of my father in the room, I had him in my mind, and I was talking to him as well as to God, as though he were a sort of intermediary. I do not mean this in any way that might be interpreted that I thought he was among the saints. I did not really know what that might mean then, and now that I do know I would hesitate to say that I thought he was in Heaven. Judging by my memory of the experience I should say it was "as if" he had been sent to me out of Purgatory. For after all, there is no reason why the souls in Purgatory should not help those on earth by their prayers and influence, just like those in Heaven: although usually they need our help more than we need theirs. But in this case, assuming my guess has some truth in it, things were the other way 'round.

However, this is not a thing on which I would place any great stress. And I do not offer any definite explanation of it. How do I know it was not merely my own imagination, or something that could be traced to a purely natural, psychological cause – I mean the part about my father? It is impossible to say. I do not offer any explanation. And I have always had a great antipathy for everything that smells of necromancy – table-turning and communications with the dead, and I would never deliberately try to enter in to any such thing. But whether it was imagination or nerves or whatever else it may have been, I can say truly that I did feel, most vividly, as if my father were present there, and the consequences that I have described followed from this, as though he had communicated to me without words an interior light from God, about the condition of my own soul – although I wasn't even sure I had a soul.

The one thing that seems to me morally certain is that this was really a grace, and a great grace. If I had only followed it through, my life might have been very different and much less miserable for the years that were to come.

Before now I had never prayed in the churches I had visited. But I remember the morning that followed this experience. I remember how I climbed the deserted Aventine, in the spring sun, with my soul broken up with contrition, but broken and clean, painful but sanitary like a lanced abscess, like a bone broken and re-set. And it was true contrition, too, for I don't think I was capable of mere attrition, since I did not believe in hell. I went to the Dominicans' Church, Santa Sabina. And it was a very definite experience, something that amounted to a capitulation, a surrender, a conversion, not without struggle, even now, to walk deliberately into the church with no other purpose than to kneel down and pray to God. Ordinarily, I never knelt in these churches, and never paid any formal or official attention to Whose house it was. But now I took holy water at the door and went straight up to the altar rail and knelt down and said, slowly, with all the belief I had in me, the Our Father.

It seems almost unbelievable to me that I did no more than this, for the memory remains in me as that of such an experience that it would seem to have implied at least a half hour of impassioned prayer and tears. The thing to remember is that I had not prayed at all for some years.

Another thing which Catholics do not realize about converts is the tremendous, agonizing embarrassment and self-consciousness which they feel about praying publicly in a Catholic Church. The effort it takes to overcome all the strange imaginary fears that everyone is looking at you, and that they all think you are crazy or ridiculous, is something that costs a tremendous effort. And that day in Santa Sabina, although the church was almost entirely empty, I walked across the stone floor mortally afraid that a poor devout old Italian woman was following me with suspicious eyes. As I knelt to pray, I wondered if she would run out and accuse me at once to the priests, with scandalous horror, for coming and praying in their church — as if Catholics were perfectly content to have a lot of heretic tourists walking about their churches with complete indifference and irreverence, and would get angry if one of them so far acknowledged God's presence there as to go on his knees for a few seconds and say a prayer!

However, I prayed, then I looked about the church, and went into a room where there was a picture by Sassoferrato, and stuck my face out a door into a tiny, simple cloister, where the sun shone down on an orange tree. After that I walked out into the open feeling as if I had been reborn, and crossed the street, and strolled through the suburban fields to another deserted church where I did not pray, being scared by some carpenters and scaffolding. I sat outside, in the sun, on a wall and tasted the joy of my own inner peace, and turned over in my mind how my life was now going to change, and how I would become better.

It was a wan hope, however. But the last week or ten days that I was in Rome were very happy and full of joy, and on one of those afternoons I took the trolley out to San Paolo, and after that got on a small rickety bus which went up a country road into a shallow saucer of a valley in the low hills south of the Tiber, to the Trappist monastery of Tre Fontane. I went in to the dark, austere old church, and liked it. But I was scared to visit the monastery. I thought the monks were too busy sitting in their graves beating themselves with disciplines. So I walked up and down in the silent afternoon, under the eucalyptus trees, and the thought grew on me: "I should like to become a Trappist monk."

There was very little danger of my doing so, then. The thought was only a daydream — and I suppose it is a dream that comes to many men, even men who don't believe in anything. Is there any man who has ever gone through a whole lifetime without dressing himself up, in his fancy, in the habit of a monk and enclosing himself in a cell where he sits magnificent in heroic austerity and solitude, while all the young ladies who hitherto were cool to his affections in the world come and beat on the gates of the monastery crying, "Come out, come out!"

Ultimately, I suppose, that is what my dream that day amounted to. I had no idea what Trappist monks were, or what they did, except that they kept silence. In fact, I also thought they lived in cells like the Carthusians, all alone.

In the bus, going back to San Paolo, I ran into a student from the American Academy whom I knew. He was riding with his mother, and introduced me to her, and we talked about the monastery, and I said I wished I were a monk. The student's mother looked at me with a horror and astonishment so extreme that I was really a little shocked by it.

The days went by. Letters came from America, telling me to take the boat and come there. Finally I bade farewell to the Italian typewriter salesman and the other inhabitants of the *pensione*, including the lady who ran the place and whose mother had been overwhelmed with thoughts of death when I played *St. Louis Blues* on the piano, sending in the maid to ask me to desist.

With sorrow in my heart I saw the last of the Piazza Barberini and the big curved boulevard that ran into it; and the last of the Pincio gardens, and St. Peter's dome in the distance and the Piazza di Spagna; but above all, I had sorrow and emptiness in my heart at leaving my beloved churches – San Pietro in Vincoli, Santa Maria Maggiore, San Giovanni in Laterano, Santa Pudenziana, Santa Prassede, Santa Sabina, Santa Maria sopra Minerva, Santa Maria in Cosmedin, Santa Maria in Trastevere, Santa Agnese, San Clemente, Santa Cecilia . . .

The train crossed the Tiber. The little pyramid and the cypresses of the English cemetery where Keats was buried disappeared. I remembered some allusion in Plautus to a big hill of rubbish and potsherds that had once stood in this part of the city. Then we came out into the bare plain between Rome and the sea. In this distance were San Paolo, and the low hills that concealed the Trappist monastery of Tre Fontane. "O Rome," I said in my heart, "will I ever see you again?"

*Much later, back in New York*
I borrowed Father Leahy's life of Hopkins from the library. It was a rainy day. I had been working in the library in the morning. I had gone to buy a thirty-five-cent lunch at one of those little pious kitchens on Broadway — the one where Professor Gerig, of the graduate school of French, sat daily in silence over a very small table, eating his Brussels sprouts. Later in the afternoon, perhaps about four, I would have to go down to Central Park West and give a Latin lesson to a youth who was sick in bed, and who ordinarily came to the tutoring school run by my landlord, on the ground floor of the house where I lived.

I walked back to my room. The rain was falling gently on the empty tennis courts across the street, and the huge old domed library stood entrenched in its own dreary greyness, arching a cyclops eyebrow at South Field.

I took up the book about Gerard Manley Hopkins. The chapter told of Hopkins at Balliol, at Oxford. He was thinking of becoming a Catholic. He was writing letters to Cardinal Newman (not yet a cardinal) about becoming a Catholic.

All of a sudden, something began to stir within me, something began to push me, to prompt me. It was a movement that spoke like a voice.

"What are you waiting for?" it said. "Why are you sitting here?

Why do you still hesitate? You know what you ought to do? Why don't you do it?"

I stirred in the chair, I lit a cigarette, looked out the window at the rain, tried to shut the voice up. "Don't act on impulses," I thought. "This is crazy. This is not rational. Read your book."

Hopkins was writing to Newman, at Birmingham, about his indecision.

"What are you waiting for?" said the voice within me again. "Why are you sitting there? It is useless to hesitate any longer. Why don't you get up and go?"

I got up and walked restlessly around the room. "It's absurd," I thought. "Anyway, Father Ford would not be there at this time of day. I would only be wasting time."

Hopkins had written to Newman, and Newman had replied to him, telling him to come and see him at Birmingham.

Suddenly, I could bear it no longer. I put down the book, and got into my raincoat, and started down the stairs. I went out into the street. I crossed over, and walked along by the grey wooden fence, towards Broadway, in the light rain.

And then everything inside me began to sing – to sing with peace, to sing with strength and to sing with conviction.

I had nine blocks to walk. Then I turned the corner of 121st Street, and the brick church and presbytery were before me. I stood in the doorway and rang the bell and waited.

When the maid opened the door, I said:

"May I see Father Ford, please?"

"But Father Ford is out."

I thought: well, it is not a waste of time, anyway. And I asked when she expected him back. I would come back later, I thought.

The maid closed the door. I stepped back into the street. And then I saw Father Ford coming around the corner from Broadway.

He approached, with his head down, in a rapid, thoughtful walk. I went to meet him and said:

"Father, may I speak to you about something?"

"Yes," he said, looking up, surprised. "Yes, sure, come into the house."

We sat in the little parlor by the door. And I said: "Father, I want to become a Catholic."

# *from* Outercourse

AS A STUDENT IN A SMALL, WORKING-CLASS CATHOLIC HIGH SCHOOL IN SCHENECTADY, New York, I was a voice crying in the wilderness when I declared that I wanted to study philosophy. Even the sensitive and generous Sister who was always encouraging me to write for publication had no way of empathizing with such an outrageous urge. Moreover, the school library had no books on the subject. Yet this Lust of my adolescent mind was such that I spun my own philosophies at home. I have no idea where I picked up that Strange propensity.

As a result of help from my parents plus winning the Bishop Gibbons scholarship (awarded on the basis of a competitive exam in religion) plus saving money from my supermarket check-out job, I managed to go to a small nearby catholic college for women. Being an inhabitant of the catholic ghetto, I had never even heard of such schools as Vassar, Radcliffe, or Smith. Even if I had heard of them, they would not have been accessible — nor would they have appeared desirable. I wanted to study *"Catholic philosophy,"* and the path of my Questing Journey led logically and realistically to The College of Saint Rose in Albany, New York.

Ironically, the college did not offer a major in philosophy, although a required minor consisting of eighteen credit hours in that subject was imposed upon all students. The difference in my case was that I loved the subject. This love persisted, despite the boringness of priest professors who opined that women could never learn philosophy, and whose lectures consisted of sitting in front of the class and reading aloud from the textbook, thereby demonstrating their ability to read English. They appeared to be thoroughly mystified by my interest, and the mystification was no doubt associated with the fact that they had never experienced enthusiasm for this pursuit in themselves. While they sat and droned, I sat and wondered at the incongruity of the situation. This wondering itself became incorporated into my own philosophical questioning. I did not yet understand that for a woman to strive to become a philosopher was to break a Terrible Taboo.

Although those professors contributed little to the furtherance of my philosophical Quest, my own experiences contributed a great deal. There had been shimmering Moments in early childhood. For example, there was the Time, when I was about five or six, that I discovered the big gleaming block of ice in the snow. There were no words for the experience. The air was crisp and it was late afternoon. There was a certain winter light and a certain winter smell when I came upon the block of ice – probably in our back yard. I was all of a sudden in touch with something awesome – which I would later call Elemental. It was a shock that awakened in me some knowing of an Other dimension and I felt within me one of the first stirrings that I can remember of the Call of the Wild. I know that my capacity for meeting ice in the snow in that way has never totally gone away, because recently, while working on this book, I went for a walk on a winter evening and it happened again. This encounter was Strangely familiar.

The shimmering Moments occurred with great intensity in early adolescence. There was the Moment, for example, when one particular clover blossom Announced its be-ing to me. It Said starkly, clearly, with utmost simplicity: "I am." It gave me an intuition of be-ing. Years later, studying the philosophy of Jacques Maritain, I knew that I was not alone with this intuition.

Yet, of course, I was unspeakably Alone with it. It was always calling me somewhere that no one else could tell me about. It would eventually lead me to cross the Atlantic, basically without any money, to obtain doctorates in theology and philosophy in a strange, medieval university where courses were taught in Latin and where my "fellow students" were catholic priests and seminarians.

The encounter with that clover blossom had a great deal to do with my becoming a Radical Feminist Philosopher. If a clover blossom could say "I am," then why couldn't I?

### Spiraling Back: Early Grades and Private Junkets

It would be difficult to convey the foreground dreariness of the forties and fifties in America, particularly for a potential Radical Feminist Philosopher with a Passion for forbidden theological and philosophical learning – it *would be* difficult if the patriarchal State of Boredom had not managed to repeat itself by belching forth the insufferable eighties and nineties, reproducing a time of dulled-out brains, souls, and passions. So I need not ask the reader to imagine or try to remember such a time; she need only look around.

In those decades, however, there was no point of comparison, no possibility of nostalgia. There was only the self-legitimating facticity of Boredom, with no apparent way out. For me, however, there was the Call of the Clover Blossom. Propelled by the idea that *I Am*, I made exploratory journeys by way of warming up for my Outercourse, which is, of course, the Direction my life has taken.

But I must Spiral back a bit, because before the Time of that existential encounter, there was "elementary school."

Let me assure the reader that I have always, that is, spasmodically, made abortive efforts to conform. For example, in the first grade at Saint John the Evangelist School in Schenectady, when I perceived that many of my classmates had dirty, secondhand readers, I spat and slobbered over the pages of my own brand-new one to make it appear used. When my teacher, Sister Mary Edmund, asked for an explanation, I was speechless. I have no idea whether she understood my motivation for the slobbering, but I do think that I myself had some idea of attempting to "fit in."

One of my classmates in the first grade, whose name was Rosemary, was hit and killed by a trolley car when she was crossing the street in front of her house. There was some confusing story about her not looking both ways and not hearing the sound of the oncoming trolley because the one she just stepped off had started to move. The whole class had to go with Sister Mary Edmund to see Rosemary "laid out." She was wearing a white dress. I did not like being there. The experience did not fit in with anything. It was like a white blob that hung there. It was impossible to understand and was worse than a nightmare.

My second grade teacher was Sister Mary Clare of the Passion, who droned a lot – too much, I thought – about "God's poor." I did not understand why the poor were God's. I had her again in the fifth grade, and I remember a feeling of deep shock when she made fun of a boy in our class who was really poor and whose name was Abram Spoor. She assaulted him with a jingle which went something like "Abram Spoor . . . and he *is* poor."

Upon reflection, I have come to the conclusion that this shocking behavior was inspired not by malice but by a passion for jingles, puns, and wordplay in general. I remember that it was Sister Mary Clare of the Passion who more than once wrote on the tops of papers I handed in to her the title of the (then) popular hymn "Daily, Daily, Sing to Mary." These words would be crossed off with a very light scribbly line – as if to indicate that she had written them there by mistake. I understood that this was meant as a game or a joke, but I did not see anything very funny about it at the time.

Upon further reflection, I Now realize that this woman had a strong creative streak. One day when I was in the fifth grade she told us all to bring in some toy that we had become sick of. The idea was that we would exchange our old toys and everyone would get something new. I brought in a tin monkey with a drum who obligingly banged this instrument when you turned the key. I was ready to discard this because it seemed much too childish for a person in the fifth grade. I remember that Abram Spoor's face lit up with sheer joy when he saw my mechanical monkey and said, "I'd like that!"

No doubt this woman had an interesting time watching all of our transactions and reactions. Personally I was delighted with my own acquisition of two oddly shaped books about "Our Gang." But the truly memorable experience of the day was the look on Abram's face and the sound of his voice when he got my monkey. Obviously he had never owned such a wondrous toy in his whole life. I am struck by the accuracy of Sister's insensitive and unfortunate pun. I Now wonder if her puns popped out uncontrollably without consideration of the consequences. Perhaps her weird and lugubrious name – which in all probability she did not freely choose – inspired her to be rather reckless and satirical with words.

Sister Mary Arthur, who was my teacher in the third and sixth grades, was a handsome young woman with shaggy black eyebrows who stormed up and down the aisles hitting the boys – only the boys – with her ruler. She had my unflagging loyalty and admiration.

These Sisters all belonged to a congregation called "Sisters of the Holy Names." Their coifs had stiff white material extending out along the sides of their faces. This headgear must have seriously affected their peripheral vision. So they had to swivel their heads quite a lot, but I didn't think of this phenomenon as too unusual, since that's how it was at Saint John the Evangelist School and I didn't know any other nuns who could serve as a point of comparison.

I missed quite a few days of school during those first six years of my formal education. Even a slight cold was an excuse for staying home in bed and reading my favorite books, such as *The Call of the Wild*, the "Raggedy Ann" stories, and the "Children of All Lands" stories by Madeline Frank Brandeis. It just seemed right to me that I could break the routine and sail off into my own private world sometimes. The special ambrosia served to me by my mother during these outer space voyages was chilled "Junket," which came in three exquisite flavors: chocolate, vanilla, and strawberry. Maybe it also came in raspberry.

The price extorted by my teachers for these blissful free days was lowering of my grade average, which reduced me to being ranked second highest in the class at the end of some weeks. The way they managed to do this was by averaging in "zeros" for tests missed on my excursion days. I thought that this was very unfair, especially because my rival, Sarah Behan, who never missed a day of school, then got to be first, even though her grades were lower. But those Times of flying free, which gave me an enduring Taste for escaping imposed routines, were worth it. I think that my mother, co-conspirator that she was, knew this.

### The World of Glowing Books and the Call of the Wild

Well, the years of elementary school skipped along in this fashion. My passion for the intellectual life burst forth at puberty, in the seventh grade to be precise. Since Saint John the Evangelist School ended with the sixth grade, I had moved on to Saint Joseph's Academy. This catholic school was attached to a working-class German parish and provided education for pupils from the first grade through high school. It was staffed by the Sisters of Saint Joseph of Carondelet. Saint Joseph's Academy no longer even exists. But for me that poor little school was the scene of Metamorphic Moments that can be Re-Called and Re-membered. For many of their hundreds of pupils, some of the Sisters who taught there, who were often unappreciated, created rich Memories of the Future. They formed/transformed our Future, which, of course, is Now.

I was an extremely willing scholar. Few understood my true motivation when I followed the high school students around worshipfully, ogling their armloads of textbooks, especially tomes of chemistry, math, and physics. What was really going on was that I was drooling with admiration and envy because they had access to these learned, fascinating books. It never crossed my mind that their attitudes toward these tomes ranged from indifference to loathing. In my own indomitable innocence I saw these as portals to paradise, as magical and infinitely enticing.

Even though, years later, I found out the less than magical qualities of many of those books, this Dis-covery was not an experience of disillusionment. My preoccupation with the high schoolers' tomes of wisdom had been grounded in a Background intuition/Realization of the Radiant Realm of Books, which was not an illusion. Therefore, there was nothing at all to be dis-illusioned about. Later on I did find out about the foreground level of most books, but that took nothing away from my knowledge of the Thisworldly/Otherworldly Reality of Books.

My parents had always given me many beautiful books as presents, especially on holidays. So the World of Glowing Books somehow entered the realm of my imagination very early and became a central focus of the Quest to be a philosopher. More than once in high school I had dreams of wondrous worlds – of being in rooms filled with colorful glowing books. I would wake up in a state of great ecstasy and knowing that this was *my* World, where I belonged.

During that early adolescent time I also Dis-covered the "celestial gleam" of nature. Since my father was a traveling salesman who sold ice cream freezers, I sometimes went with him on drives into the country when he visited his customers' ice cream stands. My awakening to the transcendental glowing light over meadows and trees happened on some of these trips. Other Moments of contact with Nature involved knowing the Call of the Wild from the mountains and purple skies and the sweet fresh smell of snow.

These invitations from Nature to my adolescent spirit were somehow intimately connected with the Call of the World of Glowing Books. My life was suffused with the desire for a kind of Great Adventure that would involve touching and exploring these strange worlds that had allowed me to glimpse their wonders and Lust for more.

### Taboo-Breaking: "The Convent" as Flyswatter

I was reasonably well equipped to follow this seemingly improbable, not fully articulated, yet crystal clear Call. For one thing I was endowed with insufferable stubbornness – a quality which never failed me. I also had the gift of being at least fifty per cent oblivious of society's expectations of me as a "normal" young woman and one hundred per cent resistant to whatever expectations I did not manage to avoid noticing. For example, I never had the slightest desire to get married and have children. Even in elementary school and in the absence of any Feminist movement I had felt that it would be intolerable to give up my own name and become "Mrs." something or other. It would obviously be a violation of mySelf. Besides, I have always really *liked* my name. I wouldn't sell it for anything. A third asset was a rock bottom self-confidence and Sense of Direction which, even in the bleakest periods, have never entirely deserted me.

Looking back, I recognize that all of these assets were gifts from my extraordinary mother. For one thing, she had always made it clear to me that she had desired only one child, and that one a daughter. I was exactly what she wanted, and all she wanted. How she managed to arrange this I was never told. At any rate my father seemed to have no serious objection. For another thing, I cannot recall that she ever once – even once – tried to promote the idea that I should marry and have a family, although she often said that she was very happily married, and indeed this seemed to be the case. She was hardly one to promote the convent either. I was the one who tossed around that threat, chiefly as a weapon against well-meaning relatives and "friends of the family" who intoned that "some day the right man would come along." I never followed through on my threat of joining the convent, but it worked well enough as a defense against society at large.

This is not to say that I never seriously considered entering the convent. I was not exactly insincere in proclaiming this as a goal. It just seemed indefinitely postponable. Perhaps if the Sisters had had the possibility of becoming great scholars, as I supposed monks did, I would have been more seriously tempted. However, I saw something of the constraints imposed upon their lives. They were deprived of the leisure to study and travel and think creatively to their fullest capacity. Even those who taught in college were confined to somewhat narrow perspectives. The Sisters were in fact assigned to be the drudges of the church. So I couldn't exactly identify with the convent as a goal and just kept moving on in my own way. Later on I read an article in which someone referred to old maidhood as a sort of "budget religious vocation" which was accorded some modicum of respect in the church, especially during the forties and fifties, and especially if the old maid in question was dedicated to her work. I am sure that message had entered my brain and seemed a pretty good deal to me. I know that some women tried to escape "love and marriage" by joining the convent – a strategy that would have worked better in the Middle Ages when many monasteries were Wild places. But I did not see it as a real Way Out. For me, to be an Old Maid/Spinster was the way to be free. Yet I could not fully articulate that idea, even to myself, because even that idea was Taboo. So I just logically acted on it, while waving the banner of "the convent" like a flyswatter when necessary.

# Chanting Faint Hymns

*You can endure the livery of a nun;*
*For aye to be in shady cloister mew'd,*
*To live a barren sister all your life,*
*Chanting faint hymns to the cold, fruitless moon.*

— A MIDSUMMER NIGHT'S DREAM

ONE OF THE FIRST THINGS I NOTED ABOUT SISTER CATHERINE OF SIENA WAS THAT SHE gave off no smell. She placed her notebook and pen on the table and sat down next to me at the long wooden conference table our first day of the seminar in hermeneutics. I was already seated, scanning the course schedule for my first semester of graduate study. Without moving my head, I took in the black habit and white wimple around her face. There was a faint smell of laundered, starched, and ironed clothing, but nothing of the body inside it. Having a nun sit next to me made me uncomfortable. I thought of moving my seat, but that would have been impolite, and the other chairs around the table were fast being filled. I wondered if having no body smell was the same as vampires having no reflection in mirrors.

The course was called Apocryphal Scripture, designed to give us an interpretation of the New Testament in the light of the stuff that didn't make the cut, like the Gnostic gospels of people like Mathias and the Magdalene, the Didache, and the Peter kerygm. The instructor was Dr. Dryer, who couldn't have been better named. A dozen students filled the chairs around the table, a few obvious priests in mufti, one rabbinical student named Herschel, who attended the nearby Hebrew Union College, and two women, Sister Catherine of Siena and a very pretty, dark-haired woman named Susan. Only Sister Catherine of Siena dressed in religious attire.

By the second session I could feel my blood quicken in anticipation of the sister's arrival. As people tend to take the same seats at subsequent sessions that they had plopped into on the first go-around, she and I remained next to each other the entire semester. By the second meeting the seminar had succumbed to a confrontational, free-wheeling style that did its best to drown out Dr. Dryer's pendantry. Herschel and I found ourselves most often on the same side of whatever argument came up, neither of us afraid to shout an occasional heresy at the wall of dogma-bound platitudes erected by our colleagues. But, to the surprise of both of us, we were quite often backed up by the urgent voice of Sister Catherine of Siena.

I looked forward to seeing this woman every Tuesday and Thursday at one-thirty. It was Susan I would walk with to the student union for a snack afterwards, arguing the whole way, but it was Sister Catherine of Siena I longed to see. During Dr. Dryer's monotonous decrescendos, I would lean back in my chair to study her form, her body pulled anxiously forward as if in fear of missing some little splotch of wisdom. The base of her skull made a faint shadow beneath the drape of the black veil. Her heavily veined hands tightened and loosened in tempo with the knitting of her heavy black eyebrows which met in the middle, giving her a look much like one of the Frida Kahlo's self-portraits.

At odd moments before and after the seminar I tried engaging her in conversation about herself, where she was from, what her real name was. Nothing. She did tell me she was working on a doctorate in theology and that she belonged — I could hear the inflection that hinted at a total belonging — to a semicloistered branch of the same Dominican order to which her fourteenth century name-sake belonged. But beyond this she would tell me nothing about herself. As the semester moved along, my longing to make some personal connection with this woman increased along with my frustration and pent-up resentment at her for holding me at arm's length. Each time I vented these feelings to Susan in the student union afterward, she'd look at me like I was nuts. Why can't you just let it go, she'd say. Do you have some kinky fetish about nuns? A point well taken, except that my attraction toward Sister Catherine of Siena was not of a sexual nature. Susan herself had of late been providing me with all the sexual distraction I needed. Why then was I wasting my time and emotional energy trying to chummy up to someone who had so obviously encapsulated herself within a medieval bubble? At night I often sat in the overstuffed chair in my room across from the campus and pondered this apparent flaw in my character.

Sister Catherine of Siena was not the first nun in my life. I had had until age fourteen that kind of marginal relationship with the sisterhood to be expected from an education in Catholic grade schools. Except for a few notable standouts, all those nuns in all those years merge together into one. Like all nuns, it seemed to me, their interactions with their charges were nothing more than merely professional. They may have administered to you but they were not truely there with you. And they did not take you into their hearts, they did not cherish you, they did not love you.

I was placed in the care of nuns at the age of three. My mother had died and my father, too old for the service — World War Two was on then — had important business, something to do with horse racing and poker games. My two brothers and I were placed in an orphan home called St. Aloysius, run by an order of Carmelite nuns. I learned quickly enough how things went in that place. My earliest memory of a nun is standing with a group of other children, waiting for something, watching this woman in white wimple and black veil reading a paper in her hand. I remember being filled with fear, and a great emptiness. One day I find myself standing beside her and taking the hand that hangs by her side.

"What?" she says, looking down at me and pulling her hand away. "What do you want?" I don't know how to tell her what I want. I want to bury my face against the side of her neck. I want to smell her hair. But she has no hair and she has no neck. She has a starched white wimple and a black veil. Her voice is not cruel or dismissive, it is matter-of-fact. "Go wait with the other children." She's not unkind, she's busy.

Senior Girls — sixth, seventh, and eighth-graders — did the day-to-day work of caring for the preschoolers, the Babies, as we were called. These girls each had their favorite, their pet. I became the pet of a girl named Helen, tall, awkwardly skinny with stringy blond hair. Helen always served me the largest piece of jelly sandwich at lunch. She took me on walks through the vegetable gardens on the back acres of the home. When no one came to see either her or me during the visiting hours on Sunday, Helen played a game of being my long-lost auntie.

But it was not Helen I wanted. I wanted the black-clad women who had no body smell, as if they were shadows of those who had died and gone to heaven. They belonged to that world to which I had been told my mother had ascended.

When I entered the first grade I stepped up one group, from the Babies to the Junior Boys. The nun in charge of the Junior Boys, Sister Dipasi, with the body of a padded hockey goalie and a face that resembled Teddy Roosevelt, maintained a constant vigil lest one of her charges slip past her into the net of eternal damnation. She was never without an eighteen-inch paddle that hung by a leather thong from her wrist. The paddle was actually a long stick, two inches wide and half an inch thick, painted red with a hole drilled in the spanking end. A college psychology class years later clued me in on the Freudian symbolism of that paddle, but as a child I learned only how much more a paddle can sting with a hole drilled in the end. We filed past her in the dormitory each night before bed, holding our hands out front for inspection. If they were not clean, a whack of the paddle. If she remembered something you had done that day for which you were not yet punished, a whack of the paddle. If she didn't like you anyhow – there were few boys she took to – a whack of the paddle. Under Sister Dipasi's reign I learned the trick of numbing down the sensation in my hands. And I learned to push from my consciousness the lingering desire to have her take me in her arms to comfort me.

On Christmas Eve, the year I was six, my father and his brother came to visit us. Daddy and Uncle Al, even though they were not twins, looked very much alike in their suits and vests, both with their pomaded hair and bright ties for the season. The looseness in their step suggested they were both a little the worse for their holiday libations. Uncle Al took me aside and explained to me in strictest confidence why we were not going to have a good Christmas that year. Apparently, Santa Claus had been trying to deliver presents to the American paratroop division my cousin Billy was currently with, in a town called Bastogne, and the Nazis had shot down Santa's helicopter.

The following day I found myself sitting on a bench in the playground pondering what my uncle had said. The day was cold, just above freezing, and still damp from the rain that had stopped during Mass that morning. The burden of the secret of Santa's death was almost too much for me to bear. I started out by thinking that the loss of Santa Claus himself was no big deal compared to being in this home with all these nuns whose embrace I longed for but could not have.

Across the playground a group of Babies were being tended by

Helen and another girl. As I watched Helen, without knowing why, I began to cry. Crying was not something held in high esteem among the Junior Boys and I was doing an admirable job of stifling myself until Helen and the Babies approached my end of the playground. When Helen left her group and walked over to wish me a Merry Christmas, I broke down completely in chest-wracking sobs. She sat down on the bench next to me and pulled me onto her lap as I buried my face in the little nook where her neck and her hair and her scratchy wool coat collar met. She held me there, asking me what was wrong. The more she held me the more I cried, but I couldn't tell her it was because Santa Claus was dead. Even when I didn't feel like crying anymore and the back of my throat ached from the sobbing, I forced myself to continue crying. As long as I cried, that's how long she would hold me.

"What are these children doing out here?" Sister Dipasi's voice came from behind the bench.

Helen jumped, startled, pushing me off her lap. "He can't stop crying. I think he must be sick or something."

"Get those Babies in out of the cold. You want them all sick?" Sister Dipasi waved her hands, shooing them away. "And what's the matter with you?" she said, looking down at me. "Here," she called Helen back, extending a handkerchief she'd taken from somewhere beneath her black cloak, indicating that Helen should clean up my face.

Helen bent and wiped the tears and the snot off my face and put her arms around me, saying, "It'll be all right." Then her head bumped into mine as Sister Dipasi whacked her from behind with the paddle.

"I said get those Babies inside." Sister Dipasi waved her hand for me to come with her. I couldn't move. The crying had left me drained and stunned. I wanted to go with Helen, but I also wanted to go with Sister Dipasi. The crying had left me defenseless against my longing to have her or any nun hold me in her embrace. Helen marched away at the head of the line of Babies. I knew with a vague sense of longing that Sister Dipasi could take me away from all this. I must have looked to her as if I were in a trance because she reached to take my hand and led me away toward the infirmary building. As we walked across the damp tarmac, Sister Dipasi's hand covering mine was filled with what I thought of as the warmth of God's love. I imagined Sister Dipasi taking me to heaven where my mother had gone. With a great feeling of relief I unveiled my secret to her. "Santa Claus is dead."

"Good," she said.

By the time the second grade started, the war was over, my cousin Billy had come home. My father remarried and brought me and my brothers back to live with him in the old neighborhood. My new stepmother was well-meaning but largely ineffectual. She tried in the beginning to provide a happy home for us, but after her own daughter was born, her role with us boys became mostly custodial. She lavished affection on her daughter but set up rules for us. My father tried hard to act like a normal family man but, ever since the death of his first wife, the only thing that could possibly bring him solace was perhaps winning the daily double at River Downs.

I never lost that conflict of desire for the embrace of each successive nun as I advanced through grade school. Each year a new nun in her black habit and white wimple and her professional air of being simultaneously there-and-not-there taught math and writing and catechism, while each day serving as my reminder that I both might and might not attain that specialness in their eyes that I so longed for. The tension between these two states of yearning and frustration never abated throughout my years in grade school. With each new year and each new nun, hope renewed itself, hope that I could become the one pupil in all her years of teaching that would become more precious to her than any she'd known. It made me jiggy around them. The longing for specialness and the anger of frustration wound tightly around each other forming a gnarled little sado-masochistic knot that determined my new relationship with each successive grade.

From the third grade on I began to verbally swipe at things they said. By the sixth grade these little comments had become reflex responses, like the way a cough is a response to a tickling in the throat. I had something to say about most everything my teacher said or did. If, for example, my third grade teacher wrote a sentence on the blackboard, I might point out that her o's and a's did not conform to the Palmer cursive method of writing she had been drilling into us. If my fifth grade teacher assured us that Jesus loved all his children, I allowed as how that was only conjecture on her part, she couldn't know that for a fact.

Each nun came to expect Smart Alec behavior from me – a term I pointed out was really trite – and thus we danced up through the eighth grade. I spent a lot of time staying after school, which left me alone in the classroom with the object of my yearnings. I also had my ears rung quite a lot from a slaps on the side of my head, and had my palms paddled regularly. Because of the hand desensitization trick I'd learned with Sister Dipasi, having my palms made red by a wooden ruler bordered on a pleasurable sensation. As the years went by, all these punishments for me became like the gold stars for the smart kids in the class, a sign of my specialness.

All this reached its acme in the eighth grade. I fell hopelessly in love with Sister Gertrude Marie, my eighth grade teacher. Not only did she teach the highest grade in the school, she was also the principal of the school. I was personally well known to her long before I ever came to grace her classroom with my daily, smart-mouthed presence.

To this day I believe that if the Blessed Virgin Mary, Mother of God, ever appeared to me like she did with the Lourdes or Fatima people, she would do so in the image of Sister Gertrude Marie. This woman was beautiful. She was tall and lithe and strong. When she laughed, her white teeth fairly glinted in the sunlight. She could line drive a softball out of the playground, and out-double-Dutch any girl in the school on the jump ropes, her skirts flapping high around her black-stockinged calves.

But she hated me. This hatred I believe began when I was in the sixth grade and grew each time I was sent to see her in her role as principal. She'd bend over me in the hallway, jabbing her finger into my chest while screaming into my face like a Marine drill sergeant.

My attraction for Sister Gertrude Marie was not sexual. That was reserved for the hero of our neighborhood kickball games, the lovely Martha Keller. And, of course, my stepmother, whose blouse I was forever peering into. No, my adoration for Sister Gertrude Marie was fueled by my age-old longing, and spiked by a recurring half-waking dream of her enfolding me in her black veil. The longing and the dream heightened my frustration at her invulnerability to what passes for normal human interaction. Because of this I couldn't shut up around her. Any normal person who adored someone as much I did this paragon might well have been tongue-tied in the glow of her presence. I was driven to even greater heights of contrariness. If she said, "Good morning, class," I'd say something from the back of the room like, "What's so good about it?" When she said, "It's a lovely autumn day," I said, "If you like that kind of thing."

Whenever we got onto religion or catechism lessons in class, where the other nuns fed us the usual dogma dumpings, Sister Gertrude Marie explored for us the fringes of the mysteries of the Faith, those unanswerable apparent contradictions that form the basis of Catholic beliefs. How is it possible that the Pope, a mere mortal like ourselves, can be infallible, she asked rhetorically.

What are the biological workings behind transubstantiation? How can the Holy Trinity be three separate individual beings and yet be three parts of the same unified being? The virgin birth question, I'm sure, she shied away from as being too volatile a subject for all the dancing hormones in an eighth grade classroom. We'd always been told by our other teachers and by the parish priest, Father Gottschalk, who could have been an early role model for Sergeant Schultz on "Hogan's Heroes," that we shouldn't bother trying to figure out these mysteries, that they would be revealed to us after we died and went to heaven. Another reason for behaving yourself in class — if you go to hell, you'll never know.

Sister Gertrude Marie not only brought up these topics on a regular basis, but wrote them out on the blackboard, analyzing different elements the way she might parse a sentence in a grammar lesson. She talked with fervor about these mysteries; as if they were not semiotics to her but were real live constructs that she wrestled with, the way a lot of fundamentalist Christians who are also scientists will try to resolve their creationist beliefs with the scientific evidence of Darwinian evolution. As far as I know, this all went right over the heads of everyone in the class except me. Not that that kept me from making a lot of smart-assed comments about things; like what about her own pretentions to infallibililty in dictating exactly what time class started in the morning; or how could the Communion Host actually be the body of a Catholic Jesus when it tasted so Protestant.

Because of her I really started thinking about this stuff in the eighth grade. At age fourteen my analytical powers weren't much better than they were at age six, when I was trying to reconcile people still getting Christmas presents even though Santa Claus had been shot down by the Nazis. But pondering the reconciliation of apparent contradictions has held a lifelong fascination for me. I don't know if I'm any better at it today than I was at age fourteen, but trying to hold in my mind an image as silly as, say, a fried ice cube or as profound as the Heisenberg uncertainty principle will also conjure up with it the image of that woman who was the first great love of my life.

My last memory of childhood association with the sisters is just a few days before our graduation from the eighth grade. A group of us boys are sitting around the classroom after school on a sunny June afternoon. Sister Gertrude Marie is relaxed at her desk in front of an open window. Her affect always seemed quicker, her laughter more spontaneous in such a setting, especially with no girls around. She easily slipped into the banter and jokes and wordplay that often characterized our budding male conversations. I am telling a joke, one that I'd heard from Lennie Meinholz, one of the others in the group, who would never have had the gall to tell such a joke in front of a nun. Sister Gertrude Marie watches me with the warring instincts of her own lingering hatred of me versus her at-the-moment inclusion in a group that is bouncing words around like a ball in a well-practiced basketball team.

The joke is about a man who is climbing out of a car wreck. He touches his forehead with his right hand, then touches his lower abdomen, his left breast and his right breast. A rescue worker, thinking the man is making the sign of the cross, asks him if he is Catholic. The man says, "No, I'm just making sure I haven't lost anything – my spectacles, testicles, wallet, and pen."

The boys in the group – even Lennie – break into into high-pitched laughter, glancing nervously at Sister Gertrude Marie. She emits a mouth-gaping, shocked bark of a laugh and then, catching herself, does something I've never seen another nun do. She blushes. She blushes, a deep crimson from one side of her starched white wimple to the other. For those few moments until that blush fades and she calls an end to our bull session, she becomes for me a full human being. My impulse in that moment is to brush her wimple aside and bury my face in her hair at the hollow of her neck.

Of course, I didn't do it. But I have carried that memory as a talisman that I had, at least once, touched something inside her. For one small moment when our eyes met in the middle of her blush I knew her as a bare human soul beyond the trappings of her sisterhood. I went on to high school, the army, college, and not until the seminar on hermeneutics in graduate school twelve years later did I have a chance to meet another nun.

On a Friday evening in the week before Thanksgiving, I spent the hours until closing, as I often did, in the rare books room of the university library. I have always loved rooms like this, windowless, climate-controlled, and possessing, I like to think, all kinds of arcane and apochryphal bits of information not known to the world at large. I was distracted in my reading by the person of Sister Catherine of Siena herself, entering through the carved oak door and scurrying in her headlong way to the end of a long table at the other side of the room. She always thrust her head forward when she walked, as if she were in training to be an automobile hood ornament. She placed her leather bookbag on the table and took off her long black overcloak. I waved at her over my pile of books but either she had turned away before seeing me or chose not to see me. The librarian unlocked a glass-fronted case and brought her the volume she'd obviously requested.

I tried to go back to my reading, but could no more ignore the black-clad figure in the corner than Poe could ignore his raven. Finally, I could stand it no longer and, picking up my own volume, carried it over to set it on the table across from her. She lifted her face to mine with a wary expression, followed by a tight smile and nod of recognition.

"I hope I'm not disturbing you, Sister, but I thought you'd be interested in what I've been reading here." It actually was coinciden- tal that she had entered the rare books room just when I had come upon one of those hidden little pieces of information that cause my heart to go pitty-pat. She said that she had a lot to accomplish and little time to do it in but, as I further insisted, finally gave her at- tention to the passage in my book, from an essay written in the sev- enteenth century concerning the origins of the New Testament.

This little node of interest had to do with the original interpre- tation of the Holy Spirit as one of the three components of the Trin- ity. In Aramaic, the language of Jesus, the word for this entity has a feminine declension. It is also translated as feminine into Archaic Greek, the language of the New Testament. Not until the Bible is translated into Latin in the early third century does the Holy Spirit become a masculine idea.

This got her full attention, as I suspected it might. She left off what she had come there to do and we fell into a prolonged discus- sion on the ramifications of changing an originally feminine spirit to a masculine one: how it may account for the morphing of an ob- scure Jewish cult that preached acceptance, surrender, and turn the other cheek, into the Holy Roman Empire, Medici Popes, the Cru- sades, Knights Templar and Spanish Inquisition. We became so wrapped and rapt in our conversation that the librarian had to come and ask us to leave since it was ten o'clock and they were clos- ing for the night.

Outside, a cold wind had kicked up into a blustery late fall eve- ning, raising dead, brown leaves in swirls. The walkway from the library was sectioned by pools of light from overhead pole lamps, almost like klieg lights on a stage. Sister Catherine of Siena and I continued our animated talk out through the front door of the li- brary, me trying to keep up with her lunging steps.

I had lost track of where I had put my reading glasses and, as we walked, I reached up to see if I'd left them on top of my head the way

I often do. Not finding them, I checked first the left breast pocket of my tweed jacket and then the right one. In the middle of this hand pattern, "Spectacles, testicles, wallet and pen" came back to me, along with the image of Sister Gertrude Marie's blushing face. The next thing to happen I can only describe as a very sudden, diamond-clear understanding of the mystery of the Holy Trinity. It appeared before me and left so fast that I saw it without really knowing what I saw. I could not explain even to myself the details or particulars of the image that flashed in front of me, but I was left with the sensation that I understood one of the Catholic religion's most abiding mysteries. In the next breath I became petrified with fear, frozen to the walkway in the dark between pools of lamplight. I stood in mortal fear for my life, thinking maybe all those nuns were right in grade school, telling us we would only understand such mysteries when we died and went to heaven.

Sister Catherine of Siena stood before me, very close, her eyes reflecting the distant lamplight and gazing intently into mine. "Are you all right?" she said. Her usual nervous state had calmed and her face, half shadowed by her wimple, was relaxed as I had never seen it, and strangely beautiful. Not knowing whether I was all right or not, I merely smiled at her. She bent and picked up my bookbag, which I was not aware of having dropped, handed it to me, and then took my free hand and led me into the nearest pool of light. There, she tilted her head back to scrutinize my face.

I felt myself to be in a fugue state, as if I'd awakened in a new place. A conflict of emotion pulled my attention in two directions. On one hand I was alarmed and confused at what had just happened to me and on the other I was entranced by the transformation in Sister Catherine of Siena. I had just gone through the eye of the needle and found her on the other side. The hand that held mine was hot, as if she'd just taken it out of a warming pan. My own hand, which I'd desensitized against the the effect of the cold wind, took in the full effect of her warmth, so that while my right hand holding the bookbag remained numb, the left tingled with sensation as if some kind of electric energy was being transferred from her to me.

Satisfied, I suppose, that I was okay, she let go of my hand and laid hers on the side of my face and neck just below my ear. For a moment I thought she might lean in and kiss me, but she only tilted her head and looked up into my eyes. Everything stopped for us there in that pool of light. I say us because for the first time in my life I experienced being part of something with another person. We were together.

And then it was over. With first the tiniest pressure of her fingers, as if she wanted to hold on, she dropped her hand, said goodnight, that she had to run. Then she turned and walked away into the night, leaving me there in the pool of light. I made no effort to stop her.

In my room, I found it impossible to sleep. But I also felt so at peace, sitting in my overstuffed chair staring at the light pattern on the sloped ceiling made by the streetlamp outside. Something had come together for me. I had no idea what the vision was I'd seen walking out of the library, and I wasn't curious to find out. Maybe I'd had a petit mal seizure, or maybe it was just a brain fart from being overtired and overemotional. The "vision" that I saw wasn't really important, at least I didn't want it to be. I thought about St. Paul and Mohammed, both having seizures and then rising up to a new vision of God. That wasn't for me. A person gives in to that kind of thinking, the next thing he knows he's making a pest out of himself running around trying to convert everybody. A new vision of God was small change compared to Sister Catherine of Siena reaching from behind her habit to take my hand.

# *from* Angela's Ashes

THE MASTER, MR. BENSON, IS VERY OLD. HE ROARS AND SPITS ALL OVER US EVERY DAY. the boys in the front row hope he has no diseases for it's the spit that carries all the diseases and he might be spreading consumption right and left. He tells us we have to know the catechism backwards, forwards and sideways. We have to know the Ten Commandments, the Seven Virtues, Divine and Moral, the Seven Sacraments, the Seven Deadly Sins. We have to know by heart all the prayers, the Hail Mary, the Our Father, the Confiteor, the Apostles' Creed, the Act of Contrition, the Litany of the Blessed Virgin Mary. We have to know them in Irish and English and if we forget an Irish word and use English he goes into a rage and goes at us with the stick. If he had his way we'd be learning our religion in Latin, the language of the saints who communed intimately with God and His Holy Mother, the language of the early Christians, who huddled in the catacombs and went forth to die on rack and sword, who expired in the foaming jaws of the ravenous lion. Irish is fine for patriots, English for traitors and informers, but it's the Latin that gains us entrance to heaven itself. It's the Latin the martyrs prayed in when the barbarians pulled out their nails and cut their skin off inch by inch. He tells us we're a disgrace to Ireland and her long sad history, that we'd be better off in Africa praying to bush or tree. He tells us we're hopeless, the worst class he ever had for First Communion but as sure as God made little apples he'll make Catholics of us, he'll beat the idler out of us and the Sanctifying Grace into us.

Brendan Quigley raises his hand. We call him Question Quigley because he's always asking questions. He can't help himself. Sir, he says, what's Sanctifying Grace?

The master rolls his eyes to heaven. He's going to kill Quigley. Instead he barks at him, Never mind what's Sanctifying Grace, Quigley. That's none of your business. You're here to learn the catechism and do what you're told. You're not here to be asking questions. There are too many people wandering the world asking questions and that's what has us in the state we're in and if I find any boy in this class asking questions I won't be responsible for what happens. Do you hear me, Quigley?

I do.

I do what?

I do, sir.

He goes on with his speech, There are boys in this class who will never know the Sanctifying Grace. And why? Because of the greed. I have heard them abroad in the schoolyard talking about First Communion day, the happiest day of your life. Are they talking about receiving the body and blood of Our Lord? Oh, no. Those greedy little blaguards are talking about the money they'll get, The Collection. They'll go from house to house in their little suits like beggars for The Collection. And will they take any of that money and send it to the little black babies in Africa? Will they think of those little pagans doomed forever for lack of baptism and knowledge of the True Faith? Little black babies denied knowledge of the Mystical Body of Christ? Limbo is packed with little black babies flying around and crying for their mothers because they'll never be admitted to the ineffable presence of Our Lord and the glorious company of saints, martyrs, virgins. Oh, no. It's off to the cinemas, our First Communion boys run to wallow in the filth spewed across the world by the devil's henchmen in Hollywood. Isn't that right, McCourt?

'Tis, sir.

Question Quigley raises his hand again. There are looks around the room and we wonder if it's suicide he's after.

What's henchmen, sir?

The master's face goes white, then red. His mouth tightens and opens and spit flies everywhere. He walks to Question and drags him from his seat. He snorts and stutters and his spit flies around the room. He flogs Question across the shoulders, the bottom, the legs. He grabs him by the collar and drags him to the front of the room.

Look at this specimen, he roars.

Question is shaking and crying. I'm sorry, sir.

The master mocks him. I'm sorry, sir. What are you sorry for?

I'm sorry I asked the question. I'll never ask a question again, sir.

The day you do, Quigley, will be the day you wish God would take you to His bosom. What will you wish, Quigley?

That God will take me to His bosom, sir.

Go back to your seat, you omadhaun, you poltroon, you thing from the far dark corner of a bog.

He sits down with the stick before him on the desk. He tells Question to stop the whimpering and be a man. If he hears a single boy in this class asking foolish questions or talking about The Collection again he'll flog that boy till the blood spurts.

What will I do, boys?

Flog the boy, sir.

Till?

Till the blood spurts, sir.

Now, Clohessy, what is the Sixth Commandment?

Thou shalt not commit adultery.

Thou shalt not commit adultery what?

Thou shalt not commit adultery, sir.

And what is adultery, Clohessy?

Impure thoughts, impure words, impure deeds, sir.

Good, Clohessy. You're a good boy. You may be slow and forgetful in the sir department and you may not have a shoe to your foot but you're powerful with the Sixth Commandment and that will keep you pure.

Paddy Clohessy has no shoe to his foot, his mother shaves his head to keep the lice away, his eyes are red, his nose always snotty. The sores on his kneecaps never heal because he picks at the scabs and puts them in his mouth. His clothes are rags he has to share with his six brothers and a sister and when he comes to school with a bloody nose or a black eye you know he had a fight over the clothes that morning. He hates school. He's seven going on eight, the biggest and oldest boy in the class, and he can't wait to grow up and be fourteen so that he can run away and pass for seventeen and join the English army and go to India where it's nice and warm and he'll live in a tent with a dark girl with the red dot on her forehead and he'll be lying there eating figs, that's what they eat in India, figs, and she'll cook the curry day and night and plonk on a ukulele and when he has enough money he'll send for the whole family and they'll all live in the tent especially his poor father who's at home coughing up great gobs of blood because of the consumption. When my mother sees Paddy on the street she says, Wisha, look at that poor child. He's a skeleton with rags and if they were making a film about the famine he'd surely be put in the middle of it.

I think Paddy likes me because of the raisin and I feel a bit guilty because I wasn't that generous in the first place. The master, Mr. Benson, said the government was going to give us the free lunch so we wouldn't have to be going home in the freezing weather. He led us down to a cold room in the dungeons of Leamy's School where the charwoman, Nellie Ahearn, was handing out the half pint of milk and the raisin bun. The milk was frozen in the bottles and we had to melt it between our thighs. The boys joked and said the bottles would freeze our things off and the master roared, Any more of that talk and I'll warm the bottles on the backs of yeer heads. We all searched our raisin buns for a raisin but Nellie said they must have forgotten to put them in and she'd inquire from the man who delivered. We searched again every day till at last I found a raisin in my bun and held it up. The boys started grousing and said they wanted a raisin and Nellie said it wasn't her fault. She'd ask the man again. Now the boys were begging me for the raisin and offering me everything, a slug of their milk, a pencil, a comic book. Toby Mackey said I could have his sister and Mr. Benson heard him and took him out to the hallway and knocked him around till he howled. I wanted the raisin for myself but I saw Paddy Clohessy standing in the corner with no shoes and the room was freezing and he was shivering like a dog that had been kicked and I always felt sad over kicked dogs so I walked over and gave Paddy the raisin because I didn't know what else to do and all the boys yelled that I was a fool and a feckin' eejit and I'd regret the day and after I handed the raisin to Paddy I longed for it but it was too late now because he pushed it right into his mouth and gulped it and looked at me and said nothing and I said in my head what kind of an eejit are you to be giving away your raisin.

Mr. Benson gave me a look and said nothing and Nellie Ahearn said, You're a great oul' Yankee, Frankie.

The priest will come soon to examine us on the catechism and everything else. The master himself has to show us how to receive Holy Communion. He tells us gather round him. He fills his hat with the *Limerick Leader* torn into little bits. He gives Paddy Clohessy the hat, kneels on the floor, tells Paddy to take one bit of paper and place it on his tongue. He shows us how to stick out the tongue, receive the bit of paper, hold it a moment, draw in the tongue, fold your hands in prayer, look toward heaven, close your eyes in adoration, wait for the paper to melt in your mouth, swallow it, and thank God for the gift, the Sanctifying Grace wafting in on the odor of sanctity. When he sticks out his tongue we have to hold in the laugh because we never saw a big purple tongue before. He opens his eyes to catch the boys who are giggling but he can't say anything because he still has God on his tongue and it's a holy moment. He gets off his knees and tells us kneel around the classroom for the Holy Communion practice. He goes around the room placing bits of paper on our tongues and mumbling in Latin. Some boys giggle and he roars at them that if the giggling doesn't stop it's not Holy Communion they'll be getting but the Last Rites and what is that sacrament called, McCourt?

Extreme Unction, sir.

That's right, McCourt. Not bad for a Yank from the sinful shores of Amerikay.

He tells us we have to be careful to stick out our tongues far enough so that the Communion wafer won't fall to the floor. He says, That's the worst thing that can happen to a priest. If the wafer slides off your tongue that poor priest has to get down on his two knees, pick it up with his own tongue and lick the floor around it in case it bounced from one spot to another. The priest could get a splinter that would make his tongue swell to the size of a turnip and that's enough to choke you and kill you entirely.

He tells us that next to a relic of the True Cross the Communion wafer is the holiest thing in the world and our First Communion is the holiest moment in our lives. Talking about First Communion makes the master all excited. He paces back and forth, waves his stick, tells us we must never forget that the moment the Holy Communion is placed on our tongues we become members of that most glorious congregation, the One, Holy, Roman, Catholic and Apostolic Church, that for two thousand years men, women and children have died for the Faith, that the Irish have nothing to be ashamed of in the martyr department. Haven't we provided martyrs galore? Haven't we bared our necks to the Protestant ax? Haven't we mounted the scaffold, singing, as if embarking on a picnic, haven't we, boys?

We have, sir.

What have we done, boys?

Bared our necks to the Protestant ax, sir.

And?

Mounted the scaffold singing, sir.

As if?

Embarking on a picnic, sir.

He says that, perhaps, in this class there is a future priest or a martyr for the Faith, though he doubts it very much for we are the laziest gang of ignoramuses it has ever been his misfortune to teach.

But it takes all kinds, he says, and surely God had some purpose when He sent the likes of ye to infest this earth. Surely God had a purpose when among us He sent Clohessy with no shoes, Quigley with his damnable questions and McCourt heavy with sin from America. And remember this, boys, God did not send His only begotten Son to hang on the cross so that ye can go around on yeer First Communion day with the paws clutching for The Collection. Our Lord died so that ye might be redeemed. It is enough to receive the gift of Faith. Are ye listening to me?

We are, sir.

And what's enough?

The gift of Faith, sir.

Good. Go home.

ANNIE CALLAN

# *from* The Anglo-Irish Treaty

YOU HEAR STORIES. WHO KNOWS WHAT REALLY WENT ON IN MY FATHER'S HEAD? YOU hear how he was driving home late one night from a rugby do, how he and she were having a row, how she raised her hand to stroke his cheek, to calm him, and he whipped his huge arm up and cracked her face open with the heft of his knuckles. How she sat back in the seat, straight as a bone, letting the blood spurt and congeal on her skin, until they came to a stop sign, and she opened that door, and walked with all the dignity she could muster, out of his life. Someone tells you that Uncle Er, the Dominican priest, urged her to leave him, that she stayed a long, sorrowful night sleepless in the Gresham Hotel, wondering who would look after their children, and next day, she went home. You hear how he didn't apologize for the blue bruise under her eye, how he said, "I thought you were going to grab the steering wheel."

It was soon after that, I think, the he signed on with the Temperance Society and pricked his lapel with a red and white Pioneer Pin, pledging never to sup on alcoholic liquids again. He didn't bother with rugby matches any more either, and eventually traded his international game passes with a doctor in Rialto in exchange for anti-depressants. Was it then that he got religious? Was it terror of the strength of his passions that seduced him into a safe, reliable love affair with the Catholic Church? Is that when he retreated from the unpredictable fireworks of his family and job and fell in love with the Legion of Mary, where the laws were plain and unquestionable, where the script was written out clearly, and all you had to do was recite it over and over and over?

Perhaps the church provided a necessary order for my father, a distraction from the chaos at home. It didn't bark at him or complain or cajole. But his newfound sanctuary did not go over well with his employers. Every chapel he popped into for a visit as he traveled the country was one less insurance policy sold, and in the end, his car was confiscated. Another story speaks of how his job was also withdrawn, and how she went down to the central office on Dawson street, a child in each arm, and one in a pram and begged them, for pity's sake, to keep him on.

I can still see him, a wide hulk of a man setting off for the office, gathering in the width of his trouser hems with elastic so they wouldn't catch in the spokes of his bicycle. At the first crack of light, he'd straddle the handlebar, and head bent down over his chest, drop into Aungiers Street for early mass, propping his bike up against the churchyard wall. He lost several bikes that way. But, being in the business he was, he had the entire family insured against everything but our crock of a bathtub.

Once his office went on strike, wanting a salary raise, and my father, a union man, sat at the round kitchen table, lecturing, "They should be damn well grateful to God that they have a job at all, and not be wasting good time marching the streets like . . ." But still he stood by them, that is, until the union failed to take a stand on the constitutional amendment to abortion, and then my father dismissed them completely. The very next day, he passed the picket, and marched into the office to work, not wanting to be associated with a group that would, even indirectly, support murder.

. . .

It is a bitterly cold February morning. The sky is sullen, the color of dishwater. The pavement is a veil of frost, slush piles huddled in alleys and doorways, relics of yesterday's snow. She walks stiffly towards the chapel door, her grey suit clinging to the hourglass of her body like a film of second skin. He stands inside the vestibule, loosening the thick strap of his watch. His woolen coat is cinched tight at the waist, collar pulled up round his neck like a gangster. She finds his hazel eyes under those coal-dark curls and sighs, "This is the man I will love."

He swallows her up in the cup of his arms, a bear hug that squeezes the breath out of her. "Margaret," he sings into her hair. He helps her out of her leather gloves, his lips puckering in a circle of love at her wrists. "This," she smiles, "is it."

A squat man with pink cheeks dancing like apples on his broad face ushers them inside. "Ah, if it isn't the bride and her groom. Come, come." A sweep of his arm towards the altar. "Now, when will yer guests be arriving?"

"There's be no guests, Father," he says.

"Then, who will ye be having for witnesses to this holy sacrament, may I ask?"

The couple shift on their heels. Dread does a sweep of her heart. He withdraws his hand from hers, and stands stiff as a coffin. "Father?"

"Ye'll be needing a couple of bodies to witness this marriage before the eyes of God. Don't ye have any guests between the pair of yis?"

They are strangers to this small English town. She is here, a nurse on locum at the hospital. He has taken the ferry and train across from Dublin. There is no friend or relative for miles. "We didn't think, Father . . ."

Suddenly, she intercepts, "Wait one moment." And she marches off to the nape of the church where a woman in a housecoat bends over floor mop. "Just finishing up, Missus. Be done in two shakes, and you'll have a clean chapel for marrying in."

Maybe the bride smiles to herself, pleased at the metaphorical aptness. Cleanliness being next to Godliness. She leans into the woman's ear, whispers some magic words, and the startled look on the woman's face soon shifts to something else, perhaps pity, and she gathers up her pail of suds and broom, nodding, nodding. The bride then heads for the main door. She blows warm air into her hands as she stands under the gothic arch, her head darting right, then left, then right.

From inside the heady heat of the vestry, the two men watch as she flags down a man in a fading crombie. He has a long shovel crooked under his arm, which he rests against the sanctuary door as she leads him inside to the warmth. "Cleanin' up the snow, I were," he mutters. "But I'd as soon be in here." And he blowing heat into the tips of his blueing fingers, as the priest settles the unlikely quartet at the altar, and blesses himself.

My mother, given away by a street cleaner, my mother, literally swept off her feet.

Four weeks earlier, when he'd proposed to her on Dun Laoghaire pier, a gypsy girl chanting emigrant songs by the lighthouse, she had felt a long shadow dance the length of her spine, a tapestry of dread. "I knew it wouldn't be easy," she told me years afterward. "Even then, I knew it would be a hard journey. But I took him on anyway."

It was November when they first met; she was a bored nurse on holiday in Harrogate. She first saw him skulking in a corner of the dancehall, "the most handsome man in the room," she said, "in the most ugly outfit imaginable." Ever the arbiter of tasteful style, she looked him up and down: pinstripe suit, sleeves too long, lapels too pointed, shoes polished like a priest. "He looked like a hoodlum," she says, "And, unquestionably Irish."

She danced with this rough hulk of an Irish man, when he asked her. His hazel eyes twinkled, his soot-colored hair a mess of curls caught behind his bruised ears. She felt light and smooth on her feet, in his grasp. Not comfortable exactly, for he held her as if she might fly away on a whim, firmly. But it wasn't until he, ever the egalitarian, asked her friend to dance and a dart shot through her spine, that she knew he'd gotten through.

He was in town for a rugby international, and was scheduled to return on the 5 o'clock ferry the following day. But he extended his stay to coincide with her holiday, and they walked together in the brisk, foggy air, weaving through the dancing ghosts of their breath, gathering up fallen chestnuts in the scoop of her skirt. This was romance, this was the foreplay to love. "The pine cones," she told me, "I kept . . . for a long time."

Months later, when she visited him in Ireland, and was introduced to his rugby pals, the captain shook her hand heartily, "Ah," he said, grinning, "so you're the fog that delayed Colum."

After the wedding, the story gets hazy (aptly perhaps, for a romance conceived in fog). She says they picked at dainty petit fours and champagne, before boarding the train to London, where they booked into The Russell Hotel in Earl's Court. "I remember asking the bellboy for 'a towel for my *husband*.' I was so proud of him." Or proud of the word, husband, deliciously swirling on her tongue like candy floss, the sugary flakes flaring and sparkling like stars out of her mouth.

He, on the other hand, contends that they went to Italy. "No doubt about it," he booms, "we went to Assisi, and sat in the square where St. Francis used to feed the birds. Sure, isn't our own house called Portiuncula, after the little chapel there?"

"Even the rain was beautiful," she says, "falling on the sycamores outside our window."

"The heat of that Roman sun would near kill you," he says. "Even in February. I came back burnt to a cinder. Never could manage the sun like your mother."

This perhaps was the first clue to my bifurcated inheritance. Upper class British blue blood vying against the fiery puces and scarlets of agricultural Ireland. Admittedly, my mother forsook her Protestant ways. (She had no choice: when she first walked through the door of his mother's house, she was greeted with, "If you want to marry my son, you'd better become a Catholic.") She pledged allegiance to Catholicism, but what she really embraced was the opposite of dogma: her fealty veered towards an untethered spiritedness, a spirituality of the heart, devoid of rituals. Still, she plied her fingers round the beads of the Rosary at night, and attended Mass every Sunday. She learned the language of my father, but spoke it only when she had to.

The tempests in my father's head: some word uttered thoughtlessly, a suggestive joke, and he would take it as a slight against Heaven, stew it around in the dark nether reaches of his mind, and you couldn't pull him back if you were Hercules himself. Say he caught one of us kids slipping in late to Mass: he'd be buying a newspaper from Gerry Redmond on his way home from the 10 o'clock, and tossing the change into his trouser pocket; he'd twist around, catching a look at your thin figure darting into the vestry out of the corner of his eye. He wouldn't mention it, not ever, but that lone observation could send him back into a black mood that would last for weeks. He'd sit solid as stone at the tea table, staring into his huge mug as if the rising steam might issue an oracle any minute.

His moodiness might manifest itself in other ways. He'd skulk about, sullen, distracted, and take off on his black bicycle up to the prefabs behind the church to count the weekly takings from the parish Planned Giving. His feet boring into the pedals like a drill, gearing up to a hefty clip, quickening, furious revolutions of his legs about the wheels. He wouldn't know his own strength, if you asked him. My mother used to shake her head in awe sometimes, saying how fortunate it was that he'd channeled his immense energies into religion. What she meant was thank God he didn't drink or get violent. There's worse things than being an industrial strength Catholic. She would intone this as a sort of consolation to herself, when letters would pour through the mail slot, all addressed to her, from various neighbors. "Mrs. Callan, could you please have a word with your husband? He rings the church bells too early and too long. I do have a headache listening to them." And, "I'm very sorry to have to tell you, Mrs. C., but Colum makes a terrible racket with them bell thingamajigs. My good china starts rattling in the cupboard some mornings." Mother would read them aloud at the tea table, to one or the other of us children, never to her husband's face. She carried her wounds privately, or at least independent from him. She had a way of confiding a dark secret about *him* in your ear, nustling up to you, all close and warm, a way of gathering you into the dark reaches of her shattered heart, and running your hands along the shards, so you'd feel the sharp edges of her grief, until you'd swear off your own father for good. "See what he's done to me now," she'd intimate with a long sigh, head bent over her slim chest. "Mrs. Callan, myself and some other parishioners have all agreed it's time to write this letter. Colum is a grand man and everything, but could you please have a word with him? He shouts his prayers so loud at Mass that we can't hear ourselves thinking. Please tell him to quieten down. Sincerely, Mrs. S., Mrs. J., Mrs. McD . . ."

The first complaint was settled when the church introduced computerized bells, and my father's job was eliminated. The second still exists: my father, on his knees in the front pew of the church, hands gripped in prayer at his throat, chin soaring upwards, lips mouthing the responses in exaggerated tones, racing everyone else to God. Mother went to see the priest, letters in hand, and he shook his head, "Sorry, Margaret, but there's nothing we can do. Best to let him be."

And so my father was let be, to inhabit a world of his own conjuring. He'd get so deep into his thoughts, you'd be helpless to pull him out. Preoccupied, he'd cycle into poles or tree trunks. Once, he pedaled at a fast clip straight through a wire clothes line, catching it in the hub of his neck, so it engraved its long shape into his skin, blood bubbling out in patches like rubies. I came home from school that day, to find a crimson necklace graven across my father's throat. He hung his head bashfully, as if a little surprised by the propulsion of his dreaming, the extent of his distractedness. He might shake his head, smiling softly, "To be honest, Anne, I don't really know what I was thinking."

The scar is still there, a thin slash banding him like a homing pigeon, but there are some who might say like a stigmata. He gathered scars on his body like trophies, nails driven through thumbs, scissors wedged into a heel. My father became a patchwork of bruises and scars, a sacrificial tapestry of gashes and clotted blood. And he accepted his fate with the equanimity, almost expectation, that he had been singled out for the receiving, specially.

In the steel-edged clouds of my childhood imaginings, I would plot wondrous itineraries, each one designed to chart a perfect path towards my father's hidden heart. One winter morning, he came lumbering in the back door, all rosy with winter frost, his eyes dancing. Pulling off his darned mittens in one swipe, he blew hot air over the tips of his fingers, and shook the ice off his boots. "Father Mulligan was talking today about the Eucharistic Congress in Australia this summer. Says each parish in Dublin will be sending two representatives . . ." I caught that wistful stare leaking out of his face.

"It's you they should be sending." my mother said, laughing, as she dished up a bowl of steaming porridge, "All those hours you put in up there." She meant the many church activities my father devoted his spare time to. "It's a gold medal they should be giving you, but they're hard pressed even to thank you. Anyway, I heard they're sending the Hennessey brothers who can pay their own passage."

"Wouldn't it be grand, though?" my father dreaming, as he eased into his chair underneath the holy water font, "Wouldn't it be a rare treat to be sitting there with all those other Catholics from so many countries? All those thousands come together in the Good Lord's name . . ."

"Colum," my mother's voice, stern, edgy. "Don't even consider it. You don't need to go to Australia for God."

"But so many people . . . This is a momentous event . . ."

"And where do you think you'll get the plane fare, tell me that!" Now her voice has risen to that pitch that could break glass. "Why don't you go into Clarke's this afternoon and buy a new pair of shoes for Paul? And a pair of uniforms for the girls while you're at it. And stop in at Whitty's, would you, and get us a slab of liver that'll feed the boys while you're gone. And after that, see how much is left in your purse for an expedition to . . . to . . . Australia." Mother spat the word out like it was a curse.

My father pulled his huge head down on his chest, like a turtle sinking into his shell.

I was only eight or so then, sitting on the upturned laundry bin in the nursery, poring over my book. Only eight, but I could read, and I could feel. And, it suddenly hit me, I could write. I loved nothing more than to seat a quire of paper on my lap and pencil exotic tales of mystical worlds where pound notes floated through air like leaves on a blustery day, where airplane tickets dripped off the eaves of every house, crying out to be plucked. I listened to the silence in the kitchen, only the cold water tap drip-dripping into the sink, and determined there and then to write a letter to the Arch Diocese of Dublin, pleading my father's case. No one I knew could deserve a seat at that conference more. If the tickets were to be issued by the quantity of prayers said, my father would win hands down.

So I pulled my best jotter out of my school satchel and wrote. And was duly invited to tea at the Archbishop of Dublin's residence. I couldn't believe my luck. I had to confide in Mother, for despite how I ambled easily through the landscapes of my mind, I knew little about navigating my way through the city I lived in. She bullied me into Mary's old cotton dress, cinching it at the waist with a wide crimson sash. She brushed all the stubborn knots out of my hair, and as I walked out the front gate, a shilling for bus fare rattling in my palm, she shouted after me, "If they offer you tea, don't scrape the bottom of the cup with your spoon, and don't take more than one sandwich on your plate — it's rude."

My heart thudded in the cave of my chest as I was ushered into the sitting room of the huge stone house on Aungiers Street. The beaming lady who sat me down kept saying, "What a girl you are! No one else in town'd get away with addressing Monsignor Ryan as *Dear Archbishop*. You should be very honored to be granted an audience."

The man himself looked a lot like Oliver Pluck, our butcher, the same scrawny look of a ravaged bird, the same beady eyes. But the emissary of God had a large crucifix dangling on his rake's chest.

When he spoke, the wafery skin would fall in folds about the hollow of his throat. He looked ill. Mostly he smiled and said over and over what a fortunate man Mr. Callan was to have such a thoughtful daughter. "And I might say, literate," he'd add at the end of each sentence, like a refrain in a children's song.

I spooned a dollop of plum jam out of the pewter jug on the tray that sat like an international border between us. I kept waiting for the important bit, for him to clear his sad throat, inhale ceremoniously before his declaration: "We're sending your father as special envoy to the Australian convocation. We'll be conveying an airline ticket within the week." I wanted to hurry him along, but instead thought of Mother waving deliriously at me from our front gate, and bit my tongue. My fingers felt sticky and awkward. The Pope's dignitary chatted quietly on, sentences spinning one after another in gentle circles, as if he were playing a recording through to its end, and then pressing Replay, when he would ease back and sneak a sip of weak tea, satisfied in the knowledge that he was fulfilling his duty.

So this is how the clergy talk, even at home, I realized: in long, meandering sermons, they deliver The Message from some impossible height that we mere humans can only aspire towards, but which we will never, no matter how zealous the groping, ever reach. Eventually I sidled out of my red velvet high-backed chair with a punctured heart. My father seemed to be embarrassed about the whole affair when he found out: Mum kept telling him to thank me.

Soon after this, my father began vigorous planning for the next convocation, which was to take place in Rome in the Holy Year of 1975. It was to be a special Jubilee year, my father said, when the common man could make reparations for other's sins, and pardons galore would be granted.

"We'll all go to Rome," he announced one evening after the Rosary. "Put a little bit by at the end of the month, can't we, Mum? The pennies'll add up over eight years, won't they?" He was rubbing his hands together like I'd seen the Artful Dodger do in Oliver Twist. And even though my mother shook her head wearily, ROME became like a hymn in our household. *Mr. Damn, Mrs. Damn and the Whole Damn Family, off we'll go a-wandering far away from home. Off we'll vaunt to Europe and all the way to Rome.*

If you'd asked me then where I'd be in 1975, I'd have sworn gravely on the Bible itself that that magic year would find me and my own blood kneeling at the foot of the Pope in the Vatican, united in abiding Catholic devotion. When all my friends were taking summer car trips to the Dingle Peninsula, or Butlins Holiday camp, I didn't care that I stayed the long sticky summer at home for I knew, I *knew*, that one year soon, I'd be jetting out of that ugly street on an airplane, maybe our own private jet, my father and mother on either side of me, my brothers and sisters filling the rows in front and behind, all of us winging like angels across the sky to convene with God.

When that glorious year finally rolled around on the calendar, it found my father in St. John of God's rest home for the second time, strolling the white corridors in his tattered plaid dressing gown, fingering the ropy belt like a rosary till it unraveled into helpless strands about his yellow feet.

"Your father isn't well, Anne," my mother would say when I'd ask after him. But about more than this, she was tight-lipped. I'll make him better, I vowed. And off I headed to the school library to pore over books on Vocations and The Religious Life. I scoured long passages about the various orders of nuns, eliminating the silent orders, for I knew even my most noble efforts to still my tongue would be fruitless, and finally settled on a convent in rural Spain where you could pluck juicy oranges out of the grove in the beating sun, and meditate on sacrifice and despair.

But I ran away from home instead, and the head nun, who wanted to expel me, only guffawed at my mother's frantic protestations, "Oh, Sister, Anne has seriously considered becoming one of your own, a nun."

"Mrs. Callan," she spoke firmly, as if she were instructing a class. "With all due respect to you, the words 'Anne' and 'nun' do not, I repeat, do not, belong in the same phylum. It's biologically impossible."

One of my father's sisters, Ann, a tall rail of a woman with a raven's beak for a nose, felt the call of God. She didn't exactly wake in the night, her bedsheets drenched and angels choiring about her violet eyes, but she was certain, in the stubborn, unquestioning way of her people, that she had received a siren call to the nunnery. She joined the Little Sisters of the Poor in Drogheda, and spent several years apprenticing to her trade. My father spoke of little else for months. Here at least, he consoled himself, was a pipeline to Heaven, and he related to it by blood, no less.

One evening after supper, he declaimed firmly, "I'm going to attend Ann's initiation into the Holy Order on Sunday." But his eyes fell on the chicken bones heaped on his plate, not on my mother's stomach, the huge swell of it, ripe with child number three.

"Colum, you can't," his wife whispered, awe in her voice with the shock of it. "I might be in labor . . ."

"The two events won't overlap, you'll see."

"Any day . . ."

"They WILL NOT overlap," he insisted, shoving his chair back so hard that chips of red paint dribbled down from the wall.

They did. On Sunday morning, she went to hospital in a taxi, her two children packed into the back seat behind her, bawling. He went to the nunnery in a rented car, where he watched his sister lower the black veil over her pale face, stitching the gaunt wraith of herself into a seam of God's harem. Within six months, she had left the convent, no longer sure of her vocation. She entered a second time several years later, but couldn't muster the wherewithal to stay, and ended up working as a secretary in the Bronx until she retired, a sad and bitter woman.

When my father drove home that evening, head craned close to the windshield to see through the rain, he was pleased to see a light on in the hallway. A hymn rose in his chest: he hadn't neglected his duty after all. For a brief flash, he felt like God: he could be a good brother, a worthy husband, a caring father. He could be everything. But what he met when he walked through the back door surprised him: a crib on the dresser, and a baby's pudgy fists gathered on a heather blanket. He could hear hoarse wails hammering down from the boys' room. He found his wife, cloaked in a lime green hospital gown, eyes aflame, standing at the kitchen table. He found a slab of meat and steaming spinach on a plate set out for him. Everything in its place.

"Smells delicious," he said, loosening his Castleknock tie.

"Good, you can have it then," my mother said, in a tone that was dulcet and calm. "Here's your tea, Colum. It's all yours." And in one swift flick of her hand, she tipped the table laden with dishes onto its side and heaved the burned supper and crockery all over him. Slowly, in silence, he knelt down and began to pick up the million shards glittering like cracked diamonds against the linoleum.

My mother's beauty was of a striking, regal kind. She had the carriage of a lady, an air of refinement and poise about her. Unlike the other housewives in the parish, who shuffled about, bodies heaving in on themselves, my mother strutted down the street like a peacock, head high, shoulders erect, a fan of color against the gray houses. You'd never find her head glutted with curlers or buried under a gaudy headscarf. No, she, if she chose to cover her diaphanous hair, would don a scarlet beret astride her forehead, say, or a suede dress hat with a wide, floaty brim, the kind you'd imagine horsey, southside women would wear on Easter Sundays. My mother assembled her wardrobe with the care of a physician preparing for surgery. Her clothes, vestiges of another life, never seemed to show their age. She would swan from one to another outfit with the grace of a queen, her bright skirt dancing about her ankles like a flower. Sometimes, if the sun caught her willowy shape from behind, her whole frame would light up and dance towards you like a silvery angel. People would stop in the street to watch her shimmer past.

This fact wasn't lost on her. For years, she would recount the story of how Mrs. Collins had once asked her if she was a model. Sipping delicately from her red-rimmed China tea cup, she would run her hands along the embroidered silk dressing gown that had been her mother's, and sigh, "A model. Me, can you imagine? With all my children?" But you knew she delighted in the attention. It seemed less important to her that her gleaming leather bag was empty save for spare buttons and loose change. What mattered hugely was that you acknowledged her particular elegance. It was all she had left of that other, English life, a window reflecting past glories and triumphs. If she could mirror that time, if she could just appear to be who she imagined she might have been then, the world was bearable.

It is true that if you put a brown paper bag over my mother's head, and carved out holes for the eyes and the mouth, that she would wear it like a fresh bride's veil. She exuded a grace rarely if ever seen in our neighborhood. And although my father was aware of this, he rarely acknowledged it. When my sister and I bought a gold satin nightdress for her, she slipped it over her ivory shoulders, twirled about the kitchen, inhaled my father's noncommittal *hmmm*, and buried the useless thing under the lavender sachets in her dresser.

My father gathered hagiophiles around him like acolytes, frenzied groupies of Religion The Loud Way, Holy Michaels and Marys, mostly Marys, bleeding out of our parish's woodwork, mongering amongst themselves about the most expedient routes to Heaven. They thought Colum Callan owned stock in the atlas. They'd cluster in droves at our doorstep, all pinched together like a dented chalice of birds, waiting for my father to issue his oratorical ravishments to their starved, cocked ears. "Colum, would you ever sign this petition to St. Jude for us, would you? Mr. Callan, have you an hour you might spare us to organize the whist drive for the Legion of Mary? Mr. C., would you mind giving the keynote talk at our Patrician meeting this Sunday?" Once the queries and requests on my father's meager time came under the rubric of religion, he would rush to comply. Like putty in the hands of his followers, my father's guidance was prodigal and democratic.

But the more he attracted local disciples, the further he pushed his own family away from him. He would appear, as if flown in the back door on a miracle, at mealtimes. He was mostly a phantom in our house, only taking on physical form when it came time to pray. Perhaps fueled by his popular receipt in certain religious circles, he began to press more firmly and weightily his own offspring, trying to engrave his insignia on his budding slabs of granite, hone us unruly kids into priests, monks, saints. After supper, in the gathering dark, he would insist we kneel around the kitchen table and recite his chosen sequence of prayers.

"Under pain of mortal sin," he would command, should any one of us resist, "Under pain of mortal sin, you MUST say the Rosary." Stifled sighs would stir on our breath, as we'd lower weary head to chest and mumble our lines. It was like a long run of a very predictable play, acted out so often that it became mindless and boring. Growing teenagers, we wanted to be out playing soccer in the garden with our dad, or pruning the hedges. We wanted to wash and wax the car, like Franner Reilly. Any task, but this dark crimping of sour mouths bleating paeans to a ruthless and threatening god. But we had no family car, and my father cared nothing for ball games after he ditched the rugby. So we knelt, seething prisoners knotted around his votive candles, longing for bedtime.

It was my brother Frank who first spoke up. In fact, he leaped up like a thunderbolt one evening and sparked through the air at my father. One minute, we were all slouched over the edge of the table, stringing beads in our hands, vaguely chanting through our script; the next minute, my father's white shirt was crushed in the heart of Frank's fist. "How dare you threaten us!" I heard my brother shouting, fury in his voice the color of fire. "I am sixteen years of age. Sixteen! How dare you bully me like a child."

My father, recovering from the surprise, pried himself free of his son's grip, cowering like a dazed animal against the wall. Sparks of light from the flickering candles leaped across his face in a chiaroscuro play of light and shadow.

"Frank," my father said, his voice gathering strength with each accruing word. "Francis, I am your father. And as my child, you shall do as I say."

"I will not!" Frank continued, his face a furnace burning. "I am not a child any more."

"Under pain of mortal sin, Frank," my father tried to go on, but Frank pounced again.

"Frank, Frank, stop that this instant!" My mother had risen from her knees, and inserted herself between the two men. "Paul, David, Mary . . . go and get the police immediately."

It was plain to see that physical damage could be wrought, and wrought quickly, but Frank, as if acknowledging the power of his unbridled rage, detached himself from his father, and, wiping his hands on the hips of his trousers as if they were stained, stated breathlessly, "No, let me go, Mum. I'll get Father Mulligan down here and let him see if you aren't overstepping the line with your threats and your bullying." And he crashed shut the back door after him, so the glass window rattled in its frame.

Poor Father Mulligan, he seemed such a pale, vulnerable figure there, standing in our hallway, sweating, embarrassed, cast unwittingly into the core of this blazing furnace, fearful perhaps of being accosted by a stray tinder. He swayed on his heels, humming and hawing. I studied this pitiful scarecrow, this missionary of the establishment, as he coughed and wheezed. I despised him in that instant, despised him for his weakness, his noncommittal wishy-washyness. Here he had an army of children blistering with rage, and a wife feverishly trying to calm them. And the husband, standing in the lintel of the kitchen, head bent down, inwards towards slouched shoulders, waiting for the pronouncements from on high.

Finally, the priest quietly declared that perhaps Mr. Callan was asking just a little bit much of his family. Everyone gave affirming nods of their heads as Father Mulligan went on, tentatively, "Perhaps, Colum, we could work out, let's say . . . a modified version of your prayers?"

Mr. Callan kept his head pinned to his chest, listening like a chastised child, silent. It was more than I could bear to see this man, for all his physical heft, my father, being instructed, even admonished, on matters so private as child-rearing. I couldn't stand silent and watch this band of smoldering furies treat him like an inferior. He standing there so quietly, so still, all his passion quashed, while the odds — 7 to 1 — were stacked against him.

Compelled to act, I pounced on Father Mulligan, thumping him vigorously on his chest, yelling every exclamative I could muster into his face. "How DARE you walk into our house," I screamed, "and tell us how to live our lives!" As he struggled to wrest himself free, to turn his sallow cheek, my brothers grabbed my flailing arms away. "You, you who don't even have a family, for God's sake. Never been married. Never had a child. Who the hell are you to tell my father how to do something you've never even done your bloody self!"

The poor priest had to be ushered out of the house as quickly as he'd been dragged in.

After that, one and then another of my siblings disappeared at prayertime, until it was only my mother, my littlest brother, and myself who pried the beads out of the prayer basket after supper. My father continued each evening to set out eight sets of rosaries on the tablecloth, and he quietly picked up four pairs, untouched, and tucked them away again, like children at bedtime.

"Anne," my father would declaim momentously, in his rare flashes of advice-giving, "If you ever marry, make sure it's to a Catholic. They're the only ones who believe in the indissolubility of marriage."

My mother had a better solution. "Anne," she would exhale sharply, sifting through change in her purse to pay Jimmy the milkman. "If you ever decide to get married," long sigh, "You probably won't because you like your freedom far too much . . ." Pause. "But . . . if you ever doooo . . ." Heave of chest, emphatically, "Please, dear, just elope."

My father dealt in spiritual tender; his was a currency of otherworldly checks and balances. A pauper would be fine for his daughter's husband, a vagabond from the poorhouse might serve as a suitable candidate, just so long as he knew The One and Only Creed. Father had no sense of pennies and pounds. Why succumb to the earthly plane of pedestrian economics when he had a (carefully chosen) wife to fret for him? Material acquisitions, no matter how necessary, hardly pierced the ethereal spinnings of his busy head. When my mother would try to cajole him to try on a new suit from the sale rack in Clery's, he would rub his hands together, eyes glinting, and say, "Sure love, why would I want a second suit when I have a good one already? I can only wear one at a time, and making decisions, well, don't you know I'm terrible at it? It isn't my strong suit (pun, pun) at all." This, even though his fading tweed jacket might be patched in leather at the elbows and the cuffs frayed with loose thread. Only his black leather boots did he cosset, and these he would polish every evening, hunkered down over old newspaper, spit-dusting them till they shone like stars.

And so it was on my mother's thin shoulders that the clouds of money management fell. And she carried that weight with the noise of a pallbearer. If her children had to starve, well then, let them – no matter how extreme the sacrifice, she held stiffly to her belief, *The Bills Must Be Paid.* For, "After all," she would tell us, over and over, "your word is everything. It's all you have in the end. Let nobody take it away from you."

My father, on the other hand, spun promises out of his nimble mouth like candy floss, all froth and sugar twittering through the air, exquisite delicacies you'd hunger after only to have them evaporate at the tip of your hand. He strung sentences together like beads, gorgeous confections, elisions floating out one after another, no beginning or end to them. His intentions were probably honorable, he *meant* what he said at the time, but the execution of his promises, the dull, practical reckoning, remained always a full stop or two, or three, beyond him. An agile dancer in the realm of ether and seraphim – which made him such a wondrous story teller – my father remained stiff and club-footed in the real world.

Between them, this awkward couple held real estate in both

realms, but rarely could they manage to meet on the same plane. When it looked as if we'd be evicted from the earthly sphere for lack of funds, it was my mother who took the Drogheda bus to visit her husband's aunt. It was she who lowered her head and begged a loan from the woman who'd married her millionaire boss in America and inherited a fortune. It was she who heard the old woman grind her false teeth together, before hissing, "Why did he have to go and marry a Sasanach anyway?"

One bitter winter day, at Dublin airport, when I was returning to America, a graduate student in impecunious straits, my father clapped his thick hands around mine, and whispered, "Anne, if you're ever in need of a few bob, just let us know . . ." I studied him there in his dilapidated rain mac, snow dancing over his shoulders like silver confetti. And then her, the slow, tired roll of her green eyes upwards, to some vacant heaven, the pale heart shape on her lapel, where her mother's diamond brooch used to sit before the pawn shop. "Just let us know," he said again, turning to his wife, "Isn't that so, Mummy?" The steady, resigned bob of her head like a seesaw a child set bouncing before walking away.

On icy winter mornings, you'll find my mother in her kitchen in a Dublin suburb, carefully extracting a grapefruit wedge with a pure silver spoon. She'll be bent softly forward, her mother's silk dressing gown sloping down the curve of her shoulders, a lace napkin puckering on her lap. She may take a sip of sweet tea from her chipped china cup, before she slices a silver knife through her soft boiled egg. The bulb overhead casts a brazen light on the scene. If you looked closely, you'd see the dingy stove and the grey sink at the edges, the peeling wooden dresser. You might see my father's huge tea mug across the table, or his callused hands sweeping the edges of his bowl with a piece of dry toast, foraging for the last bits of porridge. You might hear a loud hack from his throat as he clears away the trace of a cold. But it is to her that your eyes are always drawn, the pale contours of her willowy frame, the arch of her long neck, her accoutrements all around her like a glittering shell. She is a composition there in those cold moments of dawn, a still life of soft hues and shapes that she stubbornly sets a place for every morning, before the din of six children clattering down the staircase reels her back to true north.

# II

*Sin and Salvation*

TOBIAS WOLFF

# *from* This Boy's Life

I WAS BAPTIZED DURING EASTER ALONG WITH SEVERAL OTHERS FROM MY CATECHISM
class. To prepare ourselves for communion we were supposed to
make a confession, and Sister James appointed a time that week for
each of us to come to the rectory and be escorted by her to the confessional. She would wait outside until we were finished and then
guide us through our penance.

I thought about what to confess, but I could not break my sense
of being at fault down to its components. Trying to get a particular
sin out of it was like fishing a swamp, where you feel the tug of
something that at first seems promising and then resistant and finally hopeless as you realize that you've snagged the bottom, that
you have the whole planet on the other end of your line. Nothing
came to mind. I didn't see how I could go through with it, but in the
end I hauled myself down to the church and kept my appointment.
To have skipped it would have called attention to all my other ab-
sences and possibly provoked a visit from Sister James to my
mother. I couldn't risk having the two of them compare notes.

Sister James met me as I was coming into the rectory. She asked
if I was ready and I said I guessed so.

"It won't hurt," she said. "No more than a shot, anyway."

We walked over to the church and down the side aisle to the confessional. Sister James opened the door for me. "In you go," she
said. "Make a good one now."

I knelt with my face to the screen as we had been told to do and said, "Bless me Father, for I have sinned."

I could hear someone breathing loudly on the other side. After a time he said, "Well?"

I folded my hands together and closed my eyes and waited for something to present itself.

"You seem to be having some trouble." His voice was deep and scratchy.

"Yes, sir."

"Call me Father. I'm a priest, not a gentleman. Now then, you understand that whatever gets said in here stays in here."

"Yes, Father."

"I suppose you've thought a lot about this. Is that right?"

I said that I had.

"Well, you've just given yourself a case of nerves, that's all. How about if we try again a little later. Shall we do that?"

"Yes please, Father."

"That's what we'll do, then. Just wait outside a second."

I stood and left the confessional. Sister James came toward me from where she'd been standing against the wall. "That wasn't so bad now, was it?" she asked.

"I'm supposed to wait," I told her.

She looked at me. I could see she was curious, but she didn't ask any questions.

The priest came out soon after. He was old and very tall and walked with a limp. He stood close beside me, and when I looked up at him I saw the white hair in his nostrils. He smelled strongly of tobacco. "We had a little trouble getting started," he said.

"Yes, Father?"

"He's just a bit nervous is all," the priest said. "Needs to relax. Nothing like a glass of milk for that."

She nodded.

"Why don't we try again a little later. Say twenty minutes?"

"We'll be here, Father."

Sister James and I went to the rectory kitchen. I sat at a steel cutting table while she poured me a glass of milk. "You want some cookies?" she asked.

"That's all right, Sister."

"Sure you do." She put a package of Oreos on a plate and brought it to me. Then she sat down. With her arms crossed, hands hidden in her sleeves, she watched me eat and drink. Finally she said, "What happened, then? Cat get your tongue?"

"Yes, Sister."

"There's nothing to be afraid of."

"I know."

"Maybe you're just thinking of it wrong," she said.

I stared at my hands on the tabletop.

"I forgot to give you a napkin," she said. "Go on and lick them. Don't be shy."

She waited until I looked up, and when I did I saw that she was younger than I'd thought her to be. Not that I'd given much thought to her age. Except for the really old nuns with canes or facial hair they all seemed outside of time, without past or future. But now – forced to look at Sister James across the narrow space of this gleaming table – I saw her differently. I saw an anxious woman of about my mother's age who wanted to help me without knowing what kind of help I needed. Her good will worked strongly on me. My eyes burned and my throat swelled up. I would have surrendered to her if only I'd known how.

"It probably isn't as bad as you think it is," Sister James said. "Whatever it is, someday you'll look back and you'll see that it was natural. But you've got to bring it to the light. Keeping it in the dark is what makes it feel so bad." She added, "I'm not asking you to tell me, understand. That's not my place. I'm just saying that we all go through these things."

Sister James leaned forward over the table. "When I was your age," she said, "maybe even a little older, I used to go through my father's wallet while he was taking his bath at night. I didn't take bills, just pennies and nickels, maybe a dime. Nothing he'd miss. My father would've given me the money if I'd asked for it. But I preferred to steal it. Stealing from him made me feel awful, but I did it all the same."

She looked down at the tabletop. "I was a backbiter, too. Whenever I was with one friend I would say terrible things about my other friends, and then turn around and do the same thing to the one I had just been with. I knew what I was doing, too. I hated myself for it, I really did, but that didn't stop me. I used to wish that my mother and my brothers would die in a car crash so I could grow up with just my father and have everyone feel sorry for me."

Sister James shook her head. "I had all these bad thoughts I didn't want to let go of. Know what I mean?"

I nodded, and presented her with an expression that was meant to register dawning comprehension.

"Good!" she said. She slapped her palms down on the table. "Ready to try again?

I said that I was.

Sister James led me back to the confessional. I knelt and began again: "Bless me Father, for —"

"All right," he said. "We've been here before. Just talk plain."

"Yes, Father."

Again I closed my eyes over my folded hands.

"Come, come," he said, with a certain sharpness.

"Yes, Father." I bent close to the screen and whispered, "Father, I steal."

He was silent for a moment. Then he said, "What do you steal?"

"I steal money, Father. From my mother's purse when she's in the shower."

"How long have you been doing this?"

I didn't answer.

"Well?" he said. "A week? A year? Two years?"

I chose the one in the middle. "A year."

"A year," he repeated. "That won't do. You have to stop. Do you intend to stop?"

"Yes, Father."

"Honestly, now."

"Honestly, Father."

"All right. Good. What else?"

"I'm a backbiter."

"A backbiter?"

"I say things about my friends when they're not around."

"That won't do either," he said.

"No, Father."

"That certainly won't do. Your friends will desert you if you persist in this and let me tell you, a life without friends is no life at all."

"Yes, Father."

"Do you sincerely intend to stop?"

"Yes, Father."

"Good. Be sure that you do. I tell you this in all seriousness. Anything else?"

"I have bad thoughts, Father."

"Yes. Well," he said, "why don't we save those for next time. You have enough to work on."

The priest gave me my penance and absolved me. As I left the confessional I heard his own door open and close. Sister James came forward to meet me again, and we waited together as the priest made his way to where we stood. Breathing hoarsely, he steadied himself against a pillar. He laid his other hand on my shoulder. "That was fine," he said. "Just fine." He gave my shoulder a squeeze. "You have a fine boy here, Sister James."

She smiled. "So I do, Father. So I do."

# The Tobacco Shed

HOME WAS A TRIANGLE OF FARMLAND THE COLOR OF MILK CHOCOLATE. IT ROSE ABOVE the marshes between the Mississippi and the Gulf of Mexico, just west of New Orleans.

Our father grew tobacco. During harvest, we used to hang the stalks in sheds to dry, so we had several on our property. The sheds haunt me. Rain hammering galvanized roofs, swirls and jagged edges in the grain of weathered beams.

Because the structures were dark and mysterious, my sister Amélie and I liked to play in them. Most of all, we liked to play Church in the shed nearest the house. In this game, it was I, twelve and oldest, who played the priest.

I wore the sacred vestments: a purple maternity blouse and a knitted LSU hat with a *pompon* on top. Amélie, who was ten, wore a pleated skirt, high heels, and a straw *chapeau*. A spray of red roses hung from the black velvet band of the hat. It wasn't hard to gather these costumes. We kept them in an armoire in the attic of our house.

Amélie wore red lipstick. I put Brilliantine in my hair, making a part down the middle of my head. I wanted to look like *Grand-grand-père Florestin, Pépère Flo* we called him, who as a middle-aged man posed in a starched shirt and bow tie. The black-and-white photograph hung in an oval above the headboard in our parents' room.

We took the path from our backyard to the tobacco shed at the edge of the pasture. Poison oak covered the facade, the wild vines studded with orange trumpet blooms we dared not touch.

Inside, I stood next to the Sacred Heart nailed to the wall: His bleeding hands, His heart pierced with thorns, suspended in a corona of gold. The second floor of the shed towered over me, the topmost part of its heavy beams disappearing in vaulted darkness.

Before me, Amélie knelt as if at Mass. With a roll of mint Lifesavers in my hand, I gave her the sacred bread, saying in Latin: *Corpus Christi*. She received the Host on her tongue and then inclined her head.

As soon as the ceremony ended, we laughed and laughed and laughed. That's how we made fun of the priest of our Church, *Pépère Patin*.

*Pépère Patin*, who came from France, was all wrinkles. We thought he was a hundred years old. His fair skin and blue eyes were different from ours: olive skin and brown eyes. Patches on his temples seemed bruised and often erupted, leaving clotted blood or scabs.

"You all watch too much *télévision* – and for that, one day, you will all burn in hell!" he would say whenever he came to the house, tipsy from too much wine.

That day in the shed, I egged Amélie on, imitating *Pépère Patin*. I staggered and spat, reproaching her with my pointer finger: "One day, you will burn in hell!"

Suddenly Amélie screamed: "A snake, a snake!" The snake, coiled on a pile of tobacco stems, residue of the last harvest, was in an obscure corner of the shed. When it uncoiled and slithered, a ray of light from the window of the second floor pierced the darkness. We could see black diamonds on its back, their yellow borders on rust.

"He's looking me straight in the eye," I said. But when it slithered too close, we fled, seeking refuge in the house with Mama.

That night, Amélie and I sat on the living room floor to play cards. Between hands of *bourré*, we talked about the snake.

"Do you think it was a regular snake?" I asked.

"What do you mean?"

"Well, the way it looked at me, like it was more than just a snake."

"Maybe it's a sign," Amélie said. "A warning, you know, that we shouldn't laugh at church and *Pépère Patin* and all."

When I woke up the next morning, I thought about the snake. As much as I wanted to, I dared not tell Mama or Daddy what we had done in the shed before its appearance. Was the snake an apparition from God to instruct us?

My conscience told me Amélie was right. We had sinned, we knew it, and we would make our own penance. From then on, we would take seriously the stories *Pépère Patin* preached on Sundays: Adam and Eve in the Garden, Satan tempting Christ in the desert. . . .

To pay for our transgression, we made plans for a play based on a story we had heard countless times on Sunday. We took our little brother Jean with us. We needed him for the play.

"You'll be the most important character," I told him.

Jean smiled, his black eyes bright in his dark face.

Preparations for the play started with a gathering of *piquants*, thorns, from the *piquant-morette* tree. The tree stood near the entrance of the shed. Often, during harvest, in the heat of summer, we nailed nails at the base of tobacco stalks under the shade of this tree, then hung the stalks from the nails to dry.

We found more thorns than we needed. With thorns and *paillasse*, the hemp string we used to tie pound-sized packets of tobacco during harvest, I prepared something for the play.

"What are you doing?" asked Jean.

"You'll see," I said. I grabbed an old potato sack and ripped it at the seam.

"What are you gonna do with that?" Amélie asked.

"You'll see. Hand me the rope and the hammer on top of the barrel, *chère*."

I had found the remnants of an old telephone post standing next to a mule plough in a corner of the shed. I nailed a horizontal plank about halfway from the top of the post; a foot from the bottom, I nailed a second plank, only smaller, creating a platform. Amélie and I stood the post against the great crossbeam at the entrance of the shed.

I wrapped a piece of the sack around Jean's shorts, tied a rope around his waist to hold the cloth in place, and lifted him gently, placing his feet on the small platform at the bottom of the post. I tied Jean to the post with the rope, passing it around his waist.

Then I climbed onto an oak barrel, the kind we filled with tobacco at harvest to put leaves under pressure. I twined the rope loosely around Jean's chest and extended his arms, placing the backs of his hands against the large horizontal plank. Finally, I tied Jean's hands to the plank, providing buffers of sack between his skin and the rope.

"How's that? It doesn't hurt, does it?" I asked.

"Not at all," Jean said.

Then I put the purple and gold LSU hat, turned inside out, on his head. The hat protected him from the crown of thorns I lowered onto his brow.

"It's a game," I said. "But we don't want to be as cruel as the people in the real story of Jesus, right?"

Jean smiled timidly, and then tried to look serious, like a real actor.

Amélie and I danced around the cross. As we gained speed, I

thought of *Madame Grands-Doigts*, the stories *Mémère* used to tell. More than just a figure of folklore, *Madame Grands-Doigts* was real, ever present, and ready to gouge our eyes with her pointed fingernails whenever we misbehaved. Gathering momentum, the Holy Spirit transporting us out of this world, we sang:

Madame Grand-Doigts *will get you.*
Madame Grand-Doigts *will get you.*
*With her sharp claws, sharp claws,*
Madame Grand-Doigts *will get you.*

Jean became frightened and began to struggle against the ropes, kicking his feet on the cross, and crying, "Let me go! It hurts! I'm afraid of *Madame Grands-Doigts!*" We ignored him, continuing to laugh, to dance, and to sing:

Madame Grand-Doigts *will get you.*
Madame Grand-Doigts *will get you.*
*No use to run, no use to run,*
Madame Grand-Doigts *will get you.*

Jean's cries became desperate. He pounded the cross with his feet, and the platform holding him in place loosened.

I signaled Amélie to stop. Then I climbed quickly onto the barrel to untie Jean, but couldn't. The knots had become too tight.

We ran to the house for help, but were afraid to go to the kitchen to tell Mama what we had done. "You tell, Amélie," I said.

Amélie ran to her room, giving me an accusing look. A minute later, I hammered at her door. "Come out, come out! We've got to tell. We can't leave Jean."

Amélie burst from the room. The two of us raced to Mama. We threw ourselves at her, almost knocking her down.

When we found Jean, he was hanging from the cross, his feet having slipped from the platform. His hands were blue, and his head hung on his chest. It looked as if a woodpecker had attacked his forehead. Saliva foamed at his mouth. Twenty minutes later, the ambulance drove across the pasture.

That night, after leaving Jean at the hospital, Mama cried. "You are not my children," she said.

Daddy, equally shocked, gave us a sermon. "And you, because you're oldest, you're most responsible," he said, pointing at me.

The words of our parents hurt us terribly. They might as well have beat us with a leather belt the way Mr. Arceneaux did his children in the middle of the backyard for all the neighbors to see.

"How long will Jean be at the hospital? Will he live?" I asked myself. Despite my efforts to take *Pépère Patin* seriously, I had committed a mortal sin of the worst degree, maybe even murder.

The milk bottles in the *Baltimore Catechism* flashed before me: the first bottle, the white bottle, the soul free of sin; the second, with its few brush strokes, venial sin; and the solid black, third bottle, the lost soul of the mortal sinner. Gauges of good and evil, the milk bottles passed judgment. And now, the undeniably black bottle would send me straight to hell.

On Saturday, Amélie and I confessed our sins to *Pépère Patin*.

"Bless me, Father, for I have sinned," I began. "It has been one week since my last confession."

"What have you done, my girl?"

"I made fun of the Church, and . . ."

"What? Louder. I cannot hear you."

"Father . . . I made fun of you," I murmured.

When I had finished describing what had happened in the shed – the mock-Communion before the arrival of the snake, the episode with Jean – *Pépère Patin* was snoring. I got a whiff of stale wine on his breath. As soon as I stopped talking, he woke up. He bumped his knee on the wall of the confessional. He grunted: "Say ten Our Fathers and ten Hail *Maries*."

"What did he give you for penance, Amélie?" I asked after we had confessed.

"Ten Our Fathers and ten Hail Marys."

We looked at each other. We always compared penances. We knew that if *Pépère Patin* had really listened, he would have given me ten rosaries.

The next morning, at breakfast, Amélie and I sat on the back steps. We could smell discarded coffee grounds on the grass beside us. It started to drizzle. A breeze brought the aroma of tobacco fermenting under pressure in the shed. I couldn't swallow my *grandes pattes* and *café au lait*. I told Amélie about the nightmare I had:

*It was nighttime and the rattlesnake chased me from my bed, through the pasture, all the way to the shed. When I got there, the cross where I had hung Jean was on fire. The snake, coiled around the cross, grimaced at me. Huge teeth stuck out of his mouth. His forked tongue sprang from his throat. He rattled, and the louder he rattled the more the fire burned.*

*He hit me over the head with his rattle. Then I became the snake. My scales glowed in the firelight, my coils got bigger, and sharp teeth pushed out of my mouth.*

*Then Madame Grands-Doigts came. She reached for me with her bony fingers and sharp claws. I thought she would skin me alive.*

*But the scene changed. Jean was hanging on the cross again. Madame Grands-Doigts roared: rah! She gashed Jean's side with her claw. The blood gushed!*

"I hung my little brother. He's going to die. He's going to die, I know he's going to die."

"You didn't intend to do anything mean," Amélie said.

We thought of telling the dream to Mama, but she had disowned us, we were sure. We didn't want to make matters worse, so we kept our distance.

Three days later, Jean came back home. He was feeble, but everybody said he was going to live. Neighbors packed the living room. Mama served cake, made with a coconut she had cracked herself. And we had hand-dripped, French roast coffee – from the French Market – black, black, for those who liked it that way, or with sugar and fresh cream. When the neighbors left, I turned to Mama.

"Mama, can I please talk to Jean? I need to tell him . . ."

"I know, *chere*. He wants to talk to you, too."

I opened the door to Jean's room. I walked to the head of the bed and knelt down. Jean was dozing. I saw the rope burns on his wrists. I reached out and gently touched the red skin. Jean woke up.

"How ya doin'?"

"I'm a little tired."

"They were nice to you at the hospital?"

"Yeah."

"You're glad to be back home?"

"Yeah."

I opened my mouth to say what I wanted to say, but the words stuck on my tongue. The fan hummed on the night table. Daddy's heavy kips walked past the door. Finally, Jean spoke. "My feet slipped off the platform It's not your fault. . . ."

When I cried, Jean reached for me and held me hard on his chest. . . .

I came out of Jean's room. I hugged Mama around the waist, and she put her arms around me. Daddy brushed my hair with his hand, kissed the back of my head.

Amélie and I headed for our tree house. We walked to the cypress tree in the backyard, dodging the large cypress knees jutting from the ground. As we climbed the ladder nailed onto the trunk of the tree, sunlight filtered through moss in the branches. We sat on the floor of the tree house.

"Thank God Jean's alive!" I cried. I looked at Amélie. "I am going to take care of Jean the rest of my life."

Amélie's lips quivered.

I stopped talking. I looked straight ahead, as if in a trance. I had wanted to open Jean's pajama shirt to see the hole *Madame Grands-Doigts* had cut in his side, but I didn't. I rubbed my fingers over the floor of the tree house. My thumb found a protruding nail. I pressed back and forth against the nailhead, saying to myself, "It's going to heal, it's going to heal, I know it's going to heal."

I glanced down at the galvanized roof of the tobacco shed. Daddy's tractor droned in the distance.

SUSANN COKAL

# Immaculate Heart

WE ARE PLAYING OUR FAVORITE GAME. WE PLAY IT EVERY DAY. WE PLAY IT UNDER THE
spreading oak tree, behind the red library that used to be a barn,
west of the white statue of the Virgin where the other girls lay roses
and lilies and sticks of chewing gum. We play until the nuns come
flapping in their black-crow dresses, their tight white wimples
pinching at their red puffing faces, to chase the boys away and tell
me that this is not a good way to play at all.

I am a bad girl, they tell me. A dirty little girl. I push the hair out
of my eyes and tug at my jumper's tight collar, and try to hide the
hole in my knee sock. I'm sorry, Sister, I say, whether it's Sister Agnes or Regina or Saint-Bernard (*Bern*-ard). I go to the bathroom
and wash my hands.

Until then, we play our rushing, pushing game. I am its goal. The
boys rush at me and I stand still, push them hard to the ground if I
like them, harder still if I don't; after two or three pushes, perhaps,
I let one special boy come close, let his special lips graze my cheek,
my brow, my lips.

Seventeen boys have been special in this way. They are the seventeen boys in the fourth grade taught by Sister Regina of the Immaculate Heart of Mary, at the convent of Oak Lawn, in the town of
Lynchburg, Virginia.

First there is Stephen Miller, who is my friend outside of the
game. We are the smartest kids in the class. When we have been

good we are allowed to sit together by the goldfish pond outside the classroom, well in sight of the open French doors. We are supposed to work ahead on our Thinklab cards, but Stephen tells me stories instead – fish stories. His father is an oceanographer and Stephen has hunted and killed octopus (Bite 'em between the eyes), rescued dolphins caught in tuna nets, helped an enormous mother-whale give birth to a calf (Hold on, I'm here for you). For several months, I believe every single word of these stories.

And there is Barry Signet, the most popular boy in our class. I let him kiss me for this reason, because I already like being kissed by the most popular boy. He has broad freckled hands with square orangeish fingernails and he once told me he has a crush on Robin Tuggle, who is very short and wears sneakers with her dresses. I am a little jealous of her, but not much; after all I am the one Barry kisses.

I kiss John-Tyler Jackson, who is the only black boy in our class. I am fascinated by his liquid eyes and smooth, even skin. He is the only such boy I have seen up close, though there are two black girls behind us in the kindergarten. I wonder if my skin will feel a special tingle when he touches it. It does. I let him kiss me twice that day, then notice I tingle whenever any boy's lips touch me.

We are ten years old and it is springtime.

The nuns flap over us – over me. What would your mother say, they ask me. Go play with the girls, and while you're at it, comb your hair. I lay a stick of gum at the Virgin's feet and I continue to play. Under the oak tree, behind the library barn, west of the Virgin.

Eventually my mother is called and told of the dirty thing her daughter is doing. My mother, who will die when I am twenty-eight and still unmarried, giggles riotously and ruffles my hair, telling me she always played with the boys when she was little. She was a tomboy and very popular. She had more boyfriends than her mother could count. I have her blessing.

Then summer comes. Time lies like a blanket over my neighborhood, far from the schoolyard. I play alone.

In the fifth grade, we have the same teacher but the boys are different, more intense. They cluster behind the barn, oak leaves in their hair. They call my name. Some of them are new, but they all want to play.

Now there is Peter Seven, who is very, very thin and who will die when he is fourteen, of a disease whose name no grown-up will speak. When he kisses me his lips are cold butterfly wings.

And Timmy List, whose breath is sour and whose father is the vice president of Pepsi. He takes Sister Regina's whole class on a tour of the plant, where Mr. List treats us to warm, fizzy paper cups of soda. I drop an old peanut in mine and watch it bob up once, twice, and then sink to the bottom wearing a fuzzy coat of bubbles.

And so on, and so on. Seventeen pairs of lips.

I am already growing breasts, puffy red strawberry nipples of which I am alternately proud and ashamed. My mother shows them off. Look, she says to her friends at the grocery store and at the parties she drags me to, how Sigrid is developing. My little girl.

As I get older I will learn that when my mother was in college in the 1960s she had a scholarship but it was taken away because she was dating a black boy. And that she married because she was pregnant with me. And that I might just possibly not be the child of the man I call Daddy. I will be terrified by all this information, from the top of my uncombed head to the scuffy toes of my too-tight saddle shoes.

Meanwhile, in the lunchroom the nuns isolate me. Sisters Regina, Agnes, and Saint-Bernard line up like stern black statues. They give me a booklet called *Very Personally Yours: A Growing Girl's Guide* and tell me no girl my age has come to any good playing with boys. They don't tell me why this is dangerous and bad, only that it is. They don't tell me how the rushing game is different from sitting with Stephen, working on Thinklab cards and listening to fish stories; they just say that it is. Then they escort me to where the girls are playing on the shiny metal jungle gym (a gift from Timmy List's father) – bony knees clinging to bars, short uniform skirts flapping up and up, narrow bottoms in clean flowered panties swaying back and forth. The nuns tell me to play this way.

When the nuns have gone, the boys, led by Stephen Miller, storm the jungle gym. For a moment the girls and boys have a tug-o-war over me, girls pulling my arms, boys hauling on my legs. My saddle shoes come off. The boys of course win, and I run with them to the oak tree, my socks muddy, my breath coming short, my skin already tingling.

It is our game. We were born to play it.

And will we ever let the other girls play? Do they even try?

Not JoJo Bosiger, who is skinny and bossy and challenges the rest of us to footraces, then holds her arms out as she runs so we can't pass her: She would like to join in, but the boys refuse to rush her.

Not Caroline Tallerico, who has thick glasses and extra rolls of fat around her middle; right now I like her because she gave me, for my ninth birthday, a tiny delicate doll's tea set, which I will keep long into my adulthood and then give to my daughters to play with. In junior high Caroline will suddenly grow tall, and skinnier than JoJo, and she will make fun of me for having dirty hair and jeans that end above my ankles.

Or Robin Tuggle, who has received special permission from Sister Saint-Bernard to wear sneakers instead of saddle shoes – I think Barry would like her to play, but she is so little she can't push anyone over, and anyway she spends her lunch hour rushing from the jungle gym to the white stone Mary; reverently laying down her sticks of chewing gum and Twix bars; ecstatically swinging bottoms-up by her bony knees.

These are the girls with whom I am supposed to play. The girls who, after that jungle gym tug-o-war, will start whispering about me and turning away when I approach.

We are starting to grow up. Soon Sister Regina will take the girls aside and impart the secrets of womanhood, the secrets from which not even Mary of the Immaculate Heart was exempt. Soon Peter Seven will withdraw from school and become somebody we only pray about. And very soon, Barry Signet will give Robin Tuggle her first kiss. She will slap him and shove him, in real outrage; he will sprawl on the dirt, legs apart, looking foolish.

As she grows up Robin will shed her Catholicism and join the ministry of a famous Baptist. When he is looking to establish a home for unwed teen mothers, it will be her idea to buy the bankrupt Immaculate Heart – the old mansion where the nuns lived, the schoolrooms where we did our Thinklabs and study the textbooks called *Little Doves*.

So it will be Robin I remember best when I walk here with my husband in the old school grounds long after Barry has gone to jail and Peter and my once-beautiful, always-irresponsible mother have died and Stephen has become a real oceanographer. I will feel Robin's eyes behind every window – the eyes of the girl who was coveted (and by our most popular boy, at that) but not kissed, the girl to whom the nuns gave special privileges.

When I tell this to my husband, he will say I feel only real eyes upon me, the eyes of a couple of dozen unwed teenage girls who got themselves in trouble and whom the Lord, in His mysterious way, has turned his back on.

My husband will already know that I was actually a virgin until twenty-two, that I didn't even enjoy sex until my thirties, that mine was a long, lonely adolescence as the kids at Immaculate Heart joined the nuns in thinking I was somehow unclean. So, out loud, I say only that I still can't escape the damning eyes.

Then we will walk to the oak tree and I will put my arms around him and we will come together in one long, willing kiss in the presence of sin, even as the Immaculate Heart still beats, heavy, inside me.

ANNA QUINDLEN

# *from* How Reading Changed My Life

AS A CATHOLIC GIRL WHO GREW UP IN THE SIXTIES THE MATTER OF BANNED BOOKS HAD always fascinated me. Until Vatican II elevated individual conscience to a more central place in the faith, the church kept an Index of Forbidden Books, or Index Librorum Prohibitorum. Balzac was on the list; so were Dumas and Richardson's *Pamela*. Writing of Catholic culture, the psychologist Eugene Kennedy describes an "acceptable" Catholic novel as "generally a pious work that supported and encouraged Catholic ideals and practices and justified the institution and its control over the lives of its adherents. In such works, the good were rewarded, the erring, terribly punished." In my own Catholic home, and at the homes of my relatives, I remember the works of Bishop Fulton J. Sheen, whose radio show was enormously popular, or *The Day Christ Died* by Jim Bishop, a dramatized account of the road to Calvary. (For the more secular audience, there was also *The Day Lincoln Was Shot* by the same author.)

These books were on the bookshelves of many of our homes when I was growing up. By contrast, the dirty books – for it was a simpler, more black-and-white time, when books were not objectionable or titillating, just dirty – were almost universally to be found between the box spring and the mattress of our parents' beds. To read them – and read them we did – we had to make sure that we were alone in the house and that the bedroom door was latched, much as our parents had to do when they were actually engaged in the acts described in the books, which were far less likely to be novels than so-called marriage manuals. (In the case of my own parents, there was a copy of *Tropic of Cancer*, which I think of rather proudly today, being the only evidence I ever saw that they were forward-thinking in matters of literary taste.)

These were the books from which I learned about the mechanics of sex, but of course mechanics was not really what was wanted at all. I learned about sex, among other things, from another Catholic girl, Mary McCarthy, and the enormously popular and controversial roman à clef about her Vassar classmates entitled *The Group*. I have my original paperback copy, published in 1964, its cover softened with a smattering of daisies, and it still falls open, automatically, to the sections in which the reserved Dorothy loses her virginity and then goes to a clinic to buy a birth-control device. Both the description of female orgasm, and of the hot burning embarrassment that a clinic visit can provoke in a newly sexually active woman, remain quite vivid despite several decades and a sexual revolution. I don't know how other young women learned to identify the sensations of climax, or how mortifying a first visit to a gynecologist can be. I know I learned from Mary McCarthy. Come to think of it, she was my first introduction to lesbianism as well.

But, looking back, I realize it was not so much the sex as the sedition in the book that I found seductive. Like *Tropic of Cancer*, which I did indeed filch from my parents' bedroom, or *Portnoy's Complaint*, or *Peyton Place* or *Lady Chatterley's Lover*, the events of *The Group* were matters that I was not supposed to know about, or even be capable of understanding. The attention of our elders focused on sexual activity, but perhaps other elements were even more corrosive of the conventions: disappointment, infidelity, duplicity, hypocrisy. In all of those books, too, there was a sense of forbidden female license that translated, at some subconscious level, into female freedom. I can remember my mother poring silently over a

copy of *The Feminine Mystique*, the revolutionary book by Betty Frie-
dan describing the worm at the core of the fruit of marriage and
motherhood. But I was too young to have either husband or children; I found feminism, my eyes wide at the infinite variety of the
unknown, in *The Group*, in Kay's suicide, Lakey's lesbianism, the
sad settling that Dorothy makes of her life after her one sexual adventure. All seemed to shout, to belie those daisies on the cover by
shouting, that the lives of intelligent women had to amount to more
than this.

Sedition has been the point of the printed word almost since its
inception, certainly since Martin Luther nailed on that church
door his list of ninety-five complaints against the established
Catholic hierarchy. The printing press led to the Reformation, and
to revolutions, political and sexual. Books made atheists of believers, and made believers of millions whose ancestors knew religious
texts only as works of art, masterpieces hidden away in the monasteries.

And the opposite was true. Ignorance was the preferred condition of the people by despots. In the essay that begins her book on
multiculturalism, a movement toward more inclusionary art and
literature which has been both promulgated and ridiculed by
books, Hazel Rochman recalls the prevailing ethos of the South Af-
rican police state that led her and her husband to put their books in
a box and bury them in the backyard: "Apartheid has made us bury
our books. The Inquisition and the Nazis burned books. Slaves in
the United States were forbidden to read books. From Latin America to Eastern Europe and Asia, books have been trashed. But the
stories are still there."

For some portion of the human race, political upheaval and reform have come through experience, through the oppression of he-
reditary monarchs and the corruption of established churches,
through seats at the back of the bus in the Jim Crow South or sexual

harassment in a heretofore all-male assembly line. But that cannot explain the moral and ethical awakening of those raised in relative comfort and ease, never faced with prejudice or denigration. That was the case with me, and I suspect that it was two books that began the process of making me a liberal. One was the Bible, or at least the New Testament, in which Jesus seemed to take for granted as a necessary part of existence the need to help those who were disenfranchised. The other was by Dickens, who used the gaudy show of character and circumstance so effectively to communicate the realities of social injustice. He does it in *Bleak House* with the stranglehold of law, with debtors' prisons in *Little Dorritt*. But I remember best my first reading of *A Christmas Carol* in which Scrooge bellows, of those who would rather die than go to the workhouses, "They had better do it, and decrease the surplus population." Visions, not words, change Scrooge's mind, and his heart, but when he begs the Ghost of Christmas Present to assure him that his clerk's son, the crippled Tiny Tim, will not die, the spirit taunts him: "What then? If he be like to die, he had better do it, and decrease the surplus population.

"Man," adds the Ghost, "if man you be in heart, not adamant, forbear that wicked cant until you have discovered What the surplus is, and Where it is." A call to social action, a spiritual invocation, and a climactic moment in a wonderful, and wonderfully well wrought, bit of storytelling – so can a book be personal, political, and entertaining, all at the same time.

# *from* Chasing Grace

THE FACT THAT WOMEN WHO ENDURED TWELVE TO SIXTEEN YEARS OF CATHOLIC schools are not all virgins or prostitutes is a miracle.

The first time I consciously registered the word *sex*, I heard it from a nun. I was ten years old. It was my confirmation day. All fifth-grade girls were herded into the auditorium before the morning mass. We shivered in our lightweight polyester white gowns with red satin collars and ridiculous red beanies, ready to become "soldiers in the army of Christ." We had been instructed to wear white shoes and clear stockings. In addition, we were informed that for purposes of "modesty," which I thought meant not bragging about yourself and therefore didn't understand, we were required to wear long, full slips under our gowns. My economy-minded mother responded that it was ridiculous for prepubescent girls (whatever that meant) to be required to wear full slips. And, as the queen of improvisation, she made me try one of her half-slips with one of my regular undershirts. To say that I thought I would die is an understatement. While she was usually immune to protestations of what "every other girl" was doing, she must have registered the absolute terror on my face, because she relented. We bought a full slip, stockings, a garter belt, and flat white shoes.

The stockings and garter belt, which I had long coveted, turned out to be a huge pain in the ass, and I was relieved by the prospect of being able to return to plain socks the next day. I practiced walking in my new white shoes, consciously scuffing them on the sidewalk to prevent the occurrence of the inevitable fall whenever one hundred children walk on highly polished tile in brand-new shoes. At least one person in the class always took a sliding, flying fall in those processions. Most moments of embarrassment are felt far more personally than publicly. While they live on painfully in our own memories, most observers forget them almost immediately after they happen. But despite whatever the poor kid's parents said to comfort her or him – that it was no big deal and would be forgotten by the next day – my guess is that 98 percent of my class can still remember who took flight at our first communion.

Actually, we had two winners that year – Virginia Greeley and Marvin Miller.

Virginia took the spill, topped immediately by Marvin, who accepted his first host and then vomited in front of the entire congregation. He puked all over the highly polished tile floor and his bright white jacket, shirt, short pants, white kneesocks, white shoes, and even his little white bow tie. Other parents commiserated that it was probably the fasting. His parents claimed he had the flu. I figured he gagged on the wafer. If the priest put it way back on your tongue, it could stick to the roof of your mouth, which is why most kids come back from their first communion looking like they are rolling marbles in their mouths. The body of Christ can be difficult to swallow. Those kids are usually trying to dislodge a wafer, not having learned that you had to wait for a little saliva to soften it before you swallowed it. Otherwise, it was like trying to swallow a poker chip.

For the people still embarrassed and teased about their first-communion faux pas, confirmation offered the opportunity to be eclipsed by the next poor kid who would undoubtedly make his or her unique mark on the ceremony and would be taunted with it until eighth-grade graduation.

On the morning of our confirmation, the nuns lined us up by size, warning that they were going to conduct a full-slip inspection. The air in that room was electric with anxiety. Most of us were just at the point where we didn't want anyone to see us under our clothes, not even our mothers. Two nuns traveled down the line ferreting out the girls in half-slips. Offenders were yanked from the line and sent home in disgrace, causing them to miss the morning mass. They would be allowed to participate in the sacrament of confirmation that afternoon, provided they demonstrated proof of a full slip. I couldn't understand the concern. I didn't even know what they were so afraid that people would see. After the instant relief, a collective shame descended upon the rest of us, knowing that those girls were being punished for having something that we *all* had — only we had been more successful in covering it. The crime was not about the full slip. It was about what was under it.

We were instructed to sit down. Sister Carmelita delivered a lecture about what a holy day it was. I'll never forget her next sentence: "This is definitely not a day to be thinking about sex." *Sex*, I thought, *what's that?* It is hard to believe these days, when even three-year-old girls want to be "sexy," that we were so clueless about that word. But we were. Since second grade I had heard the euphemisms — immodest, impure, cheap, loose, dirty. But they had only the vaguest meaning.

In the paradoxical way that being told not to do something makes doing it so much more attractive, I thought about the sex thing all day. It connected with less conscious memories of the word overheard in whispers among the eighth-grade girls, or on the playgrounds with the older boys. It connected in some diffuse way to the general sense that becoming a full-grown woman was not an altogether good thing. The vigilance against betraying a woman's normal, healthy body was not stated outright to us yet. No one ever said, "Women are filth," although many of the scriptural references, such as making the name *woman* (as represented in Eve) synonymous with "the fall of man," came close. Saint Paul's blatant misogyny was recited from the pulpit without anyone trying to give it a context or qualify it in any way. The horrible things that those romantic women saints did to their developing bodies, in the name of Christ, would probably have appalled him. The sense of impending shame connected with the church's obsession with virginity, another word I still didn't understand but knew was related *only* to women and was paired with words like *immaculate, pure,* and *without sin.*

I knew it in the prohibition against "touching yourself." I knew it in the confused shame I felt after being harshly censured by a nun for linking pinkies with a favored friend. As we walked around the school yard, swinging our arms held together by our smallest fingers, she came up behind us and yelled, "What are you girls doing?"

"Nothing, Sister." Which was true.

"You will stop that immediately."

"Stop what, Sister?" I laughed anxiously, thinking that maybe she was kidding.

"Don't ever let me see you touching another girl in that way again."

*What way?*

But it connected most deeply for me in seeing how the church treated my mother. She steamed for weeks after a priest, from the pulpit, warned that women were bordering close to the brink of immodesty by wearing shorts. Not shorts *in church,* shorts in general. He wasn't talking about short, short cheek-huggers, either. He was talking about the kind of long, baggy Bermuda shorts that my mother had worn since childhood. For good measure, he also deemed sleeveless blouses and dresses immodest. My mother was usually reticent about criticizing the church in front of us. But as the priest spoke, I saw her hand – the one that didn't have a baby in it – stiffen around the pew in front to her. I could see her back straighten and her head tilt back, with her chin jutting out just a little in that wonderfully silent way of saying, *Yeah, and what are you gonna do about it?* She was quiet on the walk home. As we all retired to our separate rooms to change out of our church clothes, I could hear my mother behind her bedroom door. Despite the whispering, I could tell she was furious, and that my father was in total agreement. Hearing my parents break ranks with the church always gave me tremendous pleasure, and pride in knowing that I was on the right team. I heard my father say, "Pompous ass," which appeared to soothe my mother. She emerged several minutes later in a pair of plaid Bermuda shorts and a white sleeveless blouse.

But the worst was still to come. My mother was active in many aspects of the life of our parish, including teaching high-school Sunday school. Every week she let me grade the regular multiple-choice quizzes using a red pencil and the answer key from her textbook. It was much better than coercing my sisters and brothers into playing school. I loved marking older kids wrong. But in the middle of the year, my mother was "let go," which was a difficult thing for a Sunday school to do. It's not as if people were lined up waiting for those jobs. It was suggested to my mother that it would be better "for all concerned" if she withdrew from teaching for the rest of the year. I couldn't understand it. My mother was one of the smartest people I knew, capable of running a company, let alone a classroom. I knew kids who'd had her as a teacher and liked her. Why?

My mother was forced into an early retirement because she was pregnant – the Catholic way: five children in ten years. But I still didn't understand why that warranted early "retirement." When I asked my mother, she grimaced and answered, "Because I'm showing." My mother was pregnant so much, she was always "showing" as far as I was concerned. I didn't realize that those wise priests had determined that the vision of my mother standing in front of a high-school class would, in an "in-your-face" kind of way, be saying to her students, "Guess what I did to look like this?" No one even made a pretense of telling my mother that it was for *her* — take some time off, put your feet up. My mother carried children and grocery bags. She lugged baskets of laundry to the clothesline. She carried out the garbage, and she pushed the lawn mower. Nothing was said about what my mother might need. She wasn't "let go" for her. It wasn't for her students. It was for *them*. And even I knew it.

# Guadalupe the Sex Goddess

IN HIGH SCHOOL I MARVELED AT HOW WHITE WOMEN STRUTTED AROUND THE LOCKER room, nude as pearls, as unashamed of their brilliant bodies as the Nike of Samothrace. Maybe they were hiding terrible secrets like bulimia or anorexia, but to my naive eye then, I thought of them as women comfortable in their skin.

You could always tell us Latinas. We hid when we undressed, modestly facing a wall, or, in my case, dressing in a bathroom stall. We were the ones who still used bulky sanitary pads instead of tampons, thinking ourselves morally superior to our white classmates. *My mama said you can't use tampons till after you're married.* All Latina mamas said this, yet how come none of us thought to ask our mothers why they didn't use tampons *after* getting married?

Womanhood was full of mysteries. I was as ignorant about my own body as any female ancestor who hid behind a sheet with a hole in the center when husband or doctor called. Religion and our culture, our culture and religion, helped to create that blur, a vagueness about what went on "down there." (So ashamed was I about my own "down there" that until I was an adult I had no idea I had another orifice called the vagina; I thought my period would arrive via the urethra or perhaps through the walls of my skin.)

No wonder, then, it was too terrible to think about a doctor — a man! — looking at you down there when you could never bring yourself to look yourself. *¡Ay, nunca!* How could I acknowledge my sexuality, let alone enjoy sex, with so much guilt? In the guise of modesty my culture locked me in a double chastity belt of ignorance and *vergüenza*, shame.

I had never seen my mother nude. I had never taken a good look at myself either. Privacy for self-exploration belonged to the wealthy. In my home a private space was practically impossible; aside from the doors that opened to the street, the only room with a lock was the bathroom, and how could anyone who shared a bathroom with eight other people stay in there for more than a few minutes? Before college, no one in my family had a room of their own except me, a narrow closet just big enough for my twin bed and an oversized blond dresser we'd bought in the bargain basement of *el Sears*. The dresser was as long as a coffin and blocked the door from shutting completely. I had my own room, but I never had the luxury of shutting the door.

I didn't even see my own sex until a nurse at an Emma Goldman Clinic showed it to me — *Would you like to see your cervix? Your os is dilating. You must be ovulating. Here's a mirror, take a look.* When had anyone ever suggested I take a look or allowed me a speculum to take home and investigate myself at leisure!

I'd only been to one other birth control facility prior to the Emma Goldman Clinic, the university medical center in grad school. I was twenty-one, in a strange town far from home for the first time. I was afraid and I was ashamed to seek out a gynecologist, but I was more afraid of becoming pregnant. Still, I agonized about going for weeks. Perhaps the anonymity and distance from my family allowed me finally to take control of my life. I remember wanting to be fearless like the other women around me, to be able to have sex when I wanted, but I was too afraid to explain to a would-be lover how I'd only had one other man in my life and we'd practiced withdrawal. Would he laugh at me? How could I look anyone in the face and explain why I couldn't go see a gynecologist?

One night a classmate I liked too much took me home with him. I meant all along to say something about how I wasn't on anything, but I never quite found my voice, never the right moment to cry out – *Stop, this is dangerous to my brilliant career!* Too afraid to sound stupid, afraid to ask him to take responsibility too, I said nothing, and I let him take me like that with nothing protecting me from motherhood but luck. The days that followed were torture, but fortunately on Mother's Day my period arrived, and I celebrated my nonmaternity by making an appointment with the family-planning center.

When I see pregnant teens, I can't help but think that could've been me. In high school I would've thrown myself into love the way some warriors throw themselves into fighting. I was ready to sacrifice everything in the name of love, to do anything, even risk my own life, but thankfully there were no takers. I was enrolled at an all-girls' school. I think if I had met a boy who would have me, I would've had sex in a minute, convinced this was love. I have always had enough imagination to fall in love all by myself, then and now.

I tell you this story because I am overwhelmed by the silence regarding Latinas and our bodies. If I, as a graduate student, was shy about talking to anyone about my body and sex, imagine how difficult it must be for a young girl in middle school or high school living in a home with no lock on the bedroom door, perhaps with no door, or maybe with no bedroom, no information other than misinformation from the girlfriends and the boyfriend. So much guilt, so much silence, and such a yearning to be loved; no wonder young women find themselves having sex while they are still children, having sex without sexual protection, too ashamed to confide their feelings and fears to anyone.

What a culture of denial. Don't get pregnant! But no one tells you how not to. This is why I was angry for so many years every time I saw *la Virgen de Guadalupe,* my culture's role model for brown women like me. She was damn dangerous, an ideal so lofty and un-realistic it was laughable. Did boys have to aspire to be Jesus? I never saw any evidence of it. They were fornicating like rabbits while the Church ignored them and pointed us women toward our destiny – marriage and motherhood. The other alternative was *puta*hood.

In my neighborhood I knew only real women, neither saints nor whores, naive and vulnerable *huerquitas* like me who wanted desperately to fall in love, with the heart and soul. And yes, with the *panocha*, too.

As far as I could see, *la Lupe* was nothing but a goody two shoes meant to doom me to a life of unhappiness. Thanks but no thanks. Motherhood and/or marriage were anathema to my career. But being a bad girl, that was something I could use as a writer, a Molotov to toss at my papa and *el Papa* who had their own plans for me.

Discovering sex was like discovering writing. It was powerful in a way I couldn't explain. Like writing, you had to go beyond the guilt and shame to get to anything good. Like writing, it could take you to deep and mysterious subterranean levels. With each new depth I found out things about myself I didn't know I knew. And, like writing, for a slip of a moment it could be spiritual, the cosmos pivoting on a pin, could empty and fill you all at once like a Ganges, a Piazzolla tango, a tulip bending in the wind. I was no one, I was nothing, and I was everything in the universe little and large – twig, cloud, sky. How had this incredible energy been denied me!

When I look at *la Virgen de Guadalupe* now, she is not the Lupe of my childhood, no longer the one in my grandparents' house in Tepeyac, nor is she the one of the Roman Catholic Church, the one I bolted the door against in my teens and twenties. Like every woman who matters to me, I have had to search for her in the rubble of history. And I have found her. She is Guadalupe the sex goddess, a goddess who makes me feel good about my sexual power, my sexual energy, who reminds me I must, as Clarissa Pinkola Estés so aptly put it, "[speak] from the vulva . . . speak the most basic, honest truth," and write from my *panocha*.

In my research of Guadalupe's pre-Columbian antecedents, the she before the Church desexed her, I found Tonantzin, and inside Tonantzin a pantheon of other mother goddesses. I discovered Tlazolteotl, the goddess of fertility and sex, also referred to as Totzin, Our Beginnings, or Tzinteotl, goddess of the rump. *Putas,* nymphos, and other loose women were known as "women of the sex goddess." Tlazolteotl was the patron of sexual passion, and though she had the power to stir you to sin, she could also forgive you and cleanse you of your sexual transgressions via her priests who heard confession. In this aspect of confessor Tlazolteotl was known as Tlaelcuani, the filth eater. Maybe you've seen her; she's the one sold in the tourist markets even now, a statue of a woman squatting in childbirth, her face grimacing in pain. Tlazolteotl, then, is a duality of maternity *and* sexuality. In other words, she is a sexy mama.

To me *la Virgen de Guadalupe* is also Coatlicue, the creative/destructive goddess. When I think of the Coatlicue statue in the National Museum in Mexico City, so terrible it was unearthed and then reburied because it was too frightening to look at, I think of a woman enraged, a woman as tempest, a woman *bien berrinchuda,* and I like that. *La Lupe* as *cabrona.* Not silent and passive, but silently gathering force.

Most days I, too, feel like the creative/destructive goddess Coatlicue, especially the days I'm writing, capable of fabricating pretty tales with pretty words, as well as doing demolition work with a volley of *palabrotas* if I want to. I am the Coatlicue-Lupe whose square column of a body I see in so many Indian women, in my mother, and in myself each time I check out my thick-waisted, flat-assed torso in the mirror.

Coatlicue, Tlazolteotl, Tonantzin, *la Virgen de Guadalupe.* They are each telescoped one into the other, into who I am. And this is where *la Lupe* intrigues me – not the Lupe of 1531 who appeared to Juan Diego, but the one of the 1990s who has shaped who we are as Chicanas/*mexicanas* today, the one inside each Chicana and *mexicana*. Perhaps it's the Tlazolteotl-Lupe in me whose *malcriada* spirit inspires me to leap into the swimming pool naked or dance on a table with a skirt on my head. Maybe it's my Coatlicue-Lupe attitude that makes it possible for my mother to tell me, *No wonder men can't stand you.* Who knows? What I do know is this; I am obsessed with becoming a woman comfortable in her skin.

I can't attribute my religious conversion to a flash of lightning on the road to Laredo or anything like that. Instead, there have been several lessons learned subtly over a period of time. A grave depression and near suicide in my thirty-third year and its subsequent retrospection. Vietnamese Buddhist monk Thich Nhat Hanh's writing that has brought out the Buddha-Lupe in me. My weekly peace vigil for my friend Jasna in Sarajevo. The writings of Gloria Anzaldúa. A crucial trip back to Tepeyac in 1985 with Cherríe Moraga and Norma Alarcón. Drives across Texas talking with other Chicanas. And research for stories that would force me back inside the Church from which I'd fled.

My *Virgen de Guadalupe* is not the mother of God. She is God. She is a face for a god without a face, an *indígena* for a god without ethnicity, a female deity for a god who is genderless, but I also understand that for her to approach me, for me to finally open the door and accept her, she had to be a woman like me.

Once, watching a porn film, I saw a sight that terrified me. It was the film star's *panocha* – a tidy, elliptical opening, pink and shiny like a rabbit's ear. To make matters worse, it was shaved and looked especially childlike and unsexual. I think what startled me most was the realization that my own sex has no resemblance to this woman's. My sex, dark as an orchid, rubbery and blue purple as *pulpo*, an octopus, does not look nice and tidy, but otherworldly. I do not have little rosette nipples. My nipples are big and brown, like the Mexican coins of my childhood.

When I see *la Virgen de Guadalupe* I want to lift her dress as I did my dolls' and look to see if she comes with *chones*, and does her *panocha* look like mine, and does she have dark nipples too? Yes, I am certain she does. She is not neuter like Barbie. She gave birth. She has a womb. *Blessed art thou and blessed is the fruit of thy womb . . .* Blessed art thou, Lupe, and, therefore, blessed am I.

ROBERT LACY

# A Yellow Rose in Texas

MOTHER CONVERTED TO CATHOLICISM WHEN I WAS TWELVE AND DRAGGED ME ALONG
with her. Exactly why she did it, I have never been sure. One of the
women she worked with was Catholic, though, from an old German
family there in town, and I've always assumed that had something
to do with it. Also, I think Mother, as a widow, found comfort in the
rituals of the (pre–Vatican II) Catholic liturgy, and maybe a sense of
community in being able to count herself among the small band of
"outsiders" who made up the congregation at Saint Joseph's
Church. This was in staunchly Baptist East Texas, after all, and
many of her fellow parishioners had such distinctly un–East Texas-
sounding names as Maranto and Caccioppia and Dufresne.

My father had been killed when I was five. He was a truck driver,
among other things, and had died in a highway accident down near
Conroe on the eve of World War Two. He'd come over from Alabama
in the Depression to get rich in the Great East Texas Oil Field and
had met Mother while clerking in a grocery store. They were already separated at the time of his death. I have never known why.
"It wasn't a very good marriage, Bob," was all Mother would ever
tell me.

For a time during the war we shared a house in Houston with
Mother's younger brother and his wife and two kids, my cousins,
while mother worked as an "expediter" at Brown Shipyard (where
she managed to get her picture taken, sitting on a box with her hard

hat pushed back and a clipboard in her hands, by a Houston *Post* photographer). But mostly, in those years and ever afterwards, it was just the two of us.

After the war, back up in East Texas, with jobs suddenly scarce and money tight, Mother went to work for Darco, a lignite-processing plant on the outskirts of Marshall. I can remember, with some bitterness, that as late as 1949, with me already in junior high school, they were paying her fifty cents an hour – and working her seven days a week. This was before Texas, among the last of the states in the union to do so, passed a law against that kind of thing. All the law said back then was that you couldn't force a person to work more than fifty hours a week. So Darco had put her on seven seven-hour days.

Mother worked in their lab "down on the plant," running samples on the product, a powdery, low-grade form of coal used as a purifying agent in syrups, soft drinks, and the like. It was filthy work. She used to come home in the evenings with her coveralls caked stiff with lignite, and big, round, raccoonlike rings around her eyes where her safety goggles had been.

But Darco was also where she met Kathleen Resch, the woman from the German family, which led to her joining the Catholic Church.

The head pastor of Saint Joseph's Parish in those days was a magnificent old priest named Father Meier. A notoriously soft touch to vagrants and other strangers passing through, he could nonetheless be brutally frank in his assessments of human frailty and was a stern overseer to anyone in his charge. Father Meier practiced tough love long before the phrase became current. The church maintained a flophouse for down-and-outers across the street from its side entrance. Told one day that its current occupants had managed to clog up the plumbing yet again, and asked what should be done about it, he was said to have replied, "I don't care. Let 'em shit on the floor."

Saint Joseph's was a very poor parish, even by the standards of hardscrabble East Texas. The congregation was small, and it included few of the town's professional people, or others likely to be generous when the offering plate came around. Being chronically strapped for funds forced Father Meier to exercise ingenuity when it came to hiring his assistant pastors. What he did was recruit them from Via Coeli, the infamous sanctuary and drying-out facility for "troubled priests" out in northern New Mexico.

During my years as a member of Saint Joseph's we must have had half a dozen of these wounded souls serving in various capacities around the parish at one time or another. They were without exception able, intelligent, *interesting* men. Well-educated and much-traveled, they brought to Marshall a worldliness we weren't accustomed to. Of course, some of them brought a little too much worldliness. That had been their problem.

There was Father Kavanaugh, for instance. Compact, curly-headed, and red of face, he was a real dynamo when it came to organizing men's retreats and fund-raising spaghetti suppers. He also delivered such eloquent Sunday sermons that Father Meier, whose task it ordinarily was, would often let him celebrate the ten o'clock High Mass in his stead. Father Kavanaugh lasted with us nearly three years, his tenure coming to an end only after he locked himself into the top floor of the rectory one rainy Easter weekend and proceeded to drink two fifths of whiskey and a case of Falstaff beer.

Then there was Father Raekemper, the handyman. There was hardly anything Father Raekemper couldn't fix. He replaced all the hinges on the rectory doors and all the window screens at Saint Anne's Convent School. He also rebuilt the boiler in the church basement and fine-tuned Father Meier's old car until it was the smoothest running '48 Packard in town. But then one night he jimmied his own lock off the sacristy door and got into the Communion wine. We never saw him again after that.

And finally there was Father Gormley. He was my favorite. Born in County Cavan, Ireland, he had come over to this country as a teenager, and had gone to school, on a City of New York Scholarship, as I remember it, at Fordham. Small-boned and sprightly, and with a shock of unruly black hair, he had a lovely tenor voice and a way of speaking to you that made everything he said sound musical. All we were told about him when he arrived, in the wake of Father Raekemper's sudden departure, was that drink was not his problem.

Mother had been just twenty-seven when she was widowed, but she never remarried. Partly this was due, I think, to her unhappy experience the first time around. She'd made a mistake, she felt — her family, especially my grandmother, had let her *know* she'd made one — and she wasn't going to do so again. Partly too, though, I think, it was due to Mother's personality. She was fiercely independent, for one thing, and the same contrarian streak that had led her to join the Catholic Church in the midst of all those Protestants also made it hard for her to get along with people generally. Mother chose her friends carefully. The reason she liked Kathleen Resch, she told me once, was that "She's as mean as I am."

Not that Mother didn't go out with other men while I was growing up; she did. I remember one I especially liked. He was an insurance agent there in town and had something to do with the Texas A & M Athletic Department, as a football recruiter or scout or something, and I can recall the two of them going away on a train for a weekend in Dallas at the time of the Cotton Bowl. He was a big, cheerful man who seemed to like me, and I had no trouble at all in picturing him as a daddy. But nothing ever came of it.

She also dated for a time, just as I was entering junior high school, a gentleman named Manoogian who had come to town to manage the local overall factory. I didn't much care for him, could never get used to the smell of his cigars and the sound of his loud, cocksure laughter. And when he ultimately threw Mother over for his twenty-six-year-old secretary, I figured it was just as well. Bobby *Manoogian?* It was not a name I particularly cared to carry around with me anyway.

"Don't cry, Mama," I can remember telling her. "At least we won't have those cigars lying around the house anymore."

This was the period when Mother was converting to the Catholic Church, and we had begun to spend a lot of time, she and I, at the home of Kathleen Resch, mother's coworker out at Darco. Unmarried, and a confirmed spinster, Kathleen lived with her family in a large two-story stone house there on the square in Marshall. Her mother's maiden name had been Umdenstock and that word was worked into the wrought-iron gate out front of the premises. The Umdenstocks were among the earliest settlers in Marshall, I was told; their house had been built by slaves. On the mantel in a front room was a baroque gold clock under glass, with a plaque on it commemorating the Louisiana Purchase.

All the priests used to hang out at the Resch house. There was usually plenty to eat there (and to drink, too, now that I think of it). Lots of penny-ante poker hands got dealt around the big black table in the Resch's dining room, amid lots of cries of "You're bluffing, Father Kavanaugh!" and "Read 'em and weep, Kathleen!"

There was an upright piano in one of the rooms, and most evenings would end with whoever-all was there grouped around it, singing. This was when Father Gormley would shine. He really did have a fine tenor voice; a bit weak on the highest notes maybe, but filled with feeling, always, and purer than spring rain on the rest.

"Danny Boy" was one of his staples, of course, but he also did "Kathleen Mavourneen" in honor of our hostess; "My Love Is from the North Countree" (a James Joyce favorite, I would later learn in graduate school); the mournful Irish ballad "A Long Farewell"; and even "The Yellow Rose of Texas" from time to time, because, as he said, he liked "the lilt of it."

Mother, who was tone deaf and couldn't carry a tune in a peach basket, would usually hang back during these group singings. But I can remember seeing her more than once with her eyes shut tight and her shoulders swaying as Father Gormley moved up and down the scales on one of his ballads. His voice had that effect on people.

Although undersized and comically thin, I was doing my best at this time to excel at the game of football, it being so much a part of East Texas culture. I had tried out for and finally made the junior high school team as a ninth-grader, and as I entered high school, taller now but still too lean in the shanks, I continued to chase after gridiron glory — so much so that my grades had begun to suffer.

Into this breach stepped Father Gormley. When it wasn't occupied with cards and poker chips, he turned the Resch dinner table into a study hall for me. And while others went about their socializing all around us, he put me through my paces academically. Math and science were my weakest subjects, and these turned out to be particular strengths of his. He used to drill me endlessly on geometry theorems and the basic algebra equations.

"Ach, you may be grand at kickin' a ball around, Bobby," he'd tell me. "But you'll still need to square yoor hypotenuse."

Mother and I were living over in Pinecrest Addition at the time, having moved there to take advantage of the falling mortgage rates of the early 1950s, and he began appearing at our doorstep occasionally on weekends, to check up, he said, on my studies.

"As I was out and about in the neighborhood," he'd say, "I figured I might as well flush out any lurking scholars." (He pronounced it "loorking.")

Mother would invite him into our little living room, ask him if he'd like some iced tea or coffee, and then leave the two of us to my homework as she went about her weekend chores of scrubbing the kitchen and the bathroom. He must have stopped by half a dozen times like this over the course of several months.

And then one rainy autumn afternoon in the middle of the week I came home early from football practice to find him sitting in the living room with Mother.

"Why, here's the auld fella now!" he said, jumping up from the sofa as I walked in. "We've been waitin' for ye! Yoor mother tells me you're becomin' a dab hand at the algebra!"

Mother had risen from the sofa too when I came in, and she was saying, "Well! You're home a little early, aren't you? I thought you had a scrimmage today."

"The field's all soggy," I said. "Coach sent us home."

"Too wet to plow, is it?" Father Gormley said.

"Yes, sir," I said. "Or anything else."

"Well!" Mother said again. "Let's get you some supper fixed! Charlie, uh, Father Gormley, was just leaving." She turned to him. "Weren't you, Father?"

"Indeed, indeed," Father Gormley said. "I'd best be on my way. Father Meier will be wantin' his car back."

"Don't let me run you off," I said. "I'll just go make myself a sandwich."

"No, no, it's time to go," he said. "It's time to go. Belle will see me to the door."

My mother's name was Sally Belle. Some people called her Sally; some people called her Belle. I've always thought it was the prettiest name imaginable. At this time she would have been about forty years old and still a handsome woman. She saw Father Gormley to the door.

In the weeks and months that followed I never came home to find them on the sofa again, but I did overhear mother on the phone a time or two when she didn't seem to want to be overheard. Once, I'm fairly certain I heard her call her phonemate "Charlie."

But then one day toward Christmas of that year – funny how these things always seemed to happen around the Church's high holidays – Father Gormley was no longer there. Suddenly, over-night, he was gone. Just like Father Kavanaugh. Just like Father Raekemper. And there was never any official explanation. It was simply a matter of now you see him, now you don't.

We missed Father Gormley around the piano at the Resches, and at the poker table. And, forced to confront alone that spring the sorrowful mysteries of trigonometry, I could've used him at the coffee table in our living room. But in the aftermath of his sudden disappearance nobody seemed to want to talk about where he'd gone, or why. It was as if a conspiracy of silence had enveloped Saint Joseph's Parish, as if a great circling of the wagons had taken place as our the little Catholic community sought to cut its losses, keep its casualties hidden from the wider view.

I myself came close to bringing it up only once, one Sunday morning as mother and I were on our way to Mass. Something had caused me to remember the missing priest, and I turned to Mother and said, "Mama, I was wondering. What d'you suppose ever hap-pened to Father Gor –"

But that was as far as I got. We were in our little used Chevrolet coupe; I was driving, and the look in her eyes told me to drop the subject, right there. So I did.

This all happened in my junior year in high school. Gradually, we forgot about Father Gormley. He was just another wayfarer, after all, just another cut-rate priest Father Meier had coaxed down out of the hills of New Mexico. I managed to master trig on my own, and others arrived to fill out the poker games around the Resches table. No one could be found to hit the high notes on "Danny Boy," though, or impart the proper lilt to "The Yellow Rose of Texas."

I never saw Father Gormley again – not face to face anyway. But something did happen a couple of years later that I've turned over in my mind a few times since. In the fall of that year, having finally come into my size, I had gone off up to Paris Junior College, in the north-central part of the state, on a football scholarship. Paris was about a hundred miles from Marshall, and I used to hitchhike home on weekends with my suitcase stuffed with dirty shirts and underwear for Mother to wash.

One Friday evening my ride let me off down at the far end of our street, and as I was making my way up toward the house, suitcase in hand, I saw someone come hurrying out the front door, climb into the town's lone taxi, and leave. It was a man. He was about Father Gormley's size, and he moved with the peculiar rolling gait the little priest had. But the light wasn't good, and I couldn't see his face, and, besides, this fellow was wearing civilian clothes: some light-colored slacks and a cardigan.

Was it him? I didn't know then; I don't know now. Something told me not to bring it up with Mother, though. So I went on into the house that night, unloaded my dirty clothes on her, and never did.

Mother is dead now. She succumbed to stomach cancer several years ago. Her life was not a happy one. Through hard work and perseverence she finally managed to achieve the financial security she'd always longed for – no more days of fifty cents an hour, seven days a week – and her retirement years were well provided for. But she was alone, as she had been so much of her adult life, and she was lonely. She used to call me on the telephone late at night wherever I was – in the Marines, at college, or in one of the little university towns where I used to teach – and I could tell by the slur in her voice, usually, that she'd been drinking.

She died a devout Roman Catholic and was given the last rites and traditional burial honors of the Church. There was a Funeral Mass for her in Saint Joseph's chapel. I had flown down from Minneapolis, which is where I live these days, to be with her in her final weeks. It rained the day of the funeral – hard, cold, driving – and the priest who presided at the gravesite, a new one I had never met, wore a quilted parka over his cassock, and cowboy boots, I happened to notice, underneath it. He was a large, heavyset man, a bit wild-eyed, and though Father Meier himself was long dead by then I found myself wondering, *Via Coeli?*

In going through Mother's belongings afterward, preparatory to the estate sale that would liquidate most of them, I found in a trunk, among a lot of other stuff, some photographs I'd never seen before. They were in a big manila envelope, and most of them were of a fairly routine sort: pictures of family, of fellow workers out at Darco, of friends, and dogs, and other people's grandchildren. But one of them wasn't routine at all. It was a picture of Mother and Father Gormley that looked to have been taken about twenty-five years earlier. It showed the two of them seated side by side on a picnic table at a park somewhere. There were other people in the background, but in the picture Mother and Father Gormley were very much apart from them, and very much together. They were smiling at the camera almost impishly and the looks on their faces were identical. The looks said, "Yes, this is us, together, and we are having fun." There was such a suggestion of intimacy to the whole thing that it made me wonder who had taken the picture. Kathleen Resch?

Also in the manila envelope, protected within a little glassine envelope of its own, was a flower stem with a crisp brown leaf still attached to it. Smashed together at the bottom of the envelope were half a dozen brown petals and a white business card. The card carried the logo of an air-conditioning firm in Silver Spring, Maryland, but the name on it read "Charles A. Gormley, S. J." And underneath that were a Maryland address and two telephone numbers: the original number and another one that had been written in in pencil beneath it after the original had been lined out.

I have saved the picture, but not the card, and not the flower. I had no desire then, at that late date, to try to contact its giver. And I certainly have no wish now, at this even later date, to do so. I assume Father Gormley is long dead, too. If he's not, he's a very old man. I do take the picture out from time to time and look at it. It's such a happy shot, and such a pleasant way to remember Mother.

Did anything *untoward* ever happen between her and Father Gormley? I don't know, of course, and I have no real interest in finding out. They're both gone, and I've long since drifted away from the Church, so what could it possibly matter? Whenever the question occurs to me, though, and I confess it does occasionally, I always find myself hoping so – devoutly.

# *from* An American Requiem

I HAVE A PHOTOGRAPH IN FRONT OF ME THAT SHOWS MY FATHER IN HIS NEW UNIFORM, shiny brass buttons, flap pockets and all. He is standing on the lawn outside our Arlington apartment. I am standing next to him. He is holding my hand. I am four years old. My father in his peaked cap is looking off to the left with a benign smile that has always made me hope he is looking at my mother. I am wearing a uniform too, a fringed cowboy vest, gun belt, and boots. My eyes are in shadow, but otherwise the expression on my face is slightly stunned, as if I appreciate all that has happened to us in a few short years. Perhaps I know something else already, the other large event, the counter-vailing catastrophe that instantly and permanently undid every feeling my mother and father had of being lucky. The precise timing has always been unclear to me, but one day in this same period, my brother Joe fell down, and he could not get up again. Our mother took him to the doctor, who knew at once what to look for. Our father was summoned from his office, and this time he came. Their first-born son, the seal of a love that wasn't to have been, the issue of flesh that was weak, a child conceived in the Irish Church's idea of sin, my older brother, my lively partner in the world of radio, in the cult of bunk beds, my teacher and first friend, the one with whom I secretly shared a name – Joe had infantile paralysis, poliomyelitis, Roosevelt's disease, polio.

I remember the living room of our apartment on South Sixteenth Street, the Lady Davenport on the wall, the red couch, the figurine-laden glass shelves in the window. Four or five years old, I am sitting on the couch when they bring Joe home from the hospital for the first time. My father is carrying him. Joe smiles at me, as if privileged. I refuse at first to get off the couch, where he must lie now. My mother screams at me, the first remembered time. I run from the room, fighting off the consoling pleasure of my knowledge that Joe cannot run after me.

Behind and above my father and me, in this photograph, stands a telephone pole. This same picture sat on my table when I was a seminarian, and I recall the day I first saw that telephone pole as a crucifix. "The end of learning," Samuel Johnson wrote, "is piety." And the end, also, of a hard-won self-acceptance. There was a time in my life when I saw crucifixes everywhere – in soaring airplanes, in the joints of windowpanes, in radiator grilles, in the fall of toothpicks on a table. Polio brought the cross back into our family, where it belonged. Our religion meant one thing only, that God came onto the earth to show us, so vividly, so unforgettably, that every human being has, as Mom would never tire of saying, "a cross to bear." The phrase deflects from its own meaning, that each of us – "Drink ye all of this" – is crucified. Joe's fate – he would have a severe case of the disease, undergoing a dozen operations over the next fifteen years, forfeiting his childhood and walking with a savage limp for life – seized my parents like claws reaching up from the stockyards bog to haul them back into the fetid world from which they came, a crone chorus – Irish hags, the nuns – screeching, "Who did you think you were? How dare you think you can escape!"

After Joe got polio, our roles reversed. I did not openly claim the name in which I too had been baptized, but I usurped his place in other ways, a pseudo-older brother, sibling born to lead, to try things first, to help with chores, to mind the baby, and, later, to be the outgoing one, the Carroll boys' little representative. I did everything asked of me, and more than was expected. Yet my every success, since it came at Joe's expense, would feel like failure – a sad pattern grooved into my psyche to this day.

Mom did mute penance, nailing herself to the cross of her first son's suffering. The rest of us would compete for the dregs of her attention. His having caught one of the three viruses that caused polio – Joe and I agreed that he'd gotten it drinking from the creek that ran near our apartment house – was her fault, wasn't it? What else had she to do in life than protect her children? Or was it somehow my fault? Had I been first to slurp the forbidden water, giving him the idea? It was as if I were already older, guilty for giving bad example. I remember Joe telling me that if one of us had to get polio, he was glad it was he, a sentiment that seemed in no way noble to me. I envied him his suffering.

Mom became our own Pietà. The spontaneous, wisecracking, affectionate young woman I first knew, as it were, simply packed up and moved out, to be replaced by the Mother of Sorrows herself, a woman privileged to be in pain. Our father, meanwhile, fleeing the sure Jansenist knowledge that his own hubris, not polluted water or "germs," was the true cause of his son's polio – a perfect punishment if ever there was one, just at the time of his great achievement – he fled from us too, Joe junior for sure, a rebuke embodied; and long-suffering Mary; and also me. One might have expected that with our mother entirely taken up with Joe, I would have had more of our father to myself, his attention, talk, play; but not so. I remember sitting in the car with him, outside one hospital or another, waiting for Mom to come out from visiting Joe. He would sit at the wheel ignoring me, compulsively whistling a tune I would much later recognize as "Beautiful Dreamer." I hear it now, and it makes me sad.

Our parents would be sexually intimate again, but lovers? Propcrly unprotcctcd prophylactically, thcy would bc protected from each other in every other way from now on. I can claim only intuitive knowledge here, but my conviction is that the shock of my brother's illness broke the spell of the golden escape – the beautiful dream – they'd woven for themselves. They would be alienated from each other hereafter. She would be giving her all to her children. He would be saving the Free World from Communism. I would be the secretly beloved child of a quietly scorned woman, which would lead years later to a boundless embarrassment around sexual assertion. Now I understand my mother's forever unstated difficulty with male sexuality, mine in particular. The lesson of polio to all of us was that our bodies were plainly not to be trusted. Devastating as my brother's illness was in itself – year after year of his real agony – its resonance as a kind of Irish curse against a spoiled priest, his woman, and their children is what made it the radioactive mushroom cloud of our family. Certainly it hung over me.

Friends and relatives from Chicago stopped visiting. Mom stopped packing us into the Studebaker to go pick up Dad at night. Instead of wonder tours of Doric Washington, she did her driving now to doctors' offices and hospitals in Alexandria and Washington. Instead of past the White House and down Pennsylvania Avenue, she now drove the Studebaker every chance she got to the far northeast of D. C., an area around Catholic University called Little Rome because of its concentration of seminaries, convents, monasteries, and oratories. When Joe was in the hospital, she took me and a succession of my infant brothers to the Franciscan Monastery, where visits to the papier-mâché catacombs and concrete-over-mesh grottoes of Lourdes and Fatima earned something called "indulgences," which Mom flamboyantly "offered up," as she said, for Joe. I once asked a Friar Tuck monk why he had hair on his chin and not on his head, and the relieved pleasure I took in my mother's laughter makes me realize now that it had become unusual. Sometimes, in a wheelchair or on crutches, Joe would come with us. He could be imperious, ordering me to fetch, to wait, or to carry, but I had developed the habit of responding instantly. To do so solved the ache of my not being crippled myself.

If it wasn't the Franciscan Monastery or the Poor Clares Convent we visited, it was the National Shrine of the Immaculate Conception, in those days a crypt church still under construction. Completed, it is the largest Catholic church in North America. Even incomplete, the Shrine had a well-stocked religious goods store, where my mother bought scapulas and miraculous medals for Joe to wear, sacred oil and relics to rub on his scarred and withered legs. I went along mutely, increasingly agnostic as I saw no improvement in Joe's condition. Mainly I was learning the great lesson that religious faith has everything to do with suffering and unhappiness. I was four years old, five, six . . . eleven, twelve, going to and from these places with my mother and brothers. The Shrine especially was the North Star of my childhood. When Joe was in the hospital, it seemed we went there after every visit. I knelt below the crucifixes, all that writhing, legs as bruised as Joe's; I said my rosaries and learned carefully to deduct my time from purgatory. With the cultivated appearance of a fervor I never felt, I imitated my mother in lighting candles at the snake-ridden (virus-ridden?) feet of the Blessed Virgin Mary. After a while, and without ever believing any of it was helping Joe, I realized that these rituals had become for me what they were for my mother, a bond with her after all, and a rare – perhaps the only – source of consolation.

Latin Masses and communally recited rosaries were unintelligible rituals to me, but the act of kneeling next to her was emotionally comprehensible. I learned to bury my face in my hands, a dark focus that offered a release I had no way of understanding – and which is still available to me when, in certain circumstances and blank-minded, I assume that posture all these years later. Faith in a crucified God, son of a heartbroken mother, consoles without providing any particular hope of salvation, solution, fix, or escape – that was the first principle of my credo, and it remains the last.

Two blocks down Fourth Street from the National Shrine of the Immaculate Conception, behind a pair of looming stone pillars past which we drove every time, was a pseudo-Gothic, crenelated mausoleum that had already branded itself on my unconscious. It was St. Paul's College, a seminary. Seminary: when I first heard the word, I took it to be "cemetery," another Arlington, like the one sprawling up the hill behind my father's office at the Pentagon. Seminary: at the word I always looked for grave markers. St. Paul's College on Fourth Street was the institution where, years later, in my pathetic effort to resuscitate the mortal happiness of that fugitive young couple and their first son, their first Joseph, I would, a willing mystic Houdini, entomb myself.

"Holy Father, General and Mrs. Joseph Carroll and their sons Joseph Jr., James, Brian, Dennis and Kevin . . ."

These words are written in Gothic calligraphy in a goldframed certificate below a photograph of the smiling, large-nosed pope. In the four corners of the certificate are sketched scenes of Vatican City: St. Peter's, the Apostolic Palace, Bernini's square, the walled gardens. The framed object sits on the edge of my desk before me, leaning against the wall. I found it in one of my mother's boxes when she died two years ago, one of a matched pair of gilded frames. The other holds a color photograph of our family flanking Pope John XXIII in front of the red damask wall of his throne room in which we had our audience. In the photo, my blue father with his gleaming buttons and stars is on one side of the pope, together with Joe and Dennis. My mother, in a Lady-of-Spain mantilla, is on the other, with Brian, little Kevin, and me. I am beside her. My hair, in front, is a cresting wave, a small hint of Elvis, but my sideburns are not so long that my ears do not protrude.

The Gothic calligraphy, evoking the ghosts of Tetzel and Luther, continues, ". . . do humbly beg your fatherly and Apostolic Blessing, and a Plenary Indulgence at the hour of death on condition that being sorry for their sins but unable to confess them, or to receive Holy Viaticum, they shall at least with their lips or heart devoutly invoke the Holy Name of Jesus."

The petition is presumably answered with the scrawled signature of some monsignor and the pressed seal of the Keys of the Kingdom. This event was the absolute highlight of my parents' life, and it was something for me too. It took place in my senior year, toward the end of our time in Europe, within weeks of the chill midnight when my girlfriend and I, on the edge of the Hainerberg football field overlooking the twinkling spa city of Wiesbaden, fumbled our clothes open. The Puritan verdict "Found in Unlawful Carnal Knowledge," someone told me, gives us "fuck." My girl and I were not "found," and we did not quite consummate our "knowledge," but fucked was what, arriving in Rome, I felt. Sex was going to be my secret way out of the religion.

I have little or no memory of the papal apartments, the tapestries or great paintings. I am told that somewhere there hangs a fifteenth-century map that marks the American continent as "Terra Incognita," but I did not see it. Years later, in the statue-lined corridors of the Vatican Museums, I would notice that the male genitalia of all the Greek and Roman nudes had been chiseled off. I would learn of the artist Daniele da Volterra, ordered by Pius V — always Pius? — to cover the loins of Michelangelo's naked figures, earning for himself the sobriquet "Il Brachettone," the trouser maker. But at the time of this, my first visit to the Vatican, I was blind to such signals of the Church's genital obsessiveness, no doubt because I was so conflicted about my own. Sex evil? All I knew by then was that God was right to regard the sexual feelings of creatures as supreme competition. At times my longings obliterated the existence of everything else, including Him.

By now, the effort to recall this phase of my personal history has succeeded at least in evoking my sad pity for the affected, frightened lad in this photograph with the freckles, big ears, and mini-pompadour; his carefully constructed surface – that Windsor knot just so – layering over a seething insecurity; his dread of a future that seemed a trap or a dead end; the tumult of his hidden unbelief, sex, and filial subservience. This lad whose brothers knew nothing about him, and whose parents could see only in the unsteady light of choices they themselves had made twenty-five years before. This lad whose ability to be consoled by a sweet, pretty girl who claimed to love him, who'd trusted him with her near nakedness, was blown to smithereens by the certain knowledge that, despite himself, in every gesture of affection and word of promise he had lied to her about an open future. This lad – how, in seeing him in this photo now, I would love to embrace him, pressing in all that I have seen and learned of acceptance and forgiveness and affirmation. He is my younger self, of course, and there is nothing I can do for him.

Yet just such a thing, by a miracle of the same fresh grace that has swept the Church itself, is done then to the very same lad. It happens when Pope John turns from my brother Joe to me. He is most of a foot shorter than I, his face as red as his shoes, his cassock pure white, a gold cross, a jewel on his finger. I bend toward him, and he surprises me by reaching up and taking my shoulders firmly in his hands. His head is close to mine. I smell the scent of incense, also of soap. He holds me for a long time, pressing in all that he has seen and knows. His accent is thick, and so I do not understand what he is saying. The interpreter stays apart, as if this is private. Confession. He seems so much more affectionate with me than with my brothers that I can only assume, as with Spellman, that someone has told him of my ancient designation, my "vocation." But now instead of the claustrophobia of my hypocrisy, I feel elation. He is seeing through to the core of me, he knows my secret, and he shares it.

This is the moment of my conscription. After this encounter I will abandon the false dream of following my father into the Air Force. The romance with my girlfriend will not survive the separation following high school graduation. I will enroll at Georgetown University. In summer I will work as a clerk at the FBI, a job my father gets me. There will be other girls, and more of the panic of sex, but no more lies. I will cut short my time at college to enter the seminary – the one past which Mom drove so often when we went to lay our sorrow down at the feet of Mary. I will spend the next dozen years in a religious order, ultimately – pre-ordained? – to be ordained a priest.

Why? For a hundred reasons and for one. Here in Rome, the city itself inside a gold frame, for the first time in my life the Call feels entirely addressed to me, and not from Mom or Dad. In the person of a pope, a counter-Elvis, I glimpse the transcendence of the Church, which Michelangelo saw in flashes. The Church is a way that God has touched the earth. I know that its rituals and symbols satisfy the deepest urges of human beings because here, for a moment, this man, its chief symbol, satisfies the very thing in me. My turbulent self-consciousness is replaced for a moment – the first one – with peace. For a moment I do not think of any of this in relation to my parents.

What can we know? Why is there anything instead of nothing? What is the reason and meaning of reality? What ought we to do? Why are we here? Kant's questions, and every adolescent's, Pope

John's face is close to mine, his sweet breath blows across mine. I stop asking these questions because, for a moment — the first one — I believe in God.

Now another question: how could anything ever seem more important than this faith? To ask it is to answer it. I genuflect, and His Holiness blesses me with something not his own, not my father's, and not mine. The Hound of Heaven has me. God. And how can I not make a life of Him?

# *from* Memories of a Catholic Girlhood

WERE HE LIVING TODAY, MY PROTESTANT GRANDFATHER WOULD BE DISPLEASED TO hear that the fate of his soul had once been the occasion of intense theological anxiety with the Ladies of the Sacred Heart. While his mortal part, all unaware, went about its eighteen holes of golf, its rubber of bridge before dinner at the club, his immortal part lay in jeopardy with us, the nuns and pupils of a strict convent school set on a wooded hill quite near a piece of worthless real estate he had bought under the impression that Seattle was expanding in a northerly direction. A sermon delivered at the convent by an enthusiastic Jesuit had disclosed to us his danger. Up to this point, the disparity in religion between my grandfather and myself had given me no serious concern. The death of my parents, while it had drawn us together in many senses, including the legal one (for I became his ward), had at the same time left the gulf of a generation between us, and my grandfather's Protestantism presented itself as a natural part of the grand, granite scenery on the other side. But the Jesuit's sermon destroyed this ordered view in a single thunderclap of doctrine.

As the priest would have it, this honest and upright man, a great favorite with the Mother Superior, was condemned to eternal torment by the accident of having been baptized. Had he been a Mohammedan, a Jew, a pagan, or the child of civilized unbelievers, a place in Limbo would have been assured him; Cicero and Aristotle and Cyrus the Persian might have been his companions, and the harmless souls of unbaptized children might have frolicked about his feet. But if the Jesuit were right, all baptized Protestants went straight to Hell. A good life did not count in their favor. The baptismal rite, by conferring on them God's grace, made them also liable to His organizational displeasure. That is, baptism turned them Catholic whether they liked it or not, and their persistence in the Protestant ritual was a kind of asseverated apostasy. Thus my poor grandfather, sixty years behind in his Easter duty, actually reduced his prospects of salvation every time he sat down in the Presbyterian church.

The Mother Superior's sweet frown acknowledged me, an hour after the sermon, as I curtsied, all agitation, in her office doorway. Plainly, she had been expecting me. Madame MacIllvra, an able administrator, must have been resignedly ticking off the names of the Protestant pupils and parents all during the concluding parts of the morning's service. She had a faint worried air, when the conversation began, of depreciating the sermon: doctrinally, perhaps, correct, it had been wanting in delicacy; the fiery Jesuit, a missionary celebrity, had lived too long among the Eskimos. This disengaged attitude encouraged me to hope. Surely this lady, the highest authority I knew, could find a way out for my grandfather. She could see that he was a special case, outside the brutal rule of thumb laid down by the Jesuit. It was she, after all, in the convent, from whom all exemptions flowed, who created arbitrary holidays (called *congés* by the order's French tradition); it was she who permitted us to get forbidden books from the librarian and occasionally to receive letters unread by the convent censor. (As a rule, all slang expressions, violations of syntax, errors of spelling, as well as improper sentiments, were blacked out of our friends' communications, so unless we moved in a circle of young Addisons or Burkes, the letters we longed for came to us as fragments from which the original text could only be conjectured.) To my twelve-year-old mind, it appeared probable that Madame MacIllvra, our Mother Superior, had the power to give my grandfather *congé*, and I threw myself on her sympathies.

How could it be that my grandfather, the most virtuous person I knew, whose name was a byword among his friends and colleagues for a kind of rigid and fantastic probity – how could it be that this man should be lost, while I, the object of his admonition, the despair of his example – I, who yielded to every impulse, lied, boasted, betrayed – should, by virtue of regular attendance at the sacraments and the habit of easy penitence, be saved?

Madame MacIllvra's full white brow wrinkled; her childlike blue eyes clouded. Like many headmistresses, she loved a good cry, and she clasped me to her plump, quivering, middle-aged bosom. She understood; she was crying for my grandfather and the injustice of it too. She and my grandfather had, as a matter of fact, established a very amiable relation, in which both took pleasure. The masculine line and firmness of his character made an aesthetic appeal to her, and the billowy softness and depth of the Mother Superior struck him favorably, but, above all, it was their difference in religion that salted their conversations. Each of them enjoyed, whenever they met in her straight, black-and-white little office, a sense of broadness, of enlightenment, of transcendent superiority to petty prejudice. My grandfather would remember that he wrote a check every Christmas for two Sisters of Charity who visited his office; Madame MacIllvra would perhaps recall her graduate studies and Hume. They had long, liberal talks which had the tone of *performances*, virtuoso feats of magnanimity were achieved on both sides. Afterward, they spoke of each other in nearly identical terms: "A very fine woman," "A very fine man."

All this (and possibly the suspicion that her verdict might be repeated at home) made Madame MacIllvra's answer slow. "Perhaps

God," she murmured at last, "in His infinite mercy . . ." Yet this formulation satisfied neither of us. God's infinite mercy we believed in, but its manifestations were problematical. Sacred history showed us that it was more likely to fall on the Good Thief or the Woman Taken in Adultery than on persons of daily virtue and regular habits, like my grandfather. Our Catholic thoughts journeyed and met in a glance of alarmed recognition. Madame MacIllvra pondered. There were, of course, she said finally, other loopholes. If he had been improperly baptized . . . a careless clergyman . . . I considered this suggestion and shook my head. My grandfather was not the kind of man who, even as an infant, would have been guilty of a slovenly baptism.

It was a measure of Madame MacIllvra's intelligence, or of her knowledge of the world, that she did not, even then, when my grandfather's soul hung, as it were, pleadingly between us, suggest the obvious, the orthodox solution. It would have been ridiculous for me to try to convert my grandfather. Indeed, as it turned out later, I might have dropped him into the pit with my innocent traps (the religious books left open beside his cigar cutter, or "Grandpa, won't you take me to Mass this Sunday? I am so tired of going alone"). "Pray for him, my dear," said Madame MacIllvra, sighing, "and I will speak to Madame Barclay. The point may be open to interpretation. She may remember something in the Fathers of the Church. . . ."

A few days later, Madame MacIllvra summoned me to her office. Not only Madame Barclay, the learned prefect of studies, but the librarian and even the convent chaplain had been called in. The Benedictine view, it seemed, differed sharply from the Dominican, but a key passage in Saint Athanasius seemed to point to my grandfather's safety. The unbeliever, according to this generous authority, was not to be damned unless he rejected the true Church with sufficient knowledge and full consent of the will. Madame MacIll-vra handed me the book, and I read the passage over. Clearly, he was saved. Sufficient knowledge he had not. The Church was foreign to him; he knew it only distantly, only by repute, like the heathen Hiawatha, who had heard strange stories of missionaries, white men in black robes who bore a Cross. Flinging my arms about Madame MacIllvra, I blessed for the first time the insularity of my grandfather's character, the long-jawed, shut face it turned toward ideas and customs not its own. I resolved to dismantle at once the little altar in my bedroom at home, to leave off grace before meals, elaborate fasting, and all ostentatious practices of devotion, lest the light of my example shine upon him too powerfully and burn him with sufficient knowledge to a crisp.

# *from* Nun

THE STAGE WAS NOW SET. I HAD MASTERED MY ROLE AS GOOD GIRL AT SCHOOL, AT HOME, and in the neighborhood. I now began to look for a place where I could bring my holiness to fruition.

Just at this point, the long-robed Vocations recruiters began to appear on the scene, bringing their invitation to "Come follow Christ" to seventh and eighth graders in parish schools throughout the city. High school was near; it was time we considered the possibility that God might be calling us to spend four years in a minor seminary for boys or a convent prep school for girls. If a boy felt himself called to be a priest or a brother, or a girl "heard the call" to be a nun, such sheltered high school environments could protect the fledgling Vocation. Vocation talks were a standard part of seventh- and eighth-grade routine.

First came the recruiters for the priesthood and the brotherhood: handsome, fresh-scrubbed young men who sat on the edge of the teacher's desk and cracked jokes. We were all really impressed with their casualness: "I didn't know priests and brothers were so human!" we'd marvel to each other at recess, "and so handsome!" we'd sigh.

Recruiters spent a lot of time talking about how seminarians weren't weirdos and how they got to do normal things like play basketball and chew gum. Sometimes they'd show slides of the seminary, and 90 percent of the slides showed seminarians picnicking, playing baseball, or drinking cokes. They stressed to the boys that a Vocation was a call from God and that it was important to listen carefully in case He might be calling. "If you think He might be calling you but you're not sure, the best way to test it out is to sign up for a high school seminary. There you'll get a taste of what the priesthood is like, and then you can decide for yourself."

Nuns were similarly represented. A pretty young thing (on both scores a sharp contrast to the nuns who taught us every day) would come to talk about how she had been a red-blooded American girl too and about how she had loved nice clothes and going out on dates. "But then I began to discover that worldly pleasures left me empty and unsatisfied," she would testify with a faraway look in her eyes. "Saint Augustine exclaimed: 'Our hearts are restless till they rest in Thee, oh Lord.' Only giving myself completely to God has brought me peace and happiness." Then she would distribute brochures showing young girls, all of them radiantly beautiful and blissfully happy, strolling arm in arm across a picture-postcard campus. The brochure made it obvious that Christ wanted brides who were normal, red-blooded American girls.

After a few of these talks, no one had any confusion about what the word *Vocation* meant. Nobody came to talk to us about what it would be like to be a chemist, a social worker, or a stewardess; a *Vocation* (with a capital *V*) meant one thing: you were called by God to leave all things and to follow Christ as a nun, a priest or a brother. (I would later learn that priests and brothers hold theologically distinct places within the Church; for now I only knew that priests could celebrate Mass and hear confessions and that brothers could not.)

To have a vocation was to have a special calling. Your mom and dad would be very proud of you; *everyone* would be very proud of you. There was nothing really wrong with the way your parents lived: if they sent their kids to Catholic school, didn't use birth control, and were active in the Knights of Columbus and the Altar Society, there was a good chance they would make it to heaven too. It's just that there were higher callings, and if you *really* wanted to do something special for God and for humanity, the way to do it was to become a priest or a nun.

It was the idea of specialness that fired my imagination. Images of visiting my aunt and cousin rose up before my eyes: everyone always treated them with such respect and reverence. We'd dress up in our Sunday best and sit all prim and proper in their convent parlors, presenting them with homemade cookies and boxes of chocolates. When we went to visit other aunts and uncles, we'd wear our old clothes and play out in the backyard with their kids. The thought of *my* brothers and sisters one day bringing their children to visit the aunt who was doing something *special* with her life suddenly became very intriguing.

My parents had never suggested that I might want to be a nun someday; in fact, they always took great pains to not express career expectations to any of their children. But I knew deep down that becoming a nun was one sure way of making them proud of me. In the non-Catholic world, boys became doctors or lawyers and girls became the wives of doctors or lawyers as a way of fulfilling their parents' fondest dreams. In our Catholic world, the families that were most esteemed were those that were blessed with a priest or a nun. If I decided to become a nun, I would win for my parents the special heavenly crown reserved for those who give a daughter to the Lord.

But I still had my doubts. The thought of never having children of my own troubled me deeply. I talked to one of the recruiters about it and she assured me that nuns had children, lots of them, and that the spiritual motherhood they experienced in the classroom was every bit as satisfying as physical motherhood. I doubted that she was in a position to compare the two experiences or that she knew how sweet a newborn smells when you hold it to your heart, but I reminded myself that God doesn't give a cross without also giving the strength to carry it.

I asked the same recruiter why priests had more privileges than nuns, why they could smoke and drink and drive big cars. She seemed startled by my question, as though it had never occurred to her to ask it herself, and then she said that it was probably to make up for the fact that priests gave up more. I pondered that for a while and then realized she was again reminding me that sex wasn't really a big deal for a woman. But I knew *that* by now: knew that the word I had sometimes seen in *True Confessions, nympho*-something, referred to a woman who liked sex. I told myself that if the recruiter was right, as I now suspected she might be – if spiritual motherhood *could* eventually make up for the sacrifice of physical motherhood, if giving up sex wasn't *that* much of a sacrifice for a woman – then maybe I should give this vocation thing another look.

I entered eighth grade in 1956, and a month later a representative from the order to which my aunt and cousin belonged came to talk to our eighth-grade class. I already knew a little bit about their community, the Sisters of Blessing. I knew that their apostolate was primarily teaching and that they numbered about 1800 nuns, most of them teaching somewhere in the midwest and the south. I also knew that the order ran a prep school at their motherhouse about 100 miles away. I had often visited my aunt and cousin there at Saint Raphael's in Avington and was always moved by the simple, wooded beauty of the 150-acre campus.

Before the talk began, I introduced myself to the representative, Sister Roseanne, S. B. (Sister of Blessing), and told her that I had an aunt and a cousin in her order. She said that she knew them both and that both were "fine community women." She asked me if I had ever considered the possibility that I might have a Vocation. I told her that the thought had crossed my mind, and, smiling, she advised me to listen carefully to her talk: "You might hear Jesus calling you loud and clear."

I didn't hear Jesus, but I *did* hear Sister Roseanne and I was mesmerized by her message. She talked about the glories of serving God and His people, of helping to change the world. I was stunned: no one had ever told me that I, a mere girl, might actually be able to make a contribution to the world. Most of the women saints to whom we girls had been told to pray could boast of only one thing: they had kept their virginity intact. We read gory stories about how Saint Lucy, Saint Agnes, Maria Goretti, and the rest had been tortured, had been branded with irons, or had had their breasts cut off because they refused to surrender their virginity. As far as I could see, that was the extent of their contribution to humanity.

The men saints were the ones who inspired me: Saint Francis, who gave up everything in order to live simply; Saint Martin de Porres, the black man who worked unstintingly among the poor; Saint Vincent de Paul, who said that the poor will forgive you the good that you do them but only if you love them enough. Now here was someone saying that I, a female, could make a contribution to the world. The thought was breathtaking!

Sister Roseanne stressed that if a girl even *thought* she might have a Vocation to be a Sister of Blessing, it would probably be a good idea to test it out by attending the order's prep school. (I learned later that some nuns in this order and in others disagreed with this theory, feeling that a girl should attend a "normal" high school before making such a decision. Some orders didn't even *have* prep schools for this reason.) "Look at it this way," Sister Roseanne said. "You might go and discover that God isn't really calling you. At least you'd *know*, then; it would be a lot better than living your whole life, always wondering if you had turned your back on a Vocation."

My heart pounding, I looked at the pamphlet Sister Roseanne had given me. On the front was a picture of a church full of brides of Christ in nuptial finery; inside was information about the important work that Sisters of Blessing were doing in their various schools. As I contrasted a nun's life with the lives of the other women I saw around me, convent life began to look increasingly attractive. A teaching nun traveled all around, meeting all kinds of interesting people. But the important thing was that she was helping the world.

Sister Roseanne said that a feeling of being drawn to be a nun was a pretty clear sign of God's will and that you didn't have to hear a little voice. The feeling of being drawn was definitely there: the more I thought about it, the more I realized that this must be *it!*

And so it was decided as so many decisions are, not in one conscious moment of clear vision and choice but in many semiconscious moments that lead one into the other: I would be a nun. It was my destiny, my fate. God was calling and I would answer.

Sister Roseanne ended her talk by asking us to pray for Vocations: "The modern urge for riches, comfort, and pleasure is preventing many young men and women from following Vocations. Pray with me that more young people will find within themselves the generosity and the idealism to join Christ in His important work."

She then taught us a rousing song about Catholic Action, reminding us that we were the hope of the future. I sang with a heart bursting with excitement, with confidence that I had at last found my niche. I would commit myself to a great cause, a great mission: I would leave all things to follow Christ, to join His army of youth, to fly standards of truth, to fight for Christ the Lord.

JOANNE B. MULCAHY

# Dreams of Martyrdom

DRIVING SOUTH ALONG THE WILLAMETTE RIVER TO MY HOME IN PORTLAND, I SAW A crowd gathered on the river bank just above a row of houseboats. I parked the car and scrambled down the steep incline to the water's edge. People moved aside, recognizing the certainty of my mission. Through an arc of moving water an arm gesturing for help. I pulled my sweater overhead, kicked off my shoes, and dove. Swimming toward the figure fighting against the current, I heard a call from childhood. Sister Peter Eileen's voice reverberated through the black water: "True happiness comes only through sacrifice for others." Banishing fear, I lunged toward the the disappearing torso of the drowning man. One hand cupped under his chin, I pulled with my other arm toward shore. Coughing and spitting, I began to sink under his incessant pull. Bright light shone above me as I went down, released into the ultimate state of grace: martyrdom.

But that's not how it happened. I didn't stop; I never even slowed down. I read later that a scull had overturned. Another boat picked up the rower. The crowd dispersed within minutes, while I, worried about getting to the grocery store before it closed, anxious about the forty papers I had to grade, continued on. But not without a fantasy, one that takes over with such speed and clings with such tenacity that I've come to recognize it as a reflex.

In the fantasy, I am a savior, graceful and strong. Sometimes I'm flying, sometimes swimming, always with natural athletic fluidity.

With little thought for myself, I wildly risk all for the sake of . . . whom? As a child I longed to rescue old people and animals. Then adolescence. For an embarrassingly long period, I sought young rich and available men, future romantic partners. With time and maturity, my fantasies shifted to computer salesmen who reward me with the laptop I so covet. Pathetic, even sinful, Sister Peter Eileen would say, layering my transgressions upon one another: coveting thy neighbor's goods, fantasizing sexual encounters (in Catholicism, even desire is a sin), and worst of all, striving for personal gain. Happiness can only be attained through sacrifice; sacrifice only counts if it's pure.

My desires weren't always so profane. In fifth grade, I longed to give selflessly. I stood ready to offer all that I had for Father Devrees. My chance came on the first Friday afternoon of Lent, the forty-day ritual preparation for Easter. The sisters at St. Ursula's School outside Philadelphia hurried us through morning lessons with *The Baltimore Catechism* to allow for a full, free afternoon. The recitations of "Who made me? God made me" primed us for my favorite Lenten practice, the Stations of the Cross. After lunch, we hastened from the faded linoleum and worn brick of our schoolhouse toward the gleaming steeple and pungent incense of the stately church next door. I prayed silently though the fourteen Stations that carried me along Christ's journey to His crucifixion. "Jesus receives the Cross. Jesus falls for the first time. Jesus is met by His Blessed Mother." I always hurried to the Sixth Station, the meeting with St. Veronica where the impression of Christ's face imprints the cloth she brought to wipe away his sweat. I lingered before the image of Christ's body lowered from the cross, blood flowing from hands and feet. Each icon carried me further into the world of barefoot, white-robed, suffering Christians. Shrouds, crowns of thorns, bloodied bodies hung in agony. A world of sacred violence.

I loved the silence, the meditation, the slow, even quality of those afternoons during Lent. I didn't even mind missing Vocal, our usual Friday activity. Since the school couldn't afford musical instruments, Vocal was our compromise. For twenty-five cents, we could pass several blissful hours singing show tunes with the sisters. Memories of *Oklahoma* and *South Pacific* now merge with the ritual of the stations. The smiling, voluptuous Mary Martin on the *South Pacific* album cover melds with the image of the women of Jerusalem. I hear St. Veronica singing, "I'm gonna wash that man right out of my hair." Sacrilege, you might think, but something else alchemized on those Fridays a unique mix of secular and sacred. In our Irish-Italian neighborhood, where a walk to the nearby sewage plant on Darby Creek was a wilderness adventure, where rummage sales and bridge parties comprised social life, religion offered vistas at least as exotic as the South Pacific. Once a week, Bali Hai and Heaven merged in our suburban Philadelphia enclave. I loved everything about Friday afternoons.

On this particular Friday, we waited in our seats for Sister Eileen to announce the lines for church. John Moriarty, the scourge of the classroom, sat in front of me, pounding on the desk, ready to leap from his seat and be first in line. I hated sitting behind him. I feared touching the dandruff that settled on the greasy collar of his maroon uniform jacket. When Sister Eileen finally entered the room, a hush descended. "Class, we will not begin our Stations today as scheduled. God has another plan for us." I cringed, fearful that this might entail more time behind John Moriarty. Instead, Sister ushered the girls out into the dark hallway. Uniform check, I thought. As usual, she'd run a yardstick along the bottom edges of our skirts, calculating length and ensuring modesty. But this day was to be different. We had a mission.

"We'll begin with you girls," said Sister. "Each of you has a special gift of sight given by God." This, we knew. We heard stories almost hourly about those less fortunate than us – lepers, the blind, the maimed, and unluckiest of all, communists. Unlike the Godless communists, we knew we were blessed. Sighted, baptized, with full use of our limbs, and most important, Americans free to sacrifice our way to happiness. An additional message – implicit, never spoken – fueled our drive: as girls, we were especially suited to sacrifice. "We'll use that sight today, girls, to help us in our search." Mystified, we moved out into the schoolyard, then onto the half-mowed lawn that separated the school from the red brick church and rectory. Sister Eileen towered imposingly before us. "Our mission, class, is to find Father Devrees's finger." A collective gasp rose. I conjured up an image of Father Devrees. Of slight build, with dark, wavy hair and penetrating blue eyes, he was our newest and youngest priest, recently arrived from Russia or some Eastern European Communist country. (My mother now tells me that his name was Decries, and that he was Belgian. But I know better; there is no place on the map of Godless communism for Belgium.)

I was in love with Father Devrees. All the girls were. With his carefully trimmed goatee, he was an exotic, clerical Mitch Miller. I scanned the yard and beyond to the rectory. The real Father was nowhere in sight. That, Sister Eileen explained, was because he had his hand wrapped, awaiting the discovery of the finger he had cut off while trying to fix the lawn mower. God was cruel I decided to have maimed Father Devrees in such mundane fashion. I would find the finger. Or I would give my own. Through suffering and sacrifice, happiness would be mine.

Sister Eileen followed us outside with the boys. My fifth-grade class of sixty made a formidable search team. We formed lines of twelve and moved in single file, eyes fixed on the ground. I remembered reading about the pilgrims who prayed continuously, and began a mantra that directed my breathing, "Please, God, the finger." I had never prayed so intently. Tempted to wander off on my own, I steeled myself to stay close to the line of uniformed girls. My grade in self-control had slipped on the last report card. Earlier in the year, when President Kennedy was assassinated, my faith had wavered. Questions stacked up. How could Father, Son, and Holy Ghost be one? Why didn't the Virgin Mary get in on the Holy Trinity? Was everything a mystery? Here was the chance to strengthen my faith. Surely, adherence to Sister's orders, endless devotion, and my deep desire to sacrifice would bring me to the finger.

Pacing, I imagined the sweat on my brow wiped by St. Veronica's cloth. I mentally braced myself to cut off my own finger if necessary. My footsteps echoed my mantra "the finger, the finger." A trance state evolved – walking, praying, walking, then suddenly, a gleam of flesh. Directly below me nearly buried in the newly cut grass was the stub. Undisturbed by the sight of blood, which normally sickened me, I scooped up the finger and ran to the rectory, crying out to Father Devrees that he was saved. He came out, his bloody hand bound in rags, eyes bathed in gratitude. We got down on our knees and thanked God for our sight, our belief, and our freedom. It was my moment of glory.

But that's not how it happened. John Moriarty found the finger and I decided then that there was no God. Or if he existed, he must be a Protestant. Despite what the nuns had told us, I couldn't believe in a Catholic God that would allow the greasy, hell-raising John Moriarty to find the finger. He was a boy; what did he know about sacrifice? Even Sister Eileen looked disappointed. Her narrow face, imprisoned by her white wimple, drooped further as she ran toward the cries of glee in the far corner of the rectory lawn. John was shouting and waving wildly, "I've got it, I've got it!" "This is not a football game, John," Sister proclaimed as she retrieved the finger, the black robes of her habit flowing behind her. She carried it to the rectory, and we all watched as Father Devrees walked out to the car to be driven to St. Luke's Hospital, where the Sisters of

Mercy would attend to the bloody digit, now on ice. There would be prayers and reaffirmations of belief. Father Devrees would return grateful for full use of his appendage, and of course, his freedom.

When the commotion died down, and Sister led us back to the classroom, I pondered the meaning of the afternoon's events. If freedom and faith meant that John Moriarty could triumph on this fine spring day, achieving the happiness that was meant for me I wondered if I wasn't destined for the land of Godless communism. Nothing made sense anymore. I had not found the finger. I had not had the chance to sacrifice. And we had missed vocal *and* the Stations of the Cross.

The teachings encased in three books dominated my education at St. Ursula's. I remember each by its color – green, blue, and yellow. The three texts combined with inklike permanency to shape the story of who I would become. We began each day with lessons from the green book, *The Baltimore Catechism*. As I walked to school across the empty lot behind our house, I memorized "God made me to know him, to love him, and to serve him in this world. . . ." "Service" was the operative world. Doing for others was the path to heaven. Not to "serve" was "selfish," a term delivered with a mixture of scorn and pity, spit out rather than stated. A rival epithet was "conceited," particularly damning for girls. "Full of herself," I once heard Sister Eileen sniff to one of the other nuns, tossing her black-robed arm toward curly-haired Dawn Montgomery, the most beautiful girl in the class. I suspected the scorn for Dawn rose from her status as the only non-Catholic in the school. Her soul was damned. But worse, she was "full of herself." She would never learn to serve.

Morning prayers were followed by readings from the big blue book, *Lives of The Saints*, that Sister Eileen kept high up on a shelf. I longed to be chosen to to deliver a saints story for the day. St. Joan of Arc, for whom I was named, was my favorite. She was the star martyr, dazzling in her bravery, mysteriously androgynous. Her picture in the blue book stays imprinted in memory: Joan on horseback straight-backed, resplendent in white, leading the French army to the siege of Orleans. Joan enveloped by leaping flames after capture by the English and her refusal to deny the voices that had led her to battle. St. Ava, who when thrown to the lions, remained curiously untouched. Terese of Liseux. Not one of the great martyrs, her health precluded extreme suffering, but she endured each day by creating small trials which she recorded in *The Story of a Soul*. The blue book listed the French title, *L'Histoire D'une Ame*, in parentheses. I mouthed the words over and over, drawn in by the exotic sounds and by Terese's status as a "small martyr." Though I longed for the glamour of martyrdom, I recoiled at the thought of too much hardship.

Near the end of fourth grade, after Easter had passed, my disappointment over the finger episode lingered. Would I ever regain my belief in suffering? In late spring, the nuns introduced us to a world of potential sacrifice for all Catholic girls. On a Saturday trip to the Waverly theater, we saw enacted on the big screen a story unforgettable for those of us entering adolescence in the early 1960s: the life of St. Maria Goretti. An Italian peasant girl murdered at the turn of the century by a youth inflamed with lustful desire, Maria died of multiple stab wounds while defending her chastity. Here was a test of faith many of us would face, Sister stated without further elaboration. Since I knew little about peasants and less about sex, the real meaning of Maria's story eluded me. But the Italian girls in my neighborhood took on a special glow. A glimmer of faith had been rekindled.

For the remainder of fifth grade, our class had weekly French instruction from Helen Pineau who appeared spike-heeled and perfectly coifed on the RCA television the sisters rolled up on a wheeled tray from the convent. After French lessons, I would walk home past Darby Creek. In the privacy of the woods, I practiced my pronunciations of "Liseux," "Jeanne D'Arc" (I had discovered Joan's "real" name), and *L'Historie D'Une Ame.* I pulled on the sides of my mouth, searched for the guttural "r's" in the back of my throat, mimicking Helen Pineau's tortured movements. As I rounded the end of the creek path for home, I could smell garlic wafting from the kitchens of our Italian neighbors. Groaning out French sounds, longing for the everyday exotica of spaghetti dinners, I knew only this: that the path to sainthood was bound up with being French like St. Terese or Italian like Maria Goretti, with being something other than Irish-American, someone other than me. The person I might be if I discovered the right sacrifice, if I could somehow suffer enough.

When I was in sixth grade, Sister Mary Cyril arrived at St. Ursula's. She brought with her a steeled devotion to discipline and a passion for early Christian history and the yellow Bible study book whose stories would come to haunt me. I still see the cover faded as a wilted daffodil, worn and stained by children's hands. The scenes within detailed the suffering of the third-century Christians forced underground to worship, only to be discovered and thrown to the lions by Roman soldiers. The illustrations highlighted the horror: faces frozen in terror, human forms hurled into the Coliseum, the aftermath of mangled bodies. The thought of the catacombs made me claustrophobic; worse, I could no longer imagine martyrdom without gore.

During recess after Bible study one day, I approached Sister Mary Cyril. "Sister, that could never happen again, could it, the lions and everything?" I asked. A plea for reassurance swelled through my voice. Sister turned to her desk drawer, her face solemn. She removed a photograph. The picture showed emaciated adults in prisonlike settings, their grim visages an updated version of faces in the yellow Bible study book. "*When* do you think these people lived?" she queried. "Long ago?" I offered hopefully. Sister narrowed her eyes. "Today," she pronounced definitively. "And *where* do you think they live?" I was stuck. "The ghetto?" I puzzled, evoking that generic hub of poverty, sin, and tragedy from which we, in the blessed suburbs, were gratefully shielded. "No, dear," she returned wearily, "these unfortunate people live in Russia, where they are dying for their faith. Krushchev is the evil man responsible." I already knew about Eastern Europe from my John Nagy "Learn to Draw" sketches of Hungarian refugees. But Russia. An unimaginable place, worse than the Coliseum and the ghetto combined. Russians. They triggered both fear and the deep allure of the forbidden. Krushchev. The Devil Incarnate, destroyer of children and Christians. The Roman emperor of our age, his land the modern Coliseum. The innocent days of St. Veronica singing songs from *South Pacific* gave way to fear of lustful men with knives, the lions' jaws, Krushchev and his henchmen. No matter which way you turned, there was no shortage of tortures to endure. Suffering had lost its sheen.

When I entered junior high school, my parents decided on a seismic shift in our education. My sister Pat had developed a stomach ulcer which my parents attributed to Catholic schools. We went "public," as we referred to our neighbors who attended nonparochial schools. We had often wondered what became of those wayward, non-Catholic souls; now, we joined their ranks. At first, thin and shy, I hopped to my feet when called on by the teacher, face flushed at my inability to lose the trappings of obedience and conformity Catholic school had drilled into me. But I acculturated quickly. By eighth grade, I lingered in the bathroom after study hall, drawn by the girls in miniskirts and boots, thick black eyeliner on shaded lids, blowing Marlboro smoke through whitened lips. Sirenlike, they called to me with their smoky conversation of boys and shoplifting on Saturdays. Like Dawn Montgomery, they didn't care that their souls were damned. I yearned to be like them. Beyond the need to be good, freed from the thirst for salvation.

Through junior high and into high school, I skipped classes to smoke in the bathroom. Left alone, I read. My record was *Catcher in the Rye*, *Franny and Zooey*, and a pack of Marlboros, in the same stall on a single day. I consumed most of the reading for French class there, lost with Baudelaire and Rimbaud in a big, blue book that bore a striking resemblance to *Lives of the Saints*. Once again I went into hiding as I tortured my mouth into French pronunciation, longing for an identity more exotic than my own. Abandoning my quest for a holy self, I searched for a more alluring secular version in the world of new books.

By my junior year, the bathroom stalls had grown risky. I spent much of my time searching for places to pass school hours undetected. One day, I sought refuge in the library of a small local college. There, in the basement, I discovered an empty study room marked "smoking." Inside, a long oval table full of ashtrays stood surrounded by walls of leather-bound books. I lit a Marlboro and pulled one of the dark-red volumes from the shelf. My fingers caressed the gold inlay on blood-red leather. *Crime and Punishment* by Fyodor Dostoevsky. I yanked down one book after another, twitching with anticipation. Tolstoy, Turgenev. Russianol A surge of surprise and pleasure — the deep thrill of forbidden fruit. A world cordoned off since childhood.

I settled down to read, beginning with *Crime and Punishment*. For weeks I returned to that room, progressing to *The Idiot*, then *Notes from the Underground* working up to *The Brothers Karamazov*. I plunged deep, flirting with the dangerous, enticing edges of Dostoevskian contradiction. Saintly prostitutes. "Meek" women with steel determination who longed to rescue doomed outsiders. Dark characters like Raskolnikov, who committed murder to save the world. Gamblers and drunks, beating their brows, pacing underground, self-lacerating, longing for pain, hungering for redemption. Characters built on paradox, every dark pursuit yielding new selves. Their journeys repelled and fascinated me at the same time. Just like the mysteries of religion. From this new terrain emerged the familiar voice of Sister Eileen proclaiming "Happiness through suffering."

I turned to Tolstoy, moving from *Anna Karenina* to *War and Peace*. The female characters gripped me. I became the wildly romantic Anna, lost in the world of illicit romance and sex. In Anna, I embraced all that the sisters derided: selfishness, abandon, and carnal desire. I heaped scorn on Kitty, who lived for the happiness of others, for the fulfillment of family life — the very embodiment of the Catholic ideal. Who wanted her dull fate, built on renunciation of the self, and denial of the body? Maria Goretti be damned. Freed from the confining stories of the big green, blue, and yellow books, I entered the leather-bound world of wicked happiness.

But that's not how it happened. At least not completely. I did flirt with rebellion. I did love the wild and romantic Russian women characters. But in the end, I could not escape my deadly attraction to Dostoevsky's "meek ones," the self-sacrificing women who gave their energies to others. Theirs was the narrative of happiness for which I'd been groomed. I read and reread *Anna Karenina*, yearning to be Anna. Instead, I felt destined to the fate of self-sacrificing Kitty. Sunk into my teenage rebellion, seemingly light-years beyond my Catholic upbringing, I felt the pull of its teachings in the stories that continued to mold me.

I haven't re-read Russian novels for nearly twenty years. My shelves are lined with biographies of women — strong female characters who shape their own destinies. I banish heroines with self-sacrificing tendencies. But as I drove home along the Willamette River and felt the old story resurface, I wondered what it would take to dislodge the narrative of happiness through suffering. Almost immediately, I questioned what might replace it. If the stories of sacrifice prove unsatisfying and dangerous, so too does the self-absorption of characters like Anna Karenina. In the end, Anna K. self-destructed, flung across the cold iron tracks of a desolate Russian railroad station. Another version of the martyrdom story, one unredeemed by a higher purpose and thus even more unsavory.

What might be a new story to live by, an avenue toward fulfillment that neither negates nor glorifies the self? To imagine its contours, I begin with a revision of my past. I'm back at St. Ursula's searching for the finger. I no longer walk in single file. Forget self-control. Eyes wide open, I follow my intuition about the finger, careening in a jagged line across the lawn. I know where the finger lies. Sister Eileen tries to call me back. John Moriarty tries to follow. But I, certain of my path, risk their anger and reproach. Midway across the lawn, I stop before the finger, wrap it in my beanie cap, and return it to the rectory. John Moriarty is fuming. Father Devrees is relieved. All the other girls are proud. A victory for following one's vision, for stepping out of line in pursuit of a just cause.

What I want for young girls coming of age is the freedom to envision paths toward happiness. Then, who knows what might really happen?

# III

## *Redeeming Grace*

# *from* Memoirs of a Dutiful Daughter

ALL NATURE SPOKE TO ME OF GOD'S PRESENCE. BUT QUITE DEFINITELY IT SEEMED TO ME that he was a total stranger to the restless world of men. Just as the Pope, away inside the Vatican, hadn't to bother his head about what was going on in the world, so God, high up in the infinity of heaven, was not supposed to take any interest in the details of earthly adventures. I had long since learned to distinguish His law from secular authority. My insolence in class, and my furtive reading of banned books did not concern Him. As year followed after year, my growing piety was purified and I began to reject dry-as-dust mortality in favor of a more lively mysticism. I prayed, I meditated, I tried to make my heart aware of the divine presence. About the age of twelve I invented mortifications: locked in the water closet — my sole refuge — I would scrub my flesh with pumice stone until the blood came, and beat myself with the thin golden chain I wore around my neck. My fervor did not bear fruit. In my devotional books there was much talk about spiritual progress and exaltation; souls were supposed to stagger up rugged paths and overcome obstacles; one moment they would be trudging across barren wildernesses and then a celestial dew would fall for their refreshment: it was quite an adventure; in fact, whereas intellectually I felt I was moving ever onward and upward in my quest for knowledge, I never had the impression that I was drawing any closer to God. I longed for apparitions, ecstasies; I yearned for something to happen inside or outside me: but nothing came, and in the end my spiritual exercises were more and more like make-believe. I exhorted myself to have patience and looked forward to the day when, miraculously detached from the earth, I would find myself ensonced at the heart of eternity. Meanwhile I was able to go on living unconstrainedly on earth because my efforts set me up on spiritual peaks whose serenity could not be troubled by worldly trifles.

My complacency received a nasty shock. For the last seven years I had been making my confession to Abbé Martin twice a month; I would expatiate upon the state of my immortal soul; I would accuse myself of having taken Holy Communion without any true religious fervor, of not having thought often enough of God, and of having paid Him only lip service in my prayers; he would reply to these ethereal shortcomings with a sermon couched in very elevated terms. But one day, instead of going through the usual rigmarole, he began to speak to me in a more familiar tone of voice: "It has come to my ears that my little Simone has changed . . . that she is disobedient, noisy, that she answers back when she is reprimanded . . . From now on you must be careful about these things." My cheeks were aflame; I gazed with horror upon the impostor whom for years I had taken as the representative of God on earth; it was as if he had suddenly tucked up his cassock and revealed the skirts of one of the religious bigots; his priest's robe was only a disguise; it covered an old busybody who fed on gossip. With burning face I left the confessional, determined never to set foot in it again: from that moment on, it would have been as repugnant to me to kneel before Abbé Martin as before "the Old Scarecrow." Whenever I caught a glimpse of his black skirts swishing along a school corridor, my heart would begin to thump and I would run away: they made me feel physically sick, as if the abbé's deceit had made me his accomplice in some obscene act.

I suppose he must have been very surprised; but probably he felt himself bound by the secret of the confessional; I never heard that he told anyone of my defection; he did not attempt to have it out with me. The break had been sudden, but complete.

God emerged blameless from this episode; but only just. If I had been so prompt in disowning my spiritual director, it was in order to exercise the frightful suspicion which for a moment veiled the heavens in blackness: perhaps God Himself was as fussy and narrow-minded as a religious bigot; perhaps God was stupid! While the abbé was talking to me, a heavy hand had fallen on the back of my neck, bending my head down until it pressed my face into the ground; till the day of my death, the dead hand of stupidity would force me to crawl through life, blinded by mud and darkness; I should have to say good-bye forever to truth, liberty, and all happiness: living would be a calamity and a disgrace.

I pulled myself away from that leaden hand; I concentrated all my revulsion on the traitor who had usurped the role of divine intermediary. When I left the chapel, God had been restored to His position of omniscient majesty; I had patched up heaven again. I went wandering under the vaulted roofs of Saint-Sulpice, seeking a confessor who would not alter the messages from on high by the use of impure human words. I tried a redhead, and then a dark-haired one whom I succeeded in interesting in my soul. He suggested a few themes for meditation and lent me a *Handbook of Ascetic and Mystical Theology*. But in the great bare church I could not feel at home as I did in the school chapel. My new spiritual director had not been given to me when I was a small girl; I had chosen him, rather haphazardly: he was not a Father and I could not open up completely to him. I had passed judgment on a priest, and despised him: no other priest would ever seem to me to be like the Sovereign Judge. No one on earth was the exact incarnation of God: I was alone before Him.

And in the very depths of my being there remained unanswered some disturbing questions: who was He? what did He really want? on whose side was He?

My father was not a believer; the greatest writers and the finest thinkers shared his skepticism; on the whole, it was generally the women who went to church; I began to find it paradoxical and upsetting that the truth should be *their* privilege, when men, beyond all possible doubt, were their superiors. At the same time, I thought there was no greater disaster than to lose one's faith and I often tried to insure myself against this risk. I had reached rather an advanced stage in my religious instruction and had followed lectures in apologetics; I had subtle arguments to refute any objection that might be brought against revealed truths; but I didn't know one that could prove them. The allegory of the watch and the watchmaker did not convince me. I was too ignorant of human suffering to find in it an argument against Providence; but there was no very obvious harmony in the world. Christ and a host of saints had manifested the supernatural here on earth: I realized that the Bible, the Gospels, the miracles, and the visions were vouched for only by the authority of the Church. "The greatest miracle at Lourdes is Lourdes itself," my father used to say. The facts of religion were convincing only to those who were already convinced. Today I did not doubt that the Virgin had appeared to Bernadette in a blue-and-white robe: but tomorrow perhaps I would doubt it. Believers admitted the existence of this vicious circle since they declared that faith requires divine grace. I didn't suppose that God would play a nasty trick on me and refuse me grace forever; but I should have liked all the same to be able to get my hands on some irrefutable proof; I found only one: the voices of Joan of Arc. Joan belonged to historical fact; my father as well as my mother venerated her. She was neither a liar nor one of the illuminati so how could one deny her witness? The whole of her extraordinary adventure confirmed it: the voices had spoken to her; this was an established scientific fact and I couldn't understand how my father managed to evade it.

One evening at Meyrignac, as on so many other evenings, I was leaning out of my window; a warm fragrance was rising from the stables up to the star-sprinkled sky; my prayer rose halfheartedly and then fell back to earth. I had spent my day eating forbidden apples and reading in a book by Balzac – also forbidden – the strange idyl of a young man and a panther; before falling asleep I was going to tell myself some queer old tales which would put me in a queer state of mind. "These are sins," I told myself. It was impossible to deceive myself any longer: deliberate disobedience, systematic lies, impure imaginings such conduct could hardly be described as innocent. I dipped my hands into the freshness of the cherry-laurel leaves, I listened to the gurgling of the water, and I knew then that nothing would make me give up earthly joys. "I no longer believe in God," I told myself, with no great surprise. That was proof: if I had believed in Him, I should not have allowed myself to offend him so lightheartedly. I had always thought that the world was a small price to pay for eternity; but it was worth more than that, because I loved the world, and it was suddenly God whose price was small: from now on His name would have to be a cover for nothing more than a mirage. For a long time now the concept I had had of Him had been purified and refined, sublimated to the point where He was faceless, He no longer had any concrete link with the earth, or therefore any being. His perfection canceled out His reality. That is why I felt so little surprise when I became aware of His absence in my heart and in heaven. I was not denying Him in order to rid myself of an intruder: on the contrary, I realized that He was playing no further part in my life, and so I concluded that He had ceased to exist for me.

This liquidation had been bound to happen. I was too much of an extremist to be able to live under the eye of God and at the same time say both yes and no to life. On the other hand it would have been repugnant to me to leap without sincere belief from the profane to the sacred and to affirm my belief in Him when I was living without His presence. I could not admit any kind of compromise arrangement with heaven. However little you withheld from Him, it would be too much if God existed; and however little you gave Him, it would be too much again if He did not exist. Quibbling with one's conscience, haggling over one's pleasures – such petty bargaining disgusted me. That is why I did not attempt to use trickery. As soon as I saw the light, I made a clean break.

My father's skepticism had prepared the way for me; I would not be embarking alone upon a hazardous adventure. I even felt great relief at finding myself released from the bonds of my sex and my childhood, and in agreement with those liberal spirits I admired. The voices of Joan of Arc did not trouble me too much; I was intrigued by other enigmas: but religion had got me used to mysteries. And it was easier for me to think of a world without a creator than of a creator burdened with all the contradictions of the world. My incredulity never once wavered.

Yet the face of the universe changed. More than once during the days that followed, sitting under the copper beech or the silvery poplars I felt with anguish the emptiness of heaven. Until then, I had stood at the center of a living tableau whose colors and lighting God Himself had chosen; all things murmured softly of His glory. Suddenly everything fell silent. And what a silence! The earth was rolling through space that was unseen by any eye, and lost on its immense surface, I stood, alone, in the midst of sightless regions of the air. Alone: for the first time I understood the terrible significance of that word. Alone: without a witness, without anyone to speak to, without refuge. The breath in my body, the blood in my veins, and all this hurly-burly in my head existed for no one. I got up and ran back to the garden and sat down under the catalpa between Mama and Aunt Marguerite, so great was my need to hear a human voice.

I made another discovery. One afternoon, in Paris, I realized that I was condemned to death. I was alone in the house and I did not attempt to control my despair: I screamed and tore at the red carpet. And when, dazed, I got to my feet again, I asked myself: "How do other people manage? How shall *I* manage to . . ." It seemed to me impossible that I could live all through life with such horror gnawing at my heart. When the reckoning comes, I thought, when you're thirty or forty and you think "It'll be tomorrow," how on earth can you bear the thought? Even more than death itself I feared that terror which would soon be with me always.

Fortunately, in the course of the school year these metaphysical fulgurations were rare: I hadn't enough free time and solitude. My changed attitude did not affect my daily life. I had stopped believing in God when I discovered that God had no influence on my behavior: so this did not change in any way when I gave Him up. I had always imagined that the logical necessity of moral laws depended on Him: but they were so deeply engraved on my spirit that they remained unaltered for me after I had abolished Him. It was my respect for her which gave my mother's rulings a sacred character, and not the fact that she might owe her authority to some supernatural power. I went on submitting myself to her decisions. Everything was as before: the concept of duty; righteousness; sexual taboos.

I had no intention of revealing my spiritual turmoil to my father: it would have put him in a terribly embarrassing situation. So I bore my secret all alone and found it a heavy burden: for the first time in my life I had the feeling that good was not necesarily the same thing as truth. I couldn't help seeing myself through the eyes of others — my mother, Zaza, my school friends, my teachers even — and through the eyes of the girl I once had been. The year before, in the philosophy class, there had been an older pupil of whom it was rumored that she was an "unbeliever"; she worked well, she never expressed subversive notions, and she had not been expelled; but I would feel a sort of terror whenever, in the school corridors, I caught sight of her face, which was all the more disturbing because of the fixed intensity of a glass eye. Now it was my turn to feel I was a black sheep. My case was aggravated by deception: I still went to Mass and took Holy Communion. I would swallow the Host with complete indifference, and yet I knew that, according to the faith, I was committing a sacrilege. I was making my crime all the worse by concealing it; but how could I have dared confess it? I would have been pointed at with the finger of scorn, expelled from the school; I would have lost Zaza's friendship; and how terribly upset my mother would have been! I was condemned to live out a lie. It was no harmless fib: it was a lie that cast a shadow over my whole life, and sometimes — especially with Zaza whose forthrightness I admired — it weighed upon my spirits like a secret disease. Once again I was the victim of a spell which I couldn't manage to exorcise: I had done nothing wrong, and I felt guilty. If the grown-ups had called me a hypocrite, a blasphemer, an unnatural and crafty child, their verdict would have seemed to me at once horribly unjust and perfectly well-deserved. I could be said to be living a double life; there was no relationship between my true self and the self that others saw.

Sometimes I suffered such distress at feeling myself a marked person, an accursed outcast, that I longed to fall into error again. I had to return the *Handbook of Ascetic and Mystical Theology* to Abbé Roullin. I went back to Saint-Sulpice, knelt down in his confessional, and told him that I had not partaken of the sacraments for several months because I had lost my faith. Seeing the *Handbook* and measuring the heights from which I had fallen, the abbé was astounded, and with a disconcerting brutality asked me: "What mortal sin have you committed?" I protested that I had not committed any sin. He did not believe me and advised me to pray hard. I resigned myself to the life of an outcast.

About this time I read a novel which seemed to me to translate my spiritual exile into words: George Eliot's *The Mill on the Floss* made an even deeper impression upon me than *Little Women*. I read it in English, at Meyrignac, lying on the mossy floor of a chestnut grove. Maggie Tulliver, like myself, was torn between others and herself: I recognized myself in her. She too was dark, loved nature and books and life, was too headstrong to be able to observe the conventions of her respectable surroundings, and yet was very sensitive to the criticism of a brother she adored. Her friendship with the young hunchback who lent her books moved me just as much as that between Jo and Laurie; I longed for her to marry him. But once again love broke with childhood. Maggie fell in love with a cousin's fiancé, Stephen, whose heart she captured quite unintentionally. Compromised by him, she refused to marry him out of loyalty to Lucy: village society would have excused a treachery sanctioned by marriage, but would not forgive Maggie for having sacrificed appearances to the voice of conscience. Even her brother disowned her. The only relationship I could imagine was a love friendship; in my view, the exchange and discussion of books between a boy and a girl linked them forever; I couldn't understand the attraction Maggie felt for Stephen. But since she loved him, she should not have given him up. It was when she went back to the old mill, when she was misunderstood, calumniated, and abandoned by everyone that I felt my heart blaze with sympathy for her. I wept over her sorry fate for hours. The others condemned her because she was superior to them; I resembled her, and thenceforward I saw my isolation not as a proof of infamy but as a sign of my uniqueness. I couldn't see myself dying of loneliness. Through the heroine, I identified myself with the author: one day other adolescents would bathe with their tears a novel in which I would tell my own sad story.

I had long ago decided to devote my life to intellectual labors. Zaza shocked me when she declared, in a provocative tone of voice: "Bringing nine children into the world as Mama has done is just as good as writing books." I couldn't see any common denominator between these two modes of existence. To have children who in their turn would have more children was simply to go on playing the same old tune ad infinitum; the scholar, the artist, the writer, and the thinker created other worlds, all sweetness and light, in which everything had a purpose. That was where I wished to spend my life; I was quite determined to carve out a place for myself in those rarefied spheres. As soon as I had renounced heaven, my worldly ambitions increased: it became necessary for me to be somebody. Stretched out in a meadow, I could see at eye level the endless waves of grass, each blade identical, each submerged in a miniature jungle that concealed it from all the rest. That unending repetition of ignorance and indifference was a living death. I raised my eyes and looked at the oak tree: it dominated the landscape and there was not another like it. That, I decided, is what *I* would be like.

Why did I decide to be a writer? As a child, I had never taken my scribblings very seriously; my real aim had been to acquire knowledge; I enjoyed doing French compositions, but my teachers objected to my stilted style; I did not feel I was a "born" writer. Yet at the age of fifteen when I wrote in a friend's album the plans and preferences which were supposed to give a picture of my personality, I answered without hesitation the question "What do you want

to do later in life?" with "To be a famous author." As far as my favorite composer and my favorite flower were concerned I had invented more or less factitious preferences. But on that one point I
had no doubts at all: I had set my heart on that profession, to the ex-
clusion of everything else.

The main reason for this was the admiration I felt for writers: my
father rated them far higher than scholars, philosophers, and pro
fessors. I, too, was convinced of their supremacy: even if his name
was well-known, a specialist's monograph would be accessible to
only a small number of people; but everyone read novels: they
touched the imagination and the heart; they brought their authors
universal and intimate fame. As a woman, these dizzy summits
seemed to me much more accessible than the lowlier slopes; the
most celebrated women had distinguished themselves in literature.

I had always had a longing to communicate with others. In my
friend's album I cited as my favorite hobbies reading and conversation. I was a great talker. I would recount, or try to, everything that
had struck me in the course of the day. I dreaded night and obliv-
ion; it was agony to condemn to silence all that I had seen, felt, and
liked. Moved by the moonlight, I longed for pen and paper and the
ability to describe my feelings. When I was fifteen I loved volumes
of letters, intimate journals – for example, the diary of Eugénie de
Guérin – books that attempted to make time stand still. I had also
realized that novels, short stories, and tales are not divorced from
life but that they are, in their own way, expressions of it.

If at one time I had dreamed of being a teacher it was because I
wanted to be a law unto myself; I now thought that literature would
allow me to realize this dream. It would guarantee me an immortality that would compensate for the loss of heaven and eternity;
there no longer was a God to love me, but I would burn as a beacon
in millions of hearts. By writing a work based on my own experi-

ence I would re-create myself and justify my existence. At the same time I would be serving humanity: what finer offering could I make to it than books? I was concerned at the same time with myself and with others; I accepted the individuality of my "incarnation," but I did not wish to surrender membership in the universal. This writing project reconciled everything; it gratified all the aspirations which had been unfolding in me during the past fifteen years.

# *from* A Day in the Life of Spanish

*Basil Johnston's* Indian School Days *is the poignant autobiographical account of Native American students who were forced to attend St. Peter Claver's Indian Residential School, later called the Garnier Residential School, in Ontario, Canada. The school eventually came to be called "Spanish," after the village in which it was located.*

7:55 A.M. CLANG! CLANG! CLANG!

After grace of thanksgiving, it was outside to the recreation hall. Except for the lucky ones in Grades 1, 2 and 3, everyone went to his assigned place of work. The seniors, in Grades 6, 7 and 8, went to their permanent occupations: to the barn, to tend horses, cows, sheep, pigs and all their products; to the chicken coop, to look after chickens; to the tailor shop, shoe shop, electrical shop, carpentry shop, blacksmith shop, mill or plumber's shack. These were jobs of standing and responsibility in the adolescent community. The other boys, from grades that had no status, waited outside the storeroom for the issue of mops, pails, sponges, soap, rags, brooms, dustpans, dust-bane and other janitorial paraphernalia for performing the menial tasks of washing, sweeping, mopping, dusting, polishing toilets, corridors, refectory, chapels, kitchen, dormitory, scullery, every conceivable area.

"*Johnston!* Number *forty-three!*"

"Yes, Father."

"I have special job for you," Father said, handing me a mop, pail, soap and a peculiar, curved oval brush such as I had never before seen. Up to this time in my life the hardest and most detestable forms of work that I had performed were reluctantly carrying either wood or water for my mother. I really didn't want to work but, if work I must, it was better to begin with something special rather than with some plebeian labour.

"Come with me!"

Father Buck led me directly to the toilets, which were so vile with the reek of human waste that I nearly choked and disgorged my mush. Even Father Buck, who must have been aged about twenty-three or twenty-four, gasped as he issued his instructions: "Wash the bowls with this and the walls with this, and the urinals with this, and the floors with this, no? . . . And make clean and smell good . . . no? I come back." I thought that Father Buck staggered slightly as he went out and breathed deeply to cleanse his lungs.

I too had to go out to avoid being overcome. While I stood outside breathing in oxygen, I developed a stratagem for cleaning up the toilets without collapsing. For self-preservation the job had to be done in stages. Flush the toilets, run outside. Wash the bowls, run outside. Hold breath, wash urinals, run outside. Hold breath, wash partitions, run outside. Spread sawdust on the floor, run outside. Sweep up sawdust, run outside. The toilets may not have completely lost their miasma of dung as I swept up the last pile of sawdust, but they at least looked vastly cleaner. I staggered out, inhaling huge quantities of the "breath of life," and waited, proud of my labours . . . almost. "Achtung! You finish this, already?" Father asked as if he were astounded.

"Yes," I replied with a considerable burst of pride.

"Well! We shall see."

Father Buck didn't have to go into the lavatory to reach the conclusion that, "They not smell good." I was going to say that the smell was stuck in the walls, in the ceiling, on the floor, in the corners, everywhere, but I didn't get a chance. Father entered the lavatory and went directly into a compartment. Inside, he bent down in order to run his finger in the back of and under the bowl. He showed me a black fingertip.

"Sooooo! You like this fight but no like it work. Then you work extra week in these toilets until you learn it like work or until you learn it meaning of clean."

It was back to work.

8:55 A.M. Clang! Clang! Clang!

Line up again. According to the system then in operation half the senior boys went to class, while the other half went to work not only to practise a trade but also to provide the labour needed to run the institution. In the afternoon the seniors switched shifts. The younger boys went to classes the entire day.

"Number forty-*three!*"

There was no answer.

"Number forty-*three!*" A little louder.

Silence.

"You! Johnston!"

"Yes, Father!"

"You are number *forty-three!* Do you understand?"

I nodded.

"You answer, when I call *forty-three!*"

"Yes, Father."

"Now, you go with this Grade 5 to Father Mayhew's class."

"But Father, I'm supposed to be in Grade 6. I was in Grade 5 last year."

"Sooooo! You like it fight, you no like it work, and you like it argue! . . . sooooo!" And Father Buck fished out of his cassock pocket a black book in which he scribbled something while looking severely at me. "Soooo, you say you in Grade 6. That's what they all say. Now you be quiet. And no more trouble. You go with this Grade 5."

On the way upstairs, Ovilla Trudeau commented with a snicker, "You didn't think you'd get away with that, did you?"

"What's that teacher's name? I can't understand dat pries'."

"Father Mayhew."

After the Lord's Prayer I went directly to the teacher's desk.

"Father. Someone made a mistake. I'm supposed to be in Grade 6. I passed Grade 5 already. I tol' Father Buck, but he won't believe me."

Father Mayhew just looked at me. "I'm told you're in Grade 5. There's nothing that you can do about it."

But my appointment to Grade 5, as I learned years later, was not a product of misunderstanding but a coldly calculated decision made "for my own good." For if I had been allowed to proceed to Grade 6 as I should have been, it would have disrupted the entire promotion and graduation schedule that decreed that all boys committed to a residential school remain in the institution until age sixteen, or until their parents, if living together, arranged an early parole. If I had progressed at my normal rate through the elementary school I would have been ready for "entrance examinations" by age twelve. According to the administration it would not have been appropriate or in the best interests of society to release me or any one of my colleagues prior to age sixteen. The only solution was to have a boy repeat grades until Grade 8 and age sixteen were synchronized. I was not the only one to be so penalized.

Hence I was mired in Grade 5, forced to listen to dull and boring lessons rendered even duller and more boring by my sense of unjust treatment. What unspeakable fate I might have suffered had it not been for a collection of Tom Swift books and other volumes of doubtful merit, it is hard to say. That Father Mayhew turned a blind eye to my reading in class helped enormously; he didn't seem to mind as long as I didn't disturb the class and passed the tests. The only time I paid attention was during the reading of *The Song of Hiawatha*, whose Indian words Father Mayhew mangled and garbled. Inspired by the success of *Hiawatha*, Father Mayhew next tried to inflict *Winnie the Pooh* and *Anne of Green Gables* on us, but we denounced them as insipid so frequently that eventually Father Mayhew stopped reading them.

12:00 noon. Clang! Clang! Clang!

*"Line up! Shut up!"* The command need not have been shouted, but it was nevertheless bellowed, in the belief that a shout always obtained quicker compliance.

"Shshshshsh."

For dinner there was barley soup with other ingredients, including chunks of fat and gristle, floating about in it. Finding a chunk of fat in one's soup was like receiving a gift of manna, for it could be used to garnish the two slices of bread that came with the meal if one had lacked the foresight or the prudence to hide a chunk of lard from breakfast for one's dinner needs by sticking the lard under the table. Barley soup, pea soup (not the French or Quebec variety), green and yellow, vegetable soup, onion soup, for dinner and supper. Barley soup prepared in a hundred different combinations. "Barley soup! Don't that cook have no imagination?" Barley soup in the fall. "Hope they run outa that stuff pretty soon." Barley soup in the spring. "How much o' this stuff they plant, anyways? Hope a plague o' locusts eat all the barley this summer." Besides the soup there was a large jug of green tea diluted with milk. Clatter, clatter. "Pass the tea." Shuffle, scrape.

4:15 P.M. Clang! Clang! Clang!

By now our sole preoccupation, as hunger displaced the shapes and shadows, was food. On our way downstairs one of our colleagues expressed our collective fear: "If I starve to death, it's going to be their fault; we never have enough but they have lots for themselves."

In the recreation hall a line formed bearing in the direction of the refectory, in front of whose doors was set one of the refectory tables. Behind this makeshift counter were two boys, one of whom was lopping off the green tops of carrots with a large butcher knife which he handled like a machete, while the other distributed two raw carrots to each customer. "Collation" they called this lunch. Today it was carrots; tomorrow it would be a wedge of raw cabbage; the day after, a turnip, raw like everything else. As each boy received his ration he was directed to take his collation outside. Despite its lofty name, collation was regarded as little better than animal fodder. Nevertheless, every boy ate the fodder to stave off starvation.

Collation was intended, I guess, not only to allay hunger pains, but also to restore flagging energies. It was our first real period of leisure in a day that had begun at 6:15 A.M., but if anyone hoped for or expected an extended period of idleness, as I then did, he was soon set straight by the sight of the accursed bell in Father Buck's hand.

"Hey! Father!" an anonymous voice called out. "How come you not eating carrots like us?" To which there was no answer.

6:00 P.M. Not one second before the minute or the hour would Father ring that bell, Clang! Clang! Clang! Clangity-clang! "Hurry up! Shshshsh!" There was silence, almost absolute except for the scuffle of boots and the odd sniffle and cough. This is the way it should have been, the way that it was intended to be, the way that would have gratified and edified the prefects and the way that would have pleased Father Buck.

Father Buck nodded, as he always did, to his colleague, Father

Kehl, to open the door. In we filed and, for the next twenty minutes or a little longer, gave ourselves wholeheartedly to pea soup, bread, lard and green tea from Java. In quantity served there was just enough food to blunt the sharp edge of hunger for three or four hours, never enough to dispel hunger completely until the next meal. Every crumb was eaten, and the last morsel of bread was used to sponge up any residue of soup that might still be clinging to the sides or to the bottom of the plates, thereby leaving the plates clean and dry, the way puppies lick their dishes clean. There was the same quantity for every boy, regardless of size or need. Yet not even the "little shots," whose ingestive capacities were considerably less than those of their elders and who therefore should have required and received less, were ever heard to extol a meal with "I'm full." "I'm full" was an expression alien in our world and to our experience.

Never having the luxury of a second serving or an extra slice, the boys formed a healthy regard for food that bordered on reverence that shaped their eating habits. If they could not glut themselves, they could at least prolong the eating by carnally indulging in every morsel of food. To eat with such carnality may have constituted a sin, but we never considered it as such. Meals became rituals almost as solemn as religious services in their intensity, the only sounds the clatter of spoons on plates and mugs and the muted "Pass the mush" or "You owe me a slice"; "When you going to pay me that lard you owe me?" "I'm so hungry right now, can you wait till tomorrow?"

As deliberate as the boys were at table, few could match the solemnity or the sensuousness with which "That's the Kind" (Jim Wemigwans) presided over his meal. During the entire course of supper "That's the Kind" broke his bread, one pinch at a time, as one might nip petals off a bloom; each pinch was then deposited with delicacy on his tongue. Our colleague ate every morsel, be it barley, green beans, peas, onions, potatoes – every spoonful of every meal – with as much deliberation and relish as if it were manna or ambrosia . . . or his last meal prior to execution.

"Come on, Father! You ring that bell too soon . . . jis' when we were having fun. You don' want us to have fun."

Bells and whistles, gongs and clappers represent everything connected with sound management – order, authority, discipline, efficiency, system, organization, schedule, regimentation, conformity – and may in themselves be necessary and desirable. But they also symbolize conditions, harmony and states that must be established in order to have efficient management: obedience, conformity, dependence, subservience, uniformity, docility, surrender. In the end it is the individual who must be made to conform, who must be made to bend to the will of another.

And because prefects were our constant attendants and superintendents, regulating our time and motions, scheduling our comings and goings, supervising our work and play, keeping surveillance over deeds and words, enforcing the rules and maintaining discipline with the help of two instruments of control and oppression – bells and the black book – we came to dislike and to distrust these young men. Most were in their early twenties and had completed their novitiate of four years' study at Guelph, Ontario. Regardless of their dispositions or their attitudes toward us, they were the archenomies, simply because they held the upper hand both by virtue of their calling and by the exercise of threats. If one of our fellow inmates grew too contumacious even for the strap there was always the "reform school."

While most of these young novices (referred to as first, second or third prefects) superintended our lives by the book, a few possessed a degree of compassion. But even they were helpless to show their sympathy in a tangible way, for the prefects, too, were under the close and keen observation of the Father Superior and "the Minister," the administrator of the school. During their regency, the prefects, sometimes called "scholastics" by the priests, had to demonstrate that they had the stuff to be Jesuits.

Once one of the boys, after being warned to *"Shut up!"* continued to whisper, or perhaps just uttered one more word, which, if left unsaid, would have rendered his entire message meaningless. It must have been a very important word to risk its utterance in the presence of Father Buck. Anyway, the prefect flew into a rage and struck the offender on the head with the bell. At least, it appeared as if Father Buck had clouted the offender with the bell, for he struck our colleague with the same hand in which he held the bell — not hard enough to draw blood but forcefully enough to raise a contusion and to elicit an "Eeeeeyow!" and cause the victim to clutch his head in pain.

Even before the outcry had subsided, the senior boys at the back — Renee Cada, Tom White, Louis Mitchell, Jim Coocoo, John Latour and Louis Francis — protested: "Come on, Father! That's going too far." They wrenched the bell from Father Buck's hand and threatened to knock him on the head to "See how you'd like it. . . ."

The boy who had seized the bell raised his hand as if to strike . . . but, instead of bringing it down on Father Buck's head, returned the instrument to the disconcerted young prefect, whose face turned from ash to crimson and then back again. Had our colleague carried out his threat, he would most likely have been committed to the nearest reformatory, and also excommunicated from the church. There was a hushed silence throughout the recreation hall, both at the moment the bell was suspended over the prefect's head and afterward.

Father Buck opened the door in silence. What saved the senior boys then and other boys on other occasions from retribution was the prefect's own uneasiness about his superiors. Of course, we knew nothing of the prefects' fears.

9:00 P.M. At that hour we were dismissed from study (the babies having gone to bed at 7:30) to retire to the dormitory where everyone – or nearly everyone – loitered around the washing area, either brushing his teeth or washing . . . or just pretending to wash. Anything to waste time. While many boys dallied near and around the trough, others made their way to the infirmary, there to linger and to have their pains, bruises, aches and cuts attended to by Brother Laflamme.

9:25 P.M. The lights were switched on and off in a radical departure from bell clanging as a signal for all the boys to return to their bedsides.

"Kneel down and say your prayers."

We prayed, imploring God to allow us release from Spanish the very next day.

# *from* Unafraid of the Dark

DADDY TALKED A LOT ABOUT THE STATE OF THE NATION, AND HE LIKED WATCHING AND listening to other people talk about it, too. He watched the Sunday opinion shows as much as he was able. I grew up with the sound of Lawrence Spivak filling my house on Sundays; *Meet the Press* was Daddy's favorite show. The first big political discussions I recall – monologues delivered by my father as my mother listened with varying levels of interest – were all about the presidency of the United States. He had disliked Eisenhower's slow movement to protect black children in Little Rock, and he thought Nixon was a snake. (Even Daddy couldn't have guessed that later events would encourage him to revise his opinion of Nixon downward.) A Democrat to the core ever since the New Deal, he had admired FDR and felt even more strongly about Eleanor Roosevelt, especially her upfront support of Negroes, as in her response when Marian Anderson was denied permission to sing at Constitution Hall in Washington, D.C.

He liked John F. Kennedy, and thought it was significant that Kennedy was a Roman Catholic. That had a lot to do with why Daddy announced to Mama one day that we were all going to be raised Catholic. For him, it was a strategic decision with great implications for our future – Daddy believed strongly in strategy. From where he sat, it seemed clear that if a Catholic could be elected president, Catholics would become very powerful and influential people. He had flirted with the idea of our becoming Jewish, since he regarded Jews as the other religious group with influential members – and also viewed them as the only group of white people he could be bothered with. You could talk to Jews and reach an understanding, Daddy always said, because they were the only white people who had been through anything like what colored people were going through.

Still, Kennedy's rise was persuasive, and so was the financial incentive of being Catholic when your children were going to be sent to Catholic school. Both my parents believed that nuns would really teach us, and tuition at Catholic schools was lower for Catholics than for non-Catholics.

That's how my mother came to sign up for catechism lessons at St. Ambrose Church at Forty-seventh and Ellis. I was old enough to sit quietly with her in class, and to study the green booklet I came to know as the Baltimore Catechism. All of us were eventually baptized on the same quiet afternoon in a room of the church equipped with a marble baptismal font. Each of us had to pick a "baptismal" name. If we had been infants, our given names would have been chosen with an eye toward the saints of the Catholic Church. I chose the name Barbara, because I liked the way it sounded. I also liked the ritual of acceptance into the Church. I loved the quiet and the peace there, the smell of incense and the glow of candles and the giant echo my little footsteps made. It all seemed very godly, and I was a little girl who did a lot of praying. Part of that came from my mother, who said her prayers in front of us nearly every night. She sang spirituals all the time, especially in the morning, as she worked by herself in the kitchen before any of us were up.

Mama was raised in the Pentecostal faith, but she had no special reservations about praying in a Catholic church; for her, it was all the same God. Still, the staid Latin hymns were not the songs she sang throughout the day. On Sunday, she tuned the television to *Ju-*

*bilee Showcase* on Channel Seven. A white man named Sid Ordower was the host, and the show featured gospel singers from Chicago as well as parts of the South, including the show's "house" quartet, the Norfleet Brothers. Mama watched *Jubilee Showcase* for the same reasons many of our neighbors did: it felt familiar and personal, and it was a rare chance to see black people on television.

I learned to listen to both kinds of religious music. The Catholic hymns sounded angelic and otherworldly, a kind of visitation from on high. They were unfamiliar at first, but still incredibly beautiful. The gospel songs sounded in my head like the voices of old friends. They were vital and intense, the way people around me always seemed, and they had the added attraction of telling stories and issuing ultimatums: "Go tell that long-tongued liar, go tell that midnight rider, tell the gambler, rambler, backstabber – tell 'em: God almighty's gonna cut you down." They all seemed to offer immediate, melodic promises of justice.

But the Pentecostals had no schools to speak of, and as I turned six, in the spring of 1961, it was my parents' intention that I get a real education – something my father was convinced could never happen in the segregated Chicago public schools. He had spent hours listening to the news, mumbling under his breath about the superintendent of schools, and talking about the men in Chicago government he called "no-good sumbitches." That he would place me in the hands of such people was unthinkable. Instead, we were all placed – one by one – at the St. Ambrose School, in the firm grasp of the School Sisters of Notre Dame.

On a hazy morning in September 1961, I walked with my mother and brother to the courtyard of 1014 East Forty-seventh Street – St. Ambrose School. As we arrived, boys and girls were already lining up for the morning procession into church for eight o'clock Mass. I was dressed in the blue-and-gray jumper and white blouse that were my uniform; a white lace scarf had already been carefully fastened to my head. A scarf was a requirement for girls. If you didn't have one, the nuns would help you make do with a Kleenex tissue, but the effort would earn you a disapproving look. I lined up with the first grade and went in to Mass; it was the first time I'd been in the church on a day other than Sunday.

I loved church from the start. St. Ambrose felt beautiful to me, reverent and quiet. The floor was red-and-white linoleum tile, shining as though water were continually poured over it. In two alcoves, one on either side of the sanctuary, small altars held rows of votive candles, which flickered in white and red glass holders. Perpendicular to the altars were the confessionals, each with two small doors of carved wood on either side of a larger door, where the priests heard neighborhood sins each Saturday afternoon.

Living as we did in the waning days before Vatican II, we attended the Latin Mass each morning. The Masses were all the same: the priest in glowing vestments in the color of the liturgical season, his back turned to those of us standing in the pews. The consecration was my favorite part. I knew from the catechism that this was the magic part, where bread and wine were turned into the body and blood of Christ. A lucky altar boy rang a cluster of bells to signal the moment of transubstantiation.

Church was everything my house was not: quiet, polished, respectful, and orderly. And school, it turned out, was much the same.

I was surprised at the number of kids in my class who were Jewish. It might never have come up if it hadn't been for the fact that several of them were being confirmed, or bar mitzvahed. I had heard of confirmation; I'd been confirmed the previous year. But the solemn ceremony of the bar mitzvah was new to me. Monica wasn't going to be bas mitzvahed, but she was Jewish, too. I learned a lot that year about the High Holy Days and Jewish food (which it turned out my father knew all about from his abortive attempts at restaurants). I learned about dreidels and Purim (which I loved because it involved one of my favorite characters from the Bible, Esther) and Yom Kippur. I could appreciate the idea of having one day a year to confess every bad thing you'd done, as opposed to doing it continually, every Saturday afternoon, as Catholic kids did.

I also learned Jesus was a Jew. I cannot account for how it was that I missed that minor detail, but I did. When Monica pointed out the logic of it – how he had to be a Jew or they would never have called him Rabbi in certain parts of the New Testament – I was stunned. Monica and I were constantly having great debates over religion. We were much more preoccupied with it than with race. For a while, I kept trying to baptize her; I would wet my hands in the water fountain and chase her around the playground, reciting the words from the Baltimore Catechism: "I baptize you in the name of the Father, and of the Son, and of the Holy Ghost."

But after going to my classmates' bar mitzvahs and seeing the solemnity and beauty of the ceremony (and looking at the astounding gifts they received afterward), and after long religious discussions with Monica, I decided that I should be Jewish too. My parents had a fit. My father said: "What, being black isn't trouble enough; you want to be a Jew too?" I realize now that my desire had more to do with wanting to be like my best friend, with wanting to belong, than it did with any kind of conversion experience. But it took a particular incident to make it clear to me just how much I didn't belong.

It was the afternoon I went to play with Susie Levitt after school. She had asked me over to play earlier in the week. Because I was under strict orders to come home directly from school, going to her house required special dispensation from my parents, since I'd get home after dark. But Mama and Daddy seemed glad for once that I was making friends, and they'd agreed to let me go.

I knew the way to her house from the address: I passed within a block of where she lived each morning. I got off the bus a bit earlier than I usually did, and walked around the corner onto a street of immaculate brownstones. When I reached her address, a narrow, five-story house, I climbed the stairs and was momentarily confused. I couldn't figure out which apartment was hers; there was only one bell, with no message about how many rings would signal her. I took a chance and rang the bell once, figuring someone would direct me to where she lived.

A white woman in a uniform answered the door. When I told her I had come to see Susie, she opened the door wider and let me inside. I looked around for the mailboxes in the vestibule; there were none. I walked into the front room as Susie came downstairs. Something astounding dawned on me as we said hello: there were no apartments. The whole house was hers to live in. Susie asked if I wanted to see the house. I did. She took me through the parlor to the formal dining room and into the kitchen, where a black woman about my mother's age had her back to us. Susie asked me if I wanted a snack; I said no. The woman turned and smiled slightly at me and said hello. I said hello softly, then followed Susie out and upstairs. On the next level, another woman in uniform was ironing clothes as we passed. We walked up and up the elegant winding staircase until we reached the top floor, and Susie opened a door into what looked to me like Paradise.

In the life of every young girl, there is one fantasy. Some girls want the most beautifully dressed life-size doll. Others dream of a shining prince to take them away one day to live as his wise and beautiful queen. My fantasy was small: one day, I would have my own room. I had never even given any thought to what would be in the room; I just knew that one day I would have a room that no one was in but me. Susie already had such a room, but she had more. The room contained the decor of a little girl's dreams. Everything in it was white and gold: the dresser, the mirror frame, the vanity and most of all, the four-poster canopy bed. White curtains floated across the top, sheltering the bed like clouds.

I wanted to know where her brothers and sister slept. She cheerfully showed me her siblings' rooms – none the room of my dreams, but each separate and apart. I don't remember what we did that afternoon. I only remember feeling numb and vague. All the way home I replayed the scenes at her house. By the time I got to Forty-seventh Street to take the bus home, the contrast was evident. The noise of the train, the smells of barbecue from the shack across the street, the sporadic blare of Motown in the record shop as customers checked to be sure the 45 they wanted to buy was the right one, the strolling people in late afternoon, all dark like me, all different from those who inhabited the world I'd left only forty-five minutes earlier. I was different, too.

I walked home from the bus stop, back down Ellis Avenue, past the tansy growing in the cat lady's yard, past the blackberry bush, past Denise Young's fence. I turned on Forty-fifth Street, past the wisps of morning glory vines and the pods filled with next spring's seeds, across the alley to knock on the back door. Mama let me in and asked me if I'd had a good time. I said I had. What else could I say, when anything else would have worried her? Daddy wasn't home yet. I walked through to the front room and put down my school things, hung up my coat. My sister and brothers were playing, Mama was cooking. I walked back to the bathroom, painted a year earlier a brilliant emerald-green enamel that I now saw emphasized the cracking walls. I shut the latch tight before I sat down on the toilet and started to cry.

Being black was not the worst of it; I realized that afternoon that I was poor, too. I would not have my own room, or a white-and-gold canopy bed. Suddenly it was clear – the way my blue skirts and white blouses looked and felt so different from the other girls'. The soft wool they wore did not come from Sears or Goldblatt's, but from Marshall Field or Saks Fifth Avenue. My blouses were not cotton, they were 100 percent drip-dry polyester. I didn't have penny loafers or Bass Weejuns. I had shoes from the 2-for-$5 store. I knew the facts of all these things long before; I had joined with my mother in planning around them. But this was the day I felt it — how different, how really different I was.

When I was cried out, I wiped my face over and over with cold water until I could pass for normal. Fortunately, no one had paid much attention to how long I'd been in the bathroom. They assumed I had started reading something and lost track of time, as I always did. They were wrong this time. Something in me had broken somehow, but I was determined that they wouldn't know. For them to know, it seemed to me, would mean they would feel bad. And I didn't want Mama or Daddy or anybody to feel bad. We couldn't help being poor. It wasn't anybody's fault. And if I hadn't started going to that school, I probably wouldn't even have known. But it was too late for me; I knew that now. And in the months that followed, except when I was with a couple of people like Monica, I grew more silent and unhappy in my awareness. Now I know the feeling for what it was. I was ashamed.

KATHRYN HARRISON

# Catherine Means Pure

MY MOTHER CONVERTED TO CATHOLICISM WHEN I WAS TEN, AND I FOLLOWED IN HER
wake, seeking her even as she sought whatever it was that she had
not found in Christian Science. We had failed at even the most basic
of Mrs. Eddy's tenets, for by then we routinely sought the care of
medical doctors. At first we went only for emergencies like the accident to my chin, but then my mother developed an ulcer, and I,
never inoculated, got tetanus from a scrape, physical collapses both
stubbornly unaffected by our attempts to disbelieve in them.

In preparation for my first Communion, I was catechized by a
priest named Father Dove. Despite this felicitous name, Father
Dove was not the Holy Spirit incarnate: he chain-smoked and his
face over his white collar had a worldly, sanguine hue. Worse, I suspected that my mother was in love with him. She fell in love easily.
One Saturday, I made my first confession (that I had been rude to
my grandmother and had taken three dollars from her purse), and
the next day, I took Communion with eleven other little girls
dressed in white; and from that time forward I attended church in a
marble sanctuary filled with gilt angels, rather than in a gray-and-
blue auditorium. Light came through the stained-glass windows
and splashed colors over everything. A red circle fell on my mother's white throat. Incense roiled around us, and I looked down to
compare the shiny toes of my black patent-leather shoes to those of
hers. When we left, lining up to shake Father Dove's hand, I was

able to study the faces around me and confirm that my mother's wide hazel eyes, her long nose, and high, white forehead indeed made hers more beautiful than anyone else's.

For Christmas the following year I received, in my stocking, a boxed set of four volumes of *Lives of the Saints*, intended for children. There were two volumes of male saints, which I read once, flipping through the onionskin pages, and then left in my dresser drawer, and two of female saints, which I studied and slept with. The books contained color plates, illustrations adapted from works of the masters. Blinded Lucy. Maimed Agatha, her breasts on a platter. Beheaded Agnes. Margaret pressed to death under a door piled high with stones. Perpetua and Felicity mauled by beasts. Wellborn Clare, barefoot and wearing rags. Maria Maddalena de' Pazzi lying on the bed of splinters she made for herself in the woodshed. Veronica washing the floors with her tongue, and Angela drinking water used to bathe a leper's sores. I saw that there were those who were tortured, and those who needed no persecutors – they were enemies to their own flesh.

Saint Catherine of Siena began by saying Hail Marys on every step she climbed. Soon she slept on a board, with a brick for a pillow. She did not like her hair shirt because it smelled, so she took to wearing a little belt of nails that bit into her waist. As Catherine's *Dialogues* (dictated years later, while she was in a sustained ecstasy, which lasted weeks, even months) make clear, she believed earthly suffering was the only way to correct the intrinsic baseness of mankind.

My mother, also, held forth an ideal of perfection, an ideal for which she would suffer, but hers was beauty. For beauty she endured the small tortures of plucking and peel-off face masks, of girdles and pinched toes, of sleep sacrificed to hair rollers and meals reduced to cottage cheese. I knew, from my mother's enthusiastic response to certain pictures in magazines, to particular waifs in the movies, that the child who would best complement her vanity was dark-haired and slender and balanced on point shoes. I was blond, robust, and given to tree-climbing. By the time I was thirteen, all of what was wrong with me – the very fact of me, my presence – settled in an unavoidably obvious issue between my mother and me: how much I weighed. How much there was of me. As my conception had been accidental, as I ought not to have been there at all, it must have struck my mother as an act of defiance that I was so large a child, taller and sturdier than any other girl in my class.

I wished myself smaller. I began to dream at night of Beyond-the-Looking-Glass potions, little bottles bearing draughts that shrank me to nothing; the bit of mushroom which let me disappear between grass blades. I began, too, to dread Sunday lunches taken with my mother, who fastidiously observed my fork in its ascension to my mouth.

Saint Catherine was fourteen when her older sister Bonaventura died in childbirth. Bonaventura was the only member of Catherine's family with whom she shared any real sympathy, and Catherine blamed herself for her sister's death. She believed God had punished her and Bonaventura because Catherine had let her big sister tempt her into using cosmetics and curling her hair. She had let Bonaventura's example convince her, briefly, that a woman could embrace both heavenly and earthly desires.

Whatever buoyancy, whatever youthful resilience Saint Catherine had had, disappeared when she lost her sister. She became uncompromising in turning away from all worldly things: from food, from sleep, from men. Their mother, Lapa, a volatile woman whose choleric screams were reputedly so loud that they frightened passersby on Siena's Via dei Tintori, redoubled her efforts to marry off her uncooperative twenty-fourth child. Some accounts hold that Catherine's intended groom was Bonaventura's widowed husband, a foul-tongued and occasionally brutish man. Catherine refused; she had long ago promised herself to Christ. She cut off her hair and she fasted, eating only bread and uncooked vegetables. She began to experience ecstasies, and it is recorded that when she did, she suffered a tetanic rigor in her limbs. Then Lapa would take her daughter up from the floor where she'd fallen and almost break her bones as she tried to bend the girl's stiff arms and legs.

Though it had been ten years since my mother moved out, she had yet to find a place that suited her for any length of time, and so she received her mail at the more permanent address of her parents, and would stop by after work to pick it up. She came in the back door, cool and perfumed and impeccably dressed, and she drifted into the kitchen to find me in my rumpled school uniform, standing before the open refrigerator. One day, I turned around with a cold chicken leg in my hand. My mother had tossed her unopened bills on the counter and was slowly rereading the message inside a greeting card decorated with a drawing of two lovesick rabbits locked in a dizzy embrace. She smiled slightly – a small and self-consciously mysterious smile – and kept the content of the card averted from my eyes. When she had had her fill of it, she looked up at me. She said nothing but let her eyes rest for a moment on the meat in my hand; then she looked away, from it, from me. She did not need to speak to tell me of her disapproval, and by now my habitual response to my mother had become one of despair: muffled, mute, and stumbling. But in that moment when she looked away from me, hopelessness gave way before a sudden, visionary elation. I dropped the drumstick into the garbage can. The mouthful I had swallowed stopped in its descent, and I felt it, gelid and vile inside me as I washed the sheen of grease from my fingers. At dinnertime, after my mother had left for her apartment, I pleaded too much homework to allow time to eat at the table, and I took my plate from the kitchen to my bedroom and opened the window, dropping the food into the dark foliage of the bushes below.

Among saints, Catherine is remarkable for her will more than for her humility. One of the two women in all of history named a Doctor of the Church (the other is Saint Teresa of Ávila), she, too, confused crowns with halos, and presumed to direct the affairs of popes and kings. Even in her reports of self-flagellation, readers find the pride of the absolutist. No one believed more firmly in Catherine's baseness than did Catherine. Determined that she be the least among mortals, so also — by the topsy-turvy logic of Christian salvation — would she be assured of being the greatest. In her visions of Christ, it is Catherine alone who stands beside Him as His bride.

To earn that place was exhausting beyond mortal ability. Even as the saint tirelessly cared for plague victims, even as she exhorted thousands to convert and lobbied effectively for the return of the papacy from Avignon to Rome, she criticized, scourged, and starved herself. She allowed herself not one mortal pleasure: not food or rest, not beauty, not wealth, not marriage or children. Categorically, she rejected the very things that a mother hopes a daughter's life will hold. And reading accounts of her life, one senses how Catherine enjoyed thwarting her mother, Lapa, enjoy refusing the life her mother gave her. Biographers record that Catherine tried to eat — she wanted to do so in order to dispel accusations of demonic possession — but vomited if so much as a mouthful remained in her stomach. "She lived for years on one lettuce leaf!" was how my mother introduced me to Saint Catherine, as if she were revealing the teachings of a new diet guru.

Holiness. The idea of being consecrated, set apart. And of being whole, pure, untainted by anything. There are different kinds of purity, just as there are many reasons for rejecting life. But, no matter the motive, to the ascetic the rejection always looks the same: like salvation. Catherine would guide me to the salvation I sought. Inhumanly, she had triumphed over mortal limitations, over hunger, fatigue, and despair. She had seen demons and fought them off. And I would use her to fashion my solitary and sinful faith. Sin. A term long ago borrowed from archery: to miss the mark.

During the celebration of the Eucharist, the priest would place the Communion wafer on my tongue. I withdrew it into my mouth carefully, making the sign of the cross over myself. Back in the pew I knelt and lay my head in my arms in a semblance of devotion, stuck out my tongue, and pushed the damp wafer into my sleeve. I was a little afraid of going to hell, very afraid of swallowing bread. My rules had grown more inexorable than the Church's; they alone could save me. But the host was the host, and I could not bring myself to throw it away. So I kept it in my sock drawer with my other relics: a small fetish of my mother's hair, stolen strand by strand from the hairbrush she kept in her purse. An eye pencil from that same source. Two tiny cookies from a Christmas stocking long past, a gingerbread boy and girl, no taller than an inch. A red leather collar from my cat which had died. The trinity in my sock drawer: Mother, Death, and God in the form of weeks' worth of accumulated bits of the body of Christ which I would not eat. Despite Christian Science's early announcements to me, despite mind over matter, I remained enslaved to the material world. In my confused struggle with corpo reality I clung to these bits of rubbish, a collection that would look more at home in a trash can than in a drawer, and resisted what might better save me: food.

I still had my little books of the female saints. I looked at them before bed some nights, stared at their little portraits, at bleeding hands and feet, at exultant faces tipped up to heaven. But I read longer hagiographies now, grown-up ones. When Catherine was twenty-four she experienced a mystical death. "My soul was loosed from the body for those four hours," she told her confessor, who recorded that her heart stopped beating for that long. Though she did not want to return to her flesh, Jesus bade her go back. But henceforth, she was not as other mortals; her flesh was changed and unfit for worldly living. From that time forward she swallowed nothing she did not vomit. Her happiness was so intense that she laughed in her fits of ecstasy, she wept and laughed at the same time.

As I lost weight I watched with exultation as my bones emerged, believing that what I saw would irresistibly lure my mother's love. By the time they had failed to do that — those unlovely angles and hollows — I had so thoroughly confused the sight of them with the happiness I had hoped they would bring that I had created a satisfying, if perverse, system of rewards, one that did not require my mother's participation. I had replaced her with the bait I had hoped would entice her. I loved my transformed self. I could not look at myself enough, and I never went into the bathroom that I did not find myself helplessly undressing before the mirror. I touched myself, too. At night I lay in bed and felt each jutting rib, felt sternum and hipbone, felt my sharp jaw, and with my finger traced the orbit of my eye. Like Catherine's, mine was not a happiness that others understood, for it was the joy of power, of a private, inhuman triumph. Of a universe — my body — utterly subjugated to my will.

My life was solitary, as befits a religious. Too much of human fellowship was dictated by hunger, by taking meals in company, and what I did and did not consume separated me from others. Since I had not yet weaned myself completely from human needs, I drank coffee, tea, and Tab. I ate raw vegetables, multivitamins, No-Doz, and, when I felt very weak, tuna canned in water. When I climbed stairs, I saw stars. And when forced to eat with my grandparents, I did so, but the mask of compliance was temporary, and upstairs in my bathroom, I vomited what I had eaten. Afterward, I would lift my shirt and examine my ribs in the mirror, wanting to be sure that there was no evidence of my brief defilement.

After meals, Catherine drank cold water and gagged herself with a stalk of fennel or a quill pen. It hurt her, and she was glad. She wanted to do all her suffering on earth so that she would be spared purgatory. *This will make you pure,* I used to think when I made myself throw up. I used ipecac, the emetic kept in first-aid kits, a poison to be taken against poisons. It was worse than using my finger, perhaps even worse than a quill; at least that had to have been quick in its mechanical approach. Ipecac was suffering; it seemed to take forever and caused a reeling, sweaty nausea that made me wish I were dead. The retching was violent, but then, I intended it to be punishment.

My grandmother and grandfather, sixty-two and seventy-one at my birth, were now so old that their failing senses granted me freedom unusual for a teenager. Going blind, they did not see my thinness. Deaf, they never heard me in my bathroom. By the time I was sixteen, they depended on my driver's license for their groceries; and en route to the supermarket, I would stop at the mall. "Where did you go, Kalamazoo?" my grandmother would ask when I returned, trying to understand why I was hours late. Sometimes she accused me of secretly meeting boys; she used the word "assignation." But I had always spent my time alone. In the department stores and I went from rack to rack, garment to garment: size two, size two, size two. Each like a rosary bead: another recitation, another confirmation of my size, one more turn of the key in the lock of safety.

*Having conquered hunger, I began on sleep, and one night, in my room, very late, and in the delusional frenzy of having remained awake for nearly seventy-three hours, I began to weep with what I thought was joy. It seemed to me that I had almost gotten there; my flesh was* almost utterly turned to spirit. Soon I would not be mortal, soon I would be as invulnerable as someone who could drink pus and see God. The next day, however, I fainted and suffered a seizure that left me unable for a day to move the fingers on my right hand. I had an electroencephalogram and a number of other tests which proved inconclusive. A different nurse, a different doctor, a different wing of the hospital. But nothing had changed. my mother was making a phone call in the corridor, and I lay on a table trying not to scream, far less able to articulate the danger I sensed than when I was five.

When college gave me the opportunity to leave home, I recovered partially. At heart, I wanted to believe in a different life, and I stopped going to mass and gained a little weight — not too much, because I began taking speed and still made myself throw up sometimes. I wore my mother's clothing, castoffs and whatever I could steal from her, articles that filled the reliquary of my peculiar faith. I zipped and buttoned myself into her garments as if they could cloak me with the love I wanted from her. Like miracle seekers who would tear hair, fingers — whatever they could — from a holy person's body, I was desperate, and one September I took my mother's favorite skirt from under the dry-cleaning bag hanging in the backseat of her car. It was purple, long and narrow. I packed it in my suitcase and took it to school with me. She called me on the phone a week later. "Send it back," she said. I denied having taken it. "You're lying," she said.

Lapa did not want Catherine to scourge herself, so, although her daughter was a grown woman, Lapa took away her private bedroom and forced Catherine to sleep in bed with her. Not to be denied the mortification of her flesh, the saint dragged a plank into the bed after Lapa had fallen asleep, and she laid it between her mother's body and her own. On Lapa's side was smooth wood; on Catherine's, spikes.

I wore the skirt twice, and when it fell from the hanger, I let it remain on the dark, dirty floor of my closet. When my mother called me again, I decided to return it, but there was a stain on the waistband that the dry cleaner could not remove. For an hour I sat on my dorm bed with the skirt in my lap, considering. Finally I washed it with Woolite, and ruined it. I returned the skirt to my mother's closet when invited, during spring break, for dinner at her apartment. *Please,* I begged silently, tucking it between two other skirts. *Please don't say anything more about it. Please.* When she called me late that night at my grandparents' house, I hung up on her. Then I went into the bathroom and I sat on the floor and wept: too late, too many hours past the dinner she had fed me to make myself throw up.

Kathryn, Katherine, Catherine. All the spellings proceed from the Greek, *Katharos,* or "pure one."

Did Lapa know who her daughter would be? Did my mother know me before she named me? Did we announce ourselves to our mothers in the intimacy of the womb, flesh whispering to flesh?

Or did they make us to fit our names?

I still believe in purity, and I believe that suffering must at least prepare the way for redemption. I believe, too, in love's ability to conquer. I believe in every kiss I gave my mother, even those I scrubbed away in fear. At the end of her life, I waited for my mother to tell me how much she loved me and how good a daughter I had always been. I had faith that my mother was waiting until the end to tell me that all along she had known I had performed impossible feats of self-alchemy.

She did not, but, as faith admits no end, mine continued beyond her death. After the funeral, I packed up her apartment and looked through all her papers for a note, a letter left for me and sealed in an envelope. I closed my eyes and saw it: a meticulous, fountain-pen rendition of *Kathryn* on creamy stationery. When I didn't find that, I looked for clues to her affection. I read what correspondence she had saved. I reviewed check registers dating back ten years. I learned how much she had spent on dry-cleaning her clothes, on her cats' flea baths, and on having her car radio repaired.

The death of my mother left me with a complex religious apparatus that now lacked its object, and I expected, then, to become an atheist. I frankly looked forward to the sterile sanity of it, to what relief it would bring. But I could not do it; I could not not believe. The habit of faith, though long focused misguidedly on a mortal object, persisted; and after a few years, I found myself returning to the Church. Sporadically, helplessly, I attended mass. Having relearned to eat earthly food, now I practiced swallowing the Eucharist. Often I found myself crying out of a happiness I did not understand and which mysteriously accompanied the sense that my heart was breaking.

Rapture, too, returned. Long after I had stopped expecting it, it overcame me on a number of otherwise unnoteworthy occasions. I excused this as a fancy born of longing, as an endorphin effect brought on by exercise or pain, as craziness, pure and simple. But none of these described the experience, that same searing, light-filled, ecstatic rise, neither pleasant nor unpleasant, for no human measure applied to what I felt: transcendence.

My prayers, too, were helpless. I mouthed them in spite of myself. *Make me good. Love me. Please make me good and please love me.* For the first time, I entrusted my spiritual evolution to some power outside my self and my will; I entrusted it to God's grace. If I were going to reach any new plane, my enlightenment, it would have to be God who transported me.

In the last months of her life, Catherine lost the use of her legs. Her biographers record that for years she had lived on little more than water and what sustenance she got from chewing, not swallowing, bitter herbs. In church one night, when she was too weak to approach the altar, the Communion bread came to her. Witnesses saw bread move through the air unassisted. Catherine saw it carried by the hand of Christ.

She died at thirty-three, the same age as her Bridegroom at his death. She died in Rome, and her body was venerated from behind an iron grille in a chapel of the Church of the Minerva, so that the throngs who came would not tear her to bits, each trying to secure a wonder-working relic.

All I have left of my mother are a box of books, a china dog, two cashmere sweaters with holes in the elbows, a few photographs, and her medical records. Among the last of these is her final chest X-ray, and just over the shadow of her heart is the bright white circle cast by the saint's medal she wore on a thin gold chain. No matter how many times the technicians asked her to remove it, she would not. Not long ago, I unpacked the box of medical records, and retrieved the X ray. I held it before a light once more, trying to see the image more clearly, but of course I could make out nothing. Just a small, white circle of brightest light. A circle blocking the view of the chambers of her heart. A circle too bright to allow any vision.

I will never know, but I have decided that the medal, now with my mother in her coffin, bears a likeness of Saint Jude. I have given my mother to this saint — the patron of lost causes, the patron of last resort — just as long ago she gave me to the saint of her choosing.

# *from* Vertigo

WHEN MY MOTHER MEETS SOMEONE NEW, SHE ALWAYS MANAGES TO INTERJECT INTO the conversation the amazing fact that I started school when I was only four years old.

"Louise was only four years old when she started first grade in 1947," my mother boasts, as soon as the other mother crows about one of her child's accomplishments.

"Because she knew how to read," my mother continues. "She taught herself how to read. Before I knew what was happening, she could pick up anything at all, and read it without any help from me. And if there wasn't a book around the apartment to read, she would read the back of the cereal box. Anything. Anything at all."

My mother explains to her by-now-reluctant audience how she took me over to Sacred Heart Academy the summer before I started school, how the nuns gave me a reading test, a hard one, how they told her that, because I seemed old for my age, I was ready to start school, and they would accept me into the first grade.

My mother's story about my starting school at four is something of an exaggeration. Although it is literally true that I start school when I am four, I turn five just a few weeks later, and so it would have been more accurate if my mother had said that I was nearly five years old when I started first grade. And although I have learned to read, in my recollection, I do not learn by myself; it is my mother who teaches me. But my mother's story, her pride in describing my precocity, suggests that she had secret aspirations for me that she never openly shared. Perhaps she dreamed that I could fulfill her thwarted ambition of one day attending college, of one day becoming a writer.

My mother stands behind me while I sit on top of the telephone book at the kitchen table, "writing." I am about three, and I haven't learned how to write, really. But my mother gives me blank sheets of paper and a pencil, and I fill them with seismic shocks and waves of meaning. I am very serious. I am writing.

Years later, she tells me that when she asks me what I am doing, I reply that I am making a story.

"What's the story about?" she asks.

"I don't know," I answer, but I suspect I mean to say "I can't tell."

"When will you know?" she asks.

"When I'm finished," I answer.

"When will you be finished?" she asks.

"Yesterday," I answer.

"You mean 'tomorrow'?" she asks. I often say "yesterday" when I mean "tomorrow" and "tomorrow" when I mean "tomorrow." This confuses my mother. Time is something I haven't yet figured out. "Yesterday" and "tomorrow" are all the same to me.

That I start school when I am four years old becomes an important family story that sticks, that is told through the years, that grows true with its repetition. It means that, despite my difficult infancy, despite my difficult early childhood after my father comes home from the war, when I give my parents what seems like nothing but trouble, I have turned out all right, and I might turn out all right in the end.

The story signals that I am special. It differentiates me in my paternal grandparents' eyes from my cousins (and from my sister), none of whom, they believe, can match my intellectual accomplishments, no matter how hard they try. And my cousins will be reminded of this at every family gathering.

One Easter, my grandmother cooks a lamb's head as a special treat for the family dinner. With great ceremony, my grandfather plucks the lamb's eye out from its socket, and gives it to me to eat. I shake my head no, refusing. "You have to eat it," my father says, "it's an honor; it's for good luck." But I refuse my grandfather's offering; I can't imagine putting such an offensive thing inside my mouth, much less swallowing it. My grandfather shrugs his shoulders, pops the lamb's eye into his mouth, and pats his stomach, as if to say "Delicious," and we all laugh.

I don't know why I am singled out in this way. Nor do I know whether I would have been singled out in this way despite my accomplishments, if my father wasn't my grandparents' only son, or if I had an older brother or cousin, for, in Italian-American families, males usually get the best treatment. But in many Italian-American families, one child is often selected by family elders to carry all the hopes for success of the family. For whatever reasons, in my family, I am that child.

What this means, for me, is that my cousins treat me, not as one of a gang of eight tightly knit, rambunctious, mischievous youngsters, but as someone around whom they feel uneasy.

There I am in a family picture taken on Easter Sunday, standing off to one side, separated from the rest of them, posing like the models I have seen in magazines, one foot in front of the other, clutching at my pocketbook in front of me, looking as I always look, far too old for my years.

"Why can't the rest of you be like Louise," my grandparents harangue my cousins, in Italian.

"Louise is the smartest, she's going to go far," my grandmother says to the others, as she hands me an extra five dollars for making the honor roll.

When I start school in September 1947, when I am nearly five years old, emotionally I am not ready for school, though the nuns think I am. In public, I put on a good show; alone, I am afraid, I am always afraid, but I don't share my fears with my mother, who herself seems as afraid as I often feel.

During the first few days at school, at lunch, which is taken at long tables in the school basement, its frosted windows letting in a weak light, I sit underneath the table with my lunchbox open between my knees, trying to swallow my food through huge sobs I try to stifle in hopes that no one will hear me. No one does. No one notices I am there.

That my mother packs me off for a full day when I am so little suggests to me now that, raised in the absence of my father, and lavished with her attention and that of my grandparents, I have grown to be a very demanding child and so she wants some time away from me as soon as she can manage it. That, and she is having a hard time raising both my sister (born the previous February) and me and that she wants me out of the cramped apartment for the better part of the day.

Our tiny apartment, it is true, is barely suited for two people, and certainly not for four. There is absolutely no privacy. No doors separating the kitchen from the bedroom, or the bedroom from the parlor.

We all wash up, standing in front of the kitchen sink, in full view of everyone else. There is no bathtub, no shower.

Five of us share the toilet that is in a cubicle between two apartments, and, unless you remember to lock both doors, someone inevitably opens one when you are inside, and, when you do remember, someone knocks on the door, urgently needing their turn. No matter how fastidiously my mother or my grandmother cleans, the room always smells of someone's shit.

I am too short to reach the chain to flush. I am humiliated that I have to fetch a grown-up to pull the cord to dispose of my waste, but I get yelled at if I don't or if I forget. And I won't, I won't balance on the edges of the toilet seat so I can do it myself. Once, I had managed this. But the fear of falling into the toilet stops me from trying it a second time.

My parents, my sister, and I sleep in the same bedroom. My sister's crib, my parents' double bed, and my cot are shoved so close together that there is no room at all between my cot and my parents' bed, and barely enough room between my sister's crib and my parents' bed for them to squeeze by when it is time for them to go to sleep.

When my sister awakens in the night, she wakes us all. When I awaken in the night with a nightmare, which happens frequently, I wake everyone else.

And there is the sound of my parents' lovemaking going on so close to me, too close.

When I am awakened by their stifled moans, or by the movement of their bed, I turn my back to them, feigning a profound but restless sleep, and, to distract myself, I concentrate on the holy picture of the Sacred Heart of Jesus tucked into the corner of my mother's mirror, illuminated by the dim glow of the nightlight at the foot of my cot.

Jesus is holding his bleeding heart out in front of him on an outstretched gold plate. The sounds and smells and movements of my parents' sex, and the sight of the Sacred Heart of Jesus, bleeding on a plate, commingle.

I know that my parents' nearness upsets me because, one night, in the middle of the night, long after I am toilet-trained, I shit in my cot, which perplexes my mother and my father as they tend to me and the stinking mess I have expelled.

I remember the delight I take in the attention I am getting, and in interrupting them. And the need for some kind of release, any kind of release, as if there is too much inside me. Too much that I have seen, too much that I have heard, too much that I have felt, and too too much that has happened.

Though I grow to love school in time, initially, I hate it because I think that my mother is trying to get rid of me. I am jealous that she and my sister will be alone all day, and I wait impatiently for the day to end, so I can see my mother again.

I imagine that, while I am at school, my mother and sister are spending the day going to the playground, playing peek-a-boo, and visiting other kids on the block, as my mother and I did during the war years. But I know now that this wasn't happening. My mother has far too much work to do play games with my sister, to give her much attention at all.

She rises early to prepare breakfast. She dresses me and my sister and walks me to school. The walk to my school and back takes her over an hour. Then she starts her day's work. The washing alone takes her hours and hours. She does it all — my sister's diapers and clothes, my father's work clothes, which he changes daily, my blouse, socks, and underclothes — each day, by hand, on a washboard, in the kitchen sink. She heats the water on the stove. Leans out the window to hang the clothes to dry. Heats the iron on the stove. Starches and presses the clothes. Then, there is the cooking and cleaning. Everything she buys for us to eat, she has to cart up four flights of stairs; she has to shop every day, for our tiny kitchen has no pantry.

My mother now works hard. Too hard to enjoy my sister, too hard to be very much of a mother to her. My sister doesn't smile very much. She spends much of her day in the crib, trying to amuse herself with the toys my mother provides, so that my mother can get her day's work done before she picks me up from school.

"When Jill was a baby," my mother will later say, "she never smiled at all." And the proof is there, in the pictures of her in infancy. Eyes downcast; baby lips pulled into a frown; dull, vacant stare. I had gotten the best, the most my mother could give. My mother didn't have enough left over to give my sister.

What I like about school is being away from my mother and grandmother's battles, the vicious shouting matches between them that now erupt frequently when my father and grandfather are not there. For, by now, my mother and grandmother are enemies; they are fighting all the time. My grandmother insists that my mother shows her no respect, that she wants her dead; my mother insists that my grandmother has never loved her, never treated her as kin. When they fight, their eyes lock, their backs arch, like birds who have been trained to peck one another to death. When my mother and grandmother fight, they pay no attention to me, to Jill. We could hurt ourselves, or disappear, they wouldn't notice. Often, my mother breaks things, or hurts herself as they argue. She picks up the iron the wrong way and burns her hand. Pours the water for the washing, carelessly, and scalds herself. When this happens, she bursts into agonized cries. When, at last, one of their fights ends, it is impossible to get my mother's attention. A question, a request, provokes either no response or an angry one.

However many problems might face me in school, there are times, like when all the children are bent over their work, that it is blessedly peaceful and quiet, nothing like the maelstrom I've left behind at home. The maelstrom against which my sister grows to be a toddler.

In time, because it is such a safe, quiet place for me, I grow to love the order, the rhythm, the regularity, and predictability of the school day, its hours demarcated into periods of time devoted to penmanship, reading, spelling, arithmetic, catechism, geography. Even now, I like to plan my day in blocks of time devoted to different subjects and tasks, replicating, for comfort, this pattern that I found such a soothing respite from the whirlwind of my mother and grandmother's fights that leave my mother red in the face and in tears and unable to care for me and my sister, my grandmother, angry and distant, me, confused, because my grandmother is always kind to me when my parents are not, and my sister, withdrawn. And, during the early, hard times of my marriage, before I am able to snip away the worst things from my past, when my husband and I fight as viciously as my mother and grandmother had, I retreat then, too, to the sanctity and order of my work day.

In the Catholic grammar school that I attended, the first and second graders were taught by the same nun and were schooled in the same room. The first graders were ranged alphabetically in rows to the teacher's right; the second graders, to the teacher's left. While the first graders were receiving instruction (in spelling, math, geography, reading, or catechism), the second graders did work in their workbooks. While the second graders received instruction, the first graders did work in their workbooks. The nun who taught us (whose name I have by now forgotten but whom I will refer to by the name Sister Mary) made it a habit to write on the board directly in front of the first graders when she instructed them, and to move to the other side of the blackboard to write on the board directly in front of the second graders when she instructed them.

But because my last name began with an "S," my assigned desk was all the way in the back of the room, and right next to the first row of second graders. This meant that I couldn't see the first-grade work on the board because I was the shortest child in the class, also because we were required to "sit up straight" (no leaning to the right or left even if it was the only way we could see what was being written on the blackboard). But I could see the second-grade work on the board. Because the first graders were learning how to read and write, and I already knew how to read and write, I could complete the assignments in my workbooks quickly. Which gave me time to attend to Sister Mary teaching the second grade and learn their lessons as well.

On the first day of school, after Sister Mary settled us into our assigned places, she asked a red-headed girl in the second grade with the strange name of Miranda Panda to come up to the front of the classroom for a demonstration to which we should all pay careful attention. Miranda Panda was going to show us something that, if we were good pupils, we would be able to do by the end of the first grade.

I hated Miranda immediately. I hated her because I was petrified and because she looked so cocky and sure of herself, as she flounced to the front of the class. I hated her because she was in the second grade and I was in the first. I hated her because she wore long red banana curls and a big bow in her hair. I hated her because she was rich and lived in a big brownstone up near Stevens Institute of Technology. I hated her because she had such a stupid name and yet no one dared make fun of her. Miranda Panda was someone special, someone not to be trifled with.

I had already been laughed at for my long, unpronounceable Italian last name (which contained twelve letters in all, seven consonants and five vowels) both in the school yard when kids asked me who I was, and in the classroom when Sister Mary called the roll. I had already heard the insults that would become standard fare throughout my years of schooling.

"Hey, what kind of name is that?" from the non-Italians.

"Your name is bigger than you are" from the bigger kids.

Or the far more commonplace, "That's gotta be a Wop name; who else but a Wop would have a name like that."

By the time Miranda Panda made it to the front of the room to show the class the special thing she had learned the year before on that first day of school, I had declared her the enemy. What I felt as she stood there, waiting for further instructions from Sister Mary, was a moment of envy. Within seconds, though, I felt a keen competition. Miranda Panda had what I wanted: everyone's attention. I decided that it was very important that I beat her.

"Now, boys and girls in the first grade," Sister Mary intoned, "Miranda Panda will demonstrate for you the wonderful kinds of things you will be learning this year. How many of you know your alphabet?"

A flurry of hands from the more eager, more intelligent first graders. I kept my hands folded on my desk. Take the enemy by surprise. Don't let them know what you know.

"Boys and girls," Sister Mary gushed, with much pride in her voice, "Miranda Panda will now recite the alphabet for you, but she will recite it *backwards*."

Sister Mary stepped aside. Miranda Panda stepped forward, made a sign of the cross, took a deep breath, and began.

"Z, Y, X, W, V, U, T, S . . ."

When Miranda Panda got to the letter "R," I stopped listening. My mother had told me that I was going to learn wonderful and important and interesting things in the first grade. Sister Mary had told me that I was going to learn wonderful and important and interesting things in the first grade. And here was a display of the wonderful and important and interesting things I was slated to learn.

After Miranda was finished, Sister Mary beamed at the class.

"Now, class," she asked, "what have you learned?" And then, answering her own question, she said, "When you reach second grade, you'll know the alphabet so well, you'll be able to recite it *backwards,* just like Miranda Panda."

Miranda Panda, very pleased with herself, flounced back to her seat. I noticed that she wore ruffled socks in defiance of the Academy's strict orders that we wear only socks that were white and plain and without adornment. Yet Sister Mary had singled Miranda out as special though she broke the rules. I hated her. Whatever else Sister Mary wanted us to learn from Miranda Panda, when she settled herself smugly into her seat on the second-grade side of the classroom, I had already learned that there were insiders and there were outsiders and that it was all right for some people to break the rules.

"Now, class," Sister Mary said, "are there any questions?"

I waited a few moments, sure that every child in the first grade wanted to ask the same question I wanted to ask, but although some children moved about in their seats, no one raised a hand. I did not yet know that in certain circumstances the question "Are there any questions?" uttered by a nun or a teacher standing in front of a room did not mean "Are there any questions?" but "How can there be any questions?"

I waited a bit longer, but when it seemed that no one was going to ask my question, I shot up my hand.

Sister Mary, of course, could not yet remember my name, and so she acknowledged me with a little nod of her head.

"Sister Mary, Sister Mary," I began, having been instructed in the niceties of addressing nuns by my mother. ("You must always be very polite to the nuns. You must always use the word 'Sister' before their names.") "But *why* is it important to know the letters of the alphabet backwards as well as forward?"

I had asked the obvious, forbidden, but important question to which I wanted an honest answer, but it seemed to mock and deride what had come before.

Sister Mary paused to consider her response. And, of course, there was no legitimate answer that she could make to this question and I knew it.

I wasn't easily fooled. When I asked my question, I had already decided that reciting the alphabet backwards wasn't anything important, wasn't anything you could use, wasn't anything you had to know. It was simply a bravura display of useless knowledge. My father, a working-class utilitarian if ever there was one, repeatedly asked me, "But what good will it do you to know that? But what good will it do you to do that?" It was not just enough to know something or do something; you had to do something worthwhile with what you learned, with what you knew. His pragmatic attitude toward learning was something I had already come to share.

The truth was, I already knew the response I wanted from Sister Mary. I wanted her to admit that knowing the alphabet backwards wasn't important at all. In my mind, it was the only truly honest answer to my question. And Sister Mary couldn't answer in that way without surrendering her authority, which, of course, she wasn't prepared to do.

I do not now remember the answer that Sister Mary made to my question, if she answered it at all. But I do remember not being allowed to go to the bathroom later the same day when the need to pee was so urgent that I felt sure I would wet my pants. And I remember that Sister Mary, later in the day, after lunch, took a giant piece of Scotch tape and taped my mouth shut when she caught me asking the boy seated next to me to tell me what had been written on the blackboard because I was too short to see over the head of the tall boy seated in front of me. And Sister Mary telling me that the Scotch tape would remind me, if I could not remind myself, that, in her classroom, there was to be no whispering at any time, and no talking unless you were called upon to answer a question.

As I sat in my seat, tape over my mouth, eyes stinging with tears, staring at the birthmark on the thumb of my left hand to steady myself, I vowed that whatever else I might learn in the first grade, no matter what the cost, I would never, ever, learn how to say the letters of the alphabet backwards. I had decided that if that's what it took to gain recognition from Sister Mary, then I would forgo it. But I also decided that I would beat Miranda Pandu at the game of knowledge, but that I wouldn't do it her way. And, by the end of my first year at Sacred Heart Academy, I had beaten her. I had been selected to crown the Blessed Virgin Mary during the school's May pageant.

The nuns told us that many factors were considered in selecting the person who would crown the Virgin. First, she had to have earned good grades; second, she had to have been a model student. I had been selected, Sister Mary told the class, because I had taken it upon myself to complete the work for the second grade while I was still in the first grade; also because I was the shortest girl in the first grade and it would look very nice if I led the procession.

Before the crowning, the girls in both classes spent days decorating the classroom with blue and white crepe paper streamers, preparing the shrine of the Blessed Virgin Mary in the small garden in back of the school, decking the statue with flowers, and learning to sing "O Mary we crown thee with blossoms today/Queen of the Angels, Queen of the May." My mother sewed me a baby-blue eyelet gown with puffed sleeves and a bow that tied in front.

On the day of the crowning, the nuns gave all of us girls crowns of flowers to wear in our hair. And I was given a special tiger lily to hold for the procession. My father, very proud of me, took off a day's work, and put on his best suit to come see me.

In the picture that my father has taken of us girls standing in front of the statue of the Blessed Virgin, I am in the center, in front of the statue. Miranda Panda stands to my right, wearing a store-bought dress, her hair arranged in perfect ringlets. And though the picture is in black and white, you can see that she is wearing a trace of lipstick. She is richer than I, and older and taller, but I am smarter than she is and I know it, and I have proven it, and you can see the satisfaction on my face. And it has taken me less than a year to get what I want – Sister Mary singling me out for special merit, as she had singled out Miranda Panda on my first day at school.

In the years that I attend Catholic grammar school, in Hoboken and, later, in Ridgefield, New Jersey, after we move there, the lessons that I learn from the nuns are prodigious. They go beyond book learning. They will stay with me for a lifetime, long after I renounce my faith. They will inform my intellectual work.

I learn to see life as a titanic moral struggle between good and evil; I learn that we are all God's children; I learn the importance of neatness, order, discipline, rigor, practice, and routine in learning. The virtue of work. The spiritual, soulful nature of work. That work is another form of prayer. That you must teach others what you have learned. That you teach, too, by example. That there is beauty in the structure of a well-balanced sentence. That language must be used carefully, correctly, and precisely. I learn about the beauty of austerity and renunciation. That you are important, not for what you have, but for what you are, and for what you make of yourself. That human beings can perfect themselves but that they must constantly fight the allure of evil. That you should treat others as you wish to be treated. That generosity is a greater good than selfishness. I learn the value of intuition as a way of knowing. I learn the importance of pageantry and ceremony; I learn that having flowers nearby enriches the spirit and the soul. And that taking care of your spirit and your soul is as important as taking care of your body.

And as one nun after another after another rewarded us by reading to us after a hard day in the first and second grades, and throughout the rest of my grammar school years, I learned to listen to stories and to respect them. Although I do not now remember the names of any of these books that were read to me throughout the years, I remember that they were grown-up books, gargantuan books, that these nuns read, filled with action, with the pulse of history, or with love and passion (though never with any sex as I recall). I learn to see reading as a privilege and pleasure, and to glean the lessons to be learned from those who had taken the time to write beautifully, powerfully, and well.

But, at first, school isn't such a welcome part of my life, as it becomes in time, and, at first, I can't wait for the school day to be over.

I sit anxiously outside school on the stone steps that lead up to the huge wooden front door, waiting for my mother to pick me up, balancing, on my knees, all my books (as usual, I have much homework), and my empty lunch pail (as usual, the milk from my leaky thermos has befouled the yellow cheese sandwich, which I detest and wouldn't have eaten anyway, and I have thrown the soppy mess away). I keep my possessions close to me because I am afraid that the bigger children will snatch at them and take them from me.

I guard my blue loose-leaf binder most carefully; in it is all my homework, neatly separated by tab inserts into subjects. If you do excellent work, you get a gold star. If you do very good work, you get a red star. If you do good work, you get a blue star. If you do average work or poor work or unacceptable work (work that isn't done according to the rules), you get no star at all. Everything you do is judged and ranked and marked. And you never get a star for making an effort. (One boy, transferred from public school, asks this question.) Making an effort is expected, not rewarded.

There is a concrete statue of the Sacred Heart of Jesus (Jesus, his hand on his heart, which is circled with a crown of thorns) in the front of the school. As I await my mother, I count the times that a pigeon lands on Jesus' head. It's something that amuses me, though I know it shouldn't. When Sister Mary has heard some boys laughing at this, she has said, "Even pigeons are God's children; Jesus welcomes them to him, just as he welcomes you." Welcome or not, they make a mess, and at the beginning of the year, I watched a younger nun, sleeves rolled above her elbows, scrubbing down the statue of Jesus, making sure that he is clean. I wait to catch a glimpse of my mother coming down Washington Street, pushing my sister in her sand-colored wicker stroller. I wait to see, by the look on my mother's face, whether it has been a good or a bad day.

If my mother is a few minutes late, I become panicky, sure that she has forgotten me, sure that she has died on the way, or been captured and taken somewhere, sure that I will never see her again.

Once, when she is very late, I decide that she isn't coming, that something has happened to her, and so, dizzy and disoriented, I run all the way home. Across Washington Street, and down and left and right and down and across many, many blocks. I stop, along the way, to pick up the books and belongings that I keep dropping in my haste. Once, my looseleaf opens, and I have to put all the pages back.

It is a very long distance for a very little girl to travel, even if she has a mother beside her. And I have no mother beside me.

When I arrive at our apartment, and buzz and buzz and buzz and no one answers, I buzz my grandparents to be let in and then run up the stairs and knock and knock on my grandmother's door, only to be told that my mother has left to pick me up.

And out the door and down the stairs I fly in a panic before my grandmother can stop me, to find my mother, who, by now, has arrived at my school to find me not there. Suspecting that I have tried to walk home by myself, not believing I can find my way home alone, but not knowing what else to do, she is returning home, as quickly as she can push my sister along, but by a way different from our usual way home. She is afraid I've been kidnapped, gotten lost, been taken to the hospital. She was late. It's all her fault.

And so, we miss each other again

When my mother finally finds me around the corner from where we live, in front of Our Lady of Grace Church, she is exhausted. She kneels down and gathers me to her, sobbing and shaking in her terror at what might have happened to me.

But I am strangely calm. My earlier fear has dissipated. A bond between us has snapped, and, though I am tired and tearful, I feel good.

"What did you learn today?" my mother asks me, after she composes herself, trying to impress upon me a lesson she believes I must understand.

She expects, I think, that I will say that I have learned to wait for her patiently on the school steps even if she is late, that she will always come to get me, and that I should never again leave school until she has come for me.

"I learned that I can find my way home," I reply, which is the right answer for me, but the wrong answer for her, and I know this because she frowns at me. Still, I mean it, and I don't take the words back or change them.

She looks at me as if I am a very strange child. For, just as much as she needs me to be gone for the day, so, too, she needs to come and get me at school, needs me to wait for her there, needs to walk me back home just as I need to face the fear of losing my mother, need to make my way home without her even if it scares me, even if I have to scare myself to do it.

I have found my own way home. And I have learned that I can find my way again, anytime I need to, anytime I want to.

But my mother? What has she learned?

She has learned that she doesn't like this in me, this new bold and intrepid spirit that I have shown her on this day despite the fearfulness she knows I share with her. It is this that shall separate us. Her fear will keep her where she is. Mine will propel me, sometimes with no apparent direction, but, sometimes, with a homing instinct as sure and true as the pigeons who live in coops on the roof of our tenement display when they spiral their way down from the sky to find home.

Once I learn that I don't need my mother to make my way home, I am ready for school, truly ready, no matter how little or how afraid I am. I am ready for the lessons that I will learn.

# Trinity

I

MY FATHER LOVED ANY TOWN'S DUMP. WE VISITED THEM LIKE OTHER PEOPLE VISITED national parks, with a picnic lunch, trying hard to manufacture a sense of family togetherness that always came off better in pictures than in the moment of experience. With a strange mix of disgust and greed we would put on fuzzy orange work gloves, pile out of our van — my father, his five daughters — carefully walk over heaps of the discarded, the castoff, the left-behind. Wood was what we were looking for, dressers, end tables, and chairs especially. We would take it all home to the basement where dad would sand it, rub it, and cover it with paste, slippery white jelly, pure magic. Then to dry on the sunporch, and back to the basement for a coat of Shine in a Can.

Sometimes if a scratch was too deep or too much rain had fallen before our rescue operation, we got to keep some wooden treasure for our bedrooms or the living room. The stuff that came out of my dad's hands looking good as new went downtown to the old three-story apartment building we owned and kept fully rented, partly because it offered the only furnished units in town. Our renters were mostly new teachers coming to our small town just out of college, eager to fill our waiting blank slates, or elderly couples coming off the farm where the younger generation had taken over the farmhouse with its dining room sets, headboards, coffee tables and end pieces.

Sometimes when Dad would proclaim "no hope" for a cabinet or set of bookshelves, my sisters and I would drag it to the backyard, take our crumpled allowance to the lumberyard, and buy hideous shades of Watermelon Passion, Blueberry Hill Delight and Sundance Yellow. Stripes, polka dots, every leg two different colors, the grass around us dipped in glorious shades of July play, straight through to a ten-o'clock sunset. If I ever envied my best friend's white princess bedroom set, I never did understand why she couldn't paint it Juicy Strawberry if she woke up one day and wanted to.

My mother believed in fine fabric. She collected French decorating magazines, sent away for nubby swatches, rubbed them on her soft pink cheeks until she found one she couldn't put down. Then she sent away for a bolt. Months later it would arrive wrapped in lavender tissue paper with the name of the designer sprawled across it in fine marker. We hung the prized pastel tissue on our bedroom walls and let the frost seep through it. Our bedrooms wore the soft colorful clouds of a Minnesota winter sky.

Mom took the fabric to a custom upholstery shop in downtown Minneapolis and together, she and the clerks and eventually the soft, flushed-faced owner would decide what it should cover, a love seat, an inlaid side table, or an overstuffed sofa. Then my mother would give them her father's name and tell them to bill him at his Florida address. After all, her parents wanted her to have some nice things, even though she was who she was and had married "him." Somehow all their snobbery, of folks who actually made money during the Depression, came to her in her decorating gene.

She loved to lecture us on the difference between living with craft and living with art. How it made you different people in the end to be surrounded by things that were original, one of a kind, and things that came out of a mold, reproducible and often reproduced.

"Say something you've never said before," she would warn us. "And I am your mother, I will know the difference. I'm raising artists here, don't forget that." I guess that's why she approved of our bookshelves of fourteen different shades of green with a different variety of frog painted on each level, our wallpapering fiascoes, even our trips to the dump.

I didn't know what my first boyfriend meant when he walked into our house and said, "How can you live like this?" Until I was finally invited to his home and asked to remove my paint-dripped sneakers before stepping on the white carpet that matched the white sectional and the white lacquered entertainment center. Even then I thought I had the bigger question to ask. I began to see him as obscenely unoriginal, uncolored. When I tried to think of him before falling asleep, I couldn't picture him in my mind.

II

My mother was the first vegetarian I knew. I would come home from school to the aroma of parsnips and summer squash frying in garlic butter, artichoke hearts and goat cheese soufflé, ground apricot seeds spiced with fennel and thyme, a rich black roux and brown basmati rice. Root vegetables, she told me, ground you in the ways of the earth and eating papayas makes you grow up wise like Athena. She knew the names of seventeen different kinds of beans, seventeen different colors. How to paint a room with the juice of one ripe beet. The secret was to juice it and then thicken the purple syrup with a little ground mint leaf.

For breakfast she ate creamy rice pudding with dates and pecans. She drank wild yam tea until noon, when she switched to homemade plum wine with floating cranberries and lots of crushed ice. She taught me that drinking alcohol with crushed rainwater ice dissolved the toxicity of the drug and cleared your digestive system before dinner. Our house had the sweet smooth smell of garlic and mint dancing cheek to cheek to a Mel Tormé medley, something you couldn't help humming to even though you couldn't remember the name of the tune. It also smelled, I have come to know, like a meatless house, lighter but more pungent with an unspeakable color mist on the kitchen walls.

As a child, my father carried a rifle for three years while he walked and watched my grandfather hunt grouse, geese, ducks, prairie chickens, wild turkeys, deer and rabbits. Barrel down, elbow bent, straight-ahead, march, turn slowly, and never shout. Then finally he earned the right to carry a bullet in his breast pocket for a year and then the fifth year of rising before dawn, following behind, he was allowed to fire, to kill for food.

Division of labor was a tradition in his family. After the men shot it and the women cleaned and cooked it. Dark salty breast of duck or the gristly thigh of a grouse or deep red venison stew. All of these were home and goodness to my father. He never understood what people meant when they said, "It tastes a little too wild for me." He smoked turkeys in the garage and roasted rabbits in the backyard in forty below zero temperatures. My mother let him eat meat in her house, just not cook it.

My memories of childhood mealtimes hold the tension of a presidential debate. "You do not have to ever eat anything with eyes, feelings and a spirit that is probably near us right now, wondering why we hate it so."

"Try one bite of this neck. It's the most tender part. People pay big money to be served this in a restaurant. Your ancestors all ate what they killed. It's your heritage."

Mostly I grew up on breakfast cereal. No living thing had sacrificed its life for my selfish belly, and even Dad ate Shredded Wheat with lots of brown sugar. Before I could read, I carried animal rights posters in lines in front of the state capitol, hoping no one would mention my down-filled jacket. Sometimes, Dad would drive the kids home early so Mom could stay and get on the ten o-clock news. We would drive through McDonald's on our way out of town, sing along with the Mamas and Papas on the tape deck. We were "California Dreaming" as the steam from the cheeseburgers clouded our orange Volkswagen van windows and blocked our view of the snow-covered prairie, wide and deep as any ocean we couldn't imagine.

## III

As a child I loved the incense and bells and beautiful glistening fabrics of the priest's robes and altar cloths. Catholic was the faith of my father's childhood. At his wake a woman told a story about a skinny six-year-old boy with black hair and eyes, walking slowly with his head down around the same church, kneeling, humming, saying the Stations of the Cross. This woman, square and stooped now, was a girl then and she approached the somber little boy with a secret. *Don't say all of it. Skip the main part. Then we can play.* And the boy looked at her hurt or confused and said, *But I love the main part.* This little boy is my father.

He worshipped with a passion and dedication that left little time for attendance at college graduation speeches or grandchildren's birthday parties. If he was absent from the events that marked his children's passing lives, praying was what he did instead in relationships. Still that boy with black hair and eyes, walking the same aisle, bending his knees, chanting. *We adore Thee O Christ and we praise Thee. Because by Thy Holy Cross Thou hast redeemed the world.*

My mother became a Catholic several years into her marriage, after my older sister asked her why we couldn't all go to church together like our neighbors the Erb family, who with their long hair wound around their heads, and their flat ugly shoes, marched out of their double-wide trailer every Sunday morning looking like a true Jesus army.

So when I was eight, as a birthday present to my sister turning nine, we became a parade of long blonde hair, curled, clipped, then covered with white lace bobby-pinned in place. To the Catholic Church of the sixties, girls were impure, not allowed on the altar, wrong from the beginning, us especially, an army of five daughters with no son for my dad. Still my mother did not completely join "Mary's Team" as she called St. Leo's Women's Circle Number Five, that she was assigned to. Suddenly my gourmet, vegetarian mom was expected to bring soft macaroni and beef-based food to funerals and weddings.

At home we still faced the sectional sofa to the east after she was ready for the babies to stop coming. We sprinkled rosewater on our beds during full moon and grew pots of thyme and rosemary for her to bury her diamonds and pearls in when there was an eclipse and over the summer and winter equinoxes. There were no rocking chairs allowed in the bedrooms and no one could wear pink after midnight. We lit candles on our grandparents' graves on Christmas Eve. And we changed the words to the Sign of the Cross, season to season.

"In the name of Maia, the spring is yours, may your magic keep us well, amen."

"In the name of Isis, keeper of the day, the source of all love, fill us full, amen."

Today I call myself a Mystical Pagan Catholic. I don't see auras or care who I was in my past lives. I plant my root vegetables and potatoes on Good Friday. I sleep after Thanksgiving Dinner, drunk on tryptophan and my own homemade cranberry wine. I say the rosary when I am fighting off an anxiety attack. Sandalwood works too, but it makes me cry. The thick sweet smoke reminds me of my father loving the Stations and wondering why you would skip the main part. Adulthood stole his peaceful childhood patience, made him restless and angry in his thirties and disappointed and sarcastic in his sixties. He became pitiful to me, partly because I do not believe that angry prayer works and I cannot imagine him appealing to God out of anything but rage.

My home is an eclectic array of garage sale finds and gifts from well-traveled friends, some liberal, some artists, two old boyfriends of mine, now living together as lovers and working the land next to my husband's small grain and edible-bean farm. My children's rooms are full of color-coordinated modular furniture, purchased from a mail order company. They sleep on bunk beds with built-in computer desks surrounded by toy boxes of different sizes, filled with hotwheels, Beanie Babies, balls, paints, and construction paper. I buy them boxes of two hundred and four crayons, hues unimaginable to me when I was a child and thrilled with twenty-four – firecracker red, lapis blueberry blush, pumpkin bread pudding.

My mother died too young for me to witness the eldering of her faith, nearly twenty years before my father, before his meanness overtook him and shone through like the grain of all the wood he polished and sanded and painted, but could never completely hide. I like to imagine that had she become an old woman, she would have become even more sure of her place beside the hollyhocks and crocuses of this seamless, wide landscape. Toward the end of her short life, she became fascinated by how like the Pacific Ocean she was and how unlike the hairy human male. Still her love for my father, and his for her, has created in me an unwavering appreciation for the other, other places in the world, other ways of doing things. Together they showed their children that difference is not a reason for distance, but rather a chance to see yourself more clearly. They never changed to be like each other but they also never walked away, arms thrown in the air because they were "just so different." Agreement and intimacy are not the same thing and I am thankful for that knowing.

When my father died, I was only relieved that he was finally free from his unending chore of praying for the unsaved, especially his five daughters, who still honor him with slivers of wood under their fingernails and tuition bills to Catholic elementary schools. Holding the tuition checks in the smoke of sweet jasmine incense ensures that the teaching only gets in so far, leaving much available for the goddesses to have for themselves.

My mother's death is a terminal loss for me. I do not expect to ever get over it. She was weaving a scarf when she died, blues and purples and greens of every shade she could find in old women's sewing kits she bought at auctions and estate sales. Made from the yarn of dead strangers, the scarf was enormously long and beautiful, with no clear beginning and no sign of being finished.

# Simply to Thee I Cling

AS A YOUNG WOMAN, I SOMETIMES WALKED ACROSS MANHATTAN TO MAKE MY CONFES-
sion to a Spanish priest who did not understand English. Before
confessing my sins to this foreigner, I whittled the list down as far
as it would go. He simply listened, sparing me homilies or admoni-
tions — although I would not have understood them anyway — and
magically, I was forgiven. At first, he seemed worth the long walk
across town, but then these pilgrimages began to seem strange,
even to me. I could not understand the ways in which my soul and
my sexuality were entangled, but it was clear to me that my life and my
beliefs were not aligned. I made one last confession to the Spanish
priest and parted ways for good with the statuesque old church.

My grandmother taught me that my own native soul was wild and
knowing, but I knew from the nuns that the garden of Eden was
filled with serpents and forbidden fruit. Wildness was sin. Knowing was pride. Only God knew. Alien to all wildness, the nuns were
married to Jesus and wore his gold band on their left hand. They
chopped off their hair, hid their bodies under a loose flow of black
gabardine, squeezed their faces into strips of stiff white linen. St.
Teresa writes, "He has bound Himself to her as firmly as two human beings are joined in wedlock and will never separate Himself
from her."

To the nuns, woman was still, as she had seemed to Chrysostom, "a necessary evil, a natural temptation, a desirable calamity, a domestic peril, a deadly fascination, a painted ill."

The nuns tried to interest us in salvation by parading us through the funeral home beside the school, a dreaded place, hushed and filled with dark oiled furniture, dyed carnations, spikes of purple gladioli. Powdery odors emanated from a honeycomb of rooms. We often gathered around a corpse lying in a coffin with pearl rosary beads wound in his or her hands, skin pale and powdered, mouth lipsticked. (It seemed intriguing that only corpses were allowed to wear make-up.)

We were expected to kneel at the coffin and pray. The bridegroom would come unannounced in the middle of the night, the nuns said. Would we be ready for Him? The world was a vale of tears. Heaven alone — God's presence — would furnish bliss.

Two of my great-grandmothers were Native American, and my grandmother taught me that I should be proud of my Indian blood. Yet all I knew about native peoples were the feathered headdresses I had seen, the totem poles and bark canoes, in the Museum of Natural History. My grandmother's scant knowledge of native peoples was gleaned from her Indian friend Mary, who drank martinis and walked around New York City wrapped in a Navajo blanket.

Every house in my suburban neighborhood except mine had a woman who was a full-time mother and housekeeper. My friend's father wrote mystery novels in a dim room off the kitchen, and on the wall were enlargements of the covers of his books, all displaying large breasted women with ripped blouses. Who was Woman? Who was I?

My grandmother was more partial to taverns than churches and had never worn an apron or even lived in a house. She resided in a hotel on the corner of 29th Street and Broadway in New York City, with huge neon letters — T-R-A-N-S-I-E-N-T-S — fastened to its brick facade. She had left her toddlers to join the Navy in 1917. In the winter, every day, she flung herself into the icy Atlantic Ocean with the Polar Bear Club. Although it was something we never talked about, she was having as much trouble as I was conforming to society's image of Woman.

The prevailing stereotypes of native women in American culture have been those of the beautiful, kind princess and the filthy, violent "squaw." But in contrast to Eve, women and female spirits in Native American creation stories are sources of life, providing protection and sustenance, bestowing values like truth. The Iroquois believe they were born into the world from the mud on the back of the earth, known as Grandmother Turtle. Corn, bean and squash, the essentials of life, were given by the Three Sisters. To the Shawnee, the world was created by an old woman with grey hair, Our Grandmother.

In Native American tradition, women are associated with earth, men with sky, women with plants, men with animals.

The Hidatsa woman says, "I cannot forget our old ways. Often in summer I rise at daybreak and steal out to the cornfields, and as I hoe the corn I sing to it, as we did when I was young. No one cares for our corn songs now."

Yet even among native peoples, female sexuality was often distrusted. Menstrual blood was thought by some to be a dangerous sort of pollution that could affect the success of a hunt, spoil the crops, and weaken the spiritual powers of a man. And a Chickasaw, Sioux or Apache woman who engaged in adultery had the tip of her nose cut off — or bitten off by an irate husband.

In the seventh grade, we were given a booklet describing menstruation. Secretly excited to think of myself in this new way — as a woman, menstruating, mating, giving birth — I loved the booklet's pale blue cover and its sketches of ovaries and fallopian tubes. What awaited me the words only hinted at, but whatever it was was clearly connected to a boy in my class, Chuck Spielman, who always came to school in a white dress shirt, the kind my father wore. Manly and terrifying, he was my first sensual love.

I dreamed of being held in Chuck's arms, smoothing my fingers over the cloth of his shirt and the ribs in his back. Sex to me was something slow and deliberate, with its own exotic tastes and smells, a secret between male and female, a *connection*. But it was a distant, if fascinating realm, and I was grateful for the distance. A friend in our class said to me, "You have bedroom eyes. If only you knew how to use them!"

I was walking with my grandmother on lower Broadway one night when a thief with a knife in his hand darted out from between two parked trucks and demanded her money. Not a believer in savings accounts, she was carrying a thick wad of hundred dollar bills in a plastic purse pinned to her girdle — and she was not about to turn it over to him. She whirled around to him with a vicious look, struck him with her cane and shrieked, "What do I look like, a bank?"

He fled.

At the Barnum and Bailey circus, my grandmother laughed and laughed. I felt sorry for the fat lady and the tallest man on earth. "You should be a nurse," she said to me. In Native American cultures, women were often traders, farmers, artisans or healers, but my culture in the 1960's dispensed vocations to the girls I knew — nurse, teacher, secretary or housewife. None of them attracted me.

My friend Carol and I, on most afternoons after school, sitting on the grass halfway between our houses, dug a hole in the ground with sticks, talked about our lives, shared our secrets. Later I learned of the Hopi tradition – when a child falls on the ground, the mother soothes the child but also goes to the place of the fall to smooth over the earth with her hands.

When I read the words attributed to Duwamish Chief Sealth, I began to understand my ties to the land and its creatures.

*How can you buy the sky?*
*How can you own the rain and the wind?*
*My mother told me,*
*Every part of this earth*
*Is sacred to our people.*
*Every pine needle.*
*Every sandy shore.*
*Every mist in the dark woods.*
*Every meadow and humming insect.*
*All are holy in the memory of our people.*

I learned of the Native American girls who were sent to boarding school where their braids were cut off and they were clothed in gingham and forbidden to speak their native language. Dressed in a blue and grey wool uniform, I was expected to emulate the Blessed Virgin Mary, but instead I painted my lips and bleached my hair and reddened my pale cheeks with rouge. The nuns despised my blue eyeshadow and my long hair, a pale carrot-orange, flopping down over one eye. It was the duty of woman to stay hidden, to be ashamed. The minute they spotted me in my white piqué graduation dress with the low, swooping back, they treated me with icy disdain. But I was only a girl doing the job of an adolescent – shopping for the woman I would become.

Peter Matthiessen tells of a Native American friend of his who hated the term "wild Indian" so prevalent in history books. "We were never wild," she said. "We were just natural."

The wild mountain lion was a deity to the Native American, although my society often considers an animal an enemy if it is not tame, just as the nuns who educated me might have agreed that the only good soul is a caged soul. The animal with the golden hide – called "soft-footed brother" – was believed by some tribes to be a near relation of Sun Father and a bestower of immortality. To the nineteenth-century white man, roping the lion was a sport – the lions were pulled out of trees with ropes to be killed below by dogs, bullets or strangulation.

But all animals have souls, many native people believe. Animal eats animal, and one creature vanishes into another. The shaman says, "Life's greatest danger lies in the fact that man's food consists entirely of souls."

What did it mean to have, as my grandmother said, the blood of the red people? I looked in the mirror. My skin was white. I blushed easily. My eyes were blue. My temperament was fiery and brooding. Yet even in suburbia, I sought out nature, spending a good deal of time perched in the tops of maple trees. My connection to the land felt primitive, attuned to the deepest human needs and the turning earth.

> The voice of my grandmother said to me
> Teach our children what
> You have been taught.
> The earth is our mother.
> What befalls the earth befalls
> All the sons and daughters of the earth.

The first time I had sexual intercourse with a man, my *no* was clear, but his *yes* prevailed. I was eighteen, he was twenty-five. We had been dating all summer and were about to return to our distant col-leges. Making love was nothing like I had imagined it would be when I first sat studying the contours of Chuck's shoulders beneath his white shirt. It was a quick and odd encounter – not magical or even pleasant, not frightening, just disappointing – in the bed-room off the living room, while my father slept upstairs. Virginity had been made into a goddess in my youth, and to have stepped be-yond that personage – to have actually jeopardized my soul – was suddenly such an *ordinary* event, I wanted to be chanted into adult-hood by my tribe. I wanted to know the oneness of two souls unit-ing, to see in his eyes his recognition of *me* – not to feel terrified of pregnancy and seized by guilt, remorse, and regret.

My culture taught me to be accommodating to men; the nuns taught me to be accommodating to God. I slept with a young teacher at Yale because he thought it was a nice Saturday ritual, like going to the football game and having a sherry party afterward in his book-lined apartment. I confessed this fornication to the Spanish priest – but the sin to me was not the sex but my absence of emo-tion during this loveless encounter. To me it felt wrong to be only a body in bed and not a whole, complex woman – body, mind and soul offering and receiving love. I wanted a man to seek not only my body but this being under my skin – my soul, that silent part of me begging to be known.

After I married, we packed up a Ryder truck and moved to the country where daisies and thistle bloomed at the sides of the roads and no one mowed them down. Everywhere there were old apple orchards, pastures, swamps full of weasels and marsh marigolds, black-and-white Holstein cows, great blue mountains that made us feel both sheltered and frail. Coyotes barked at night. I had never seen so much wildness – wild cherries and pear trees, bats circling the house at twilight, porcupines with hollow, dark quills, red squirrels in the attic. Violets sprang up under my toes. The brook bloomed with mint and yellow lilies and horseradish.

A black bird flew into the living room. A snake crawled up through a hole in the floor. The apple trees I planted were eaten by rabbits and deer. Noises outside alarmed me. I was a New Yorker, more accustomed to burglars than bears.

Before the move to the farm, I had been shadowy, tentative, a half-formed creature. Now I was far away from everything I knew. I had left my religion behind, but I had not found a new one. I had married, but I had not taken the vows of my mother and grandmothers and great-grandmothers.

In the kitchen of the farmhouse was a woolly needlepoint hanging, SIMPLY TO THEE I CLING, and a black iron Kalamazoo woodstove. Country women knew how to master such contraptions, adjusting the draughts and the flue in the stovepipe, adding green wood to keep the fire steady and cool, serving up big Sunday dinners at noon. My attempts at cooking filled the house with smoke. I imagined long-haired women in summer kitchens, canning peaches, making jam, women moving through candlelit rooms in white lisle, women digging in the earth, gathering parsnips in March, stacking apples and potatoes in the root cellar, women making love. What kind of a woman was I? What could I create?

I sewed curtains for the house, planted a garden filled with vegetables and hyssop and lemon balm. I taught myself to make bread and jam and corn fritters and dreamed of writing a novel. Thin trails of moonlight brushed through the kitchen, the sun in the mornings glittered on the bubbled glass. The mountains changed from lavender to grey to dusty blue.

I jumped naked into a stream, climbed a mountain, cleared the land to plant my own food. I picked some lilies and put them in a vase and found myself becoming a full being, a woman.

I got up in the morning and braided my hair as the sun trailed onto the windowsill. I swam under the culvert with the rainbow trout. I learned that yellow dye could be made from boiling porcupine quills and moss, or by peeling the inner bark out of the wild rose, and that I could redden my cheeks with the roots of white forget-me-nots. The peeper frogs sang in the spring, and their song was one of longing to be connected, the same song that I felt.

My great-grandmothers, Nona Walsh Quinlan and Frances Embley Colfer MacBride, vanished with their religion, their rituals, their names, into the heritage of their Irish husbands. The mountain is covered with ripe blackberries and yellow lady's-slipper and bright red Indian turnip and black cohosh and dark blue cucumber berries, and as I climb I can see myself as I am, as I long to be – the spirit that nourishes, the heart that knows. My grandmother and my great-grandmothers are with me as I walk.

I remember the story of the native woman who gave a man a Polaroid snapshot of her, together with the gift of a handmade pot. The pot and the photograph are one, she told him, as is the clay of the pot, containing the dust of her ancestors.

# Faith: A Primer

I REMEMBER YEARS AGO GOING TO SEE THE FILM *THE LAST TEMPTATION OF CHRIST,* based on Nikos Kazantzakis's book of the same name. It was opening in San Francisco, and the theater was being picketed by those who couldn't quite see Jesus as being the *incarnation* (that is, the fleshly presence) of God on this earth. In their theology, spirit didn't mingle with flesh.

I had arrived at the theater early because I had heard that we would be searched for weapons before being allowed to enter. With forty-five minutes to wait before the film started, I began chatting with the young man seated next to me. He had dark good looks, an Italian I thought. And I was right — Italian Catholic, as it turned out. He made it clear to me right away that in spite of his strong Catholic upbringing, in spite of his years serving as an altar boy, he was, in his words, "not religious" and he "didn't believe in that stuff." He was, however, interested in Jesus, he said. And then he began to unburden himself, passionately confessing the Faith he claimed to have lost, continuing in a virtual monologue until the film began.

What is it about Catholicism that takes such firm hold of its adherents — whether loyal or lapsed — and will not let us go? This phenomenon of "once a Catholic, always a Catholic" reminds me of those trick birthday candles that look like their more innocuous counterparts, but when the celebrant blows out the flame, it only *seems* to be out: it flares up again and again, ever brighter.

I myself am now a Unitarian Universalist minister, by route of Catholicism, by further route of the Southern Baptist faith. It has been quite a journey. But I have to say that, like most other people who were raised Catholic, I've never been able to get it out of my bones. I don't even want to anymore.

My mother was the Catholic in the family. Because of my early years under her tutelage, Catholicism entered my being more deeply that I could have guessed. I went to Catholic school for two years, did my First Communion, was confirmed. I sinned, confessed, had my forehead spread with Lenten ashes, and was forgiven. I smelled the incense and heard the ringing of the bell during the Mass. I saw the robes of the priest, with their gold and green, and I saw the Host as it was raised into the air. As do all Catholics, I knew my Faith not just through my mind but through my body, through my very flesh.

I also knew that as a female I was to serve – and that I was willing to do – but I was never to see myself as equal to a male. Like Mary, the Mother of God, I was to give birth, to nurture both man and child, to be there when the crosses appeared, and to mourn at the tomb.

One quiet summer day – a very ordinary day it was, as I remember – my grandfather and my uncle, who were from Louisiana, arrived at our house in Cincinnati. My mother wasn't at home. My father took a sheet and threw it in the middle of the floor, dumped our clothes inside, threw the bundle in the trunk of the Studebaker, and we headed south. I had to leave my bride doll behind – it was too big, Daddy said. And my new puppy. We drove fast over the back roads to my grandparents' home in rural North Louisiana.

Mother didn't write or call for over a year, and I had no idea why. It turned out that she had gone into a mental hospital after we were taken from her. We children were not told. We were being protected, I suppose. I was nine years old when it happened. I remember little of my childhood before that day. Just a few scattered images remain.

I continued to be the good girl that I was and to take my younger brother and sister to St. Margaret's, the little white frame church of my faith – the only one in our small Southern town. But by the time I was twelve or so, I was beginning to have serious problems with some of the tenets of the Church – like transubstantiation, for example. I had been taught that the Host and the wine become the body and blood of Jesus as they are ingested by the believer. I asked the priest, "Do you mean they actually, physically, change into the flesh and blood of Jesus?" The priest assured me that, yes, they did. I tried to imagine the wafer actually turning into human flesh as it slipped into my stomach, but try as I would, I could not. I could not believe. For a Catholic, that is a major problem.

And then there was the problem of the confessional. My sins were small potatoes – all of them venial, in the language of the Church. But there was a rule that if you failed during confession to express a known venial sin, you then were slapped with a mortal sin, which could of course send you to hell. It just so happened that some of my sins were in bad taste, I felt, and so I was reluctant to confess them to anyone, much less a priest. So I was stockpiling quite a few mortal sins this way, thus ensuring that I would spend an eternity in hell. Not only would I be going there, but my father, with his drinking and his women, would surely go there, too. My problem, again, was one of belief. It was not that I believed that I was too good to go to hell, nor certainly that my father was too good, but that God was too good to send anyone to a burning pit of fire. Especially for eternity. Eternity is a long time. And burning hurts more than anything. No, it could not be so. So really for want of metaphor, I left the Church.

When I failed to show up at Mass Sunday after Sunday, the priest called my grandparents and asked if he could come talk with me. I remember his visit well. I was thirteen. My grandparents left me alone in the living room with him. Now the living room was never used in our home – or that is to say it was used only at Christmas and Thanksgiving when my aunts and uncles came. Otherwise it stood empty. It was a forlorn and musty space. Father Goubeaux sat at one end of the sofa and I at the other. He had on his black cassock and his cross. His silver hair, unruly as it was, stood out in spikes, and his teeth shone. He leaned forward. "Marilyn Jane," he said quietly, "Marilyn Jane, if you don't come back to the Church, you are going to hell."

I took a deep breath. Hell. He said I was going to hell. Well, maybe he's right. But there's nothing to be done. "Father," I said.

"Yes, my child?"

"Do you believe that God knows everything?"

"Yes, of course, my child." He was hopeful. He saw that I was struggling toward salvation.

"Well, then God would know what is in my heart. I don't believe. So even if I went back to church, it wouldn't do me any good." Father Goubeaux sighed. He sat there for a moment staring at this hands, and then moved toward the door, shaking his head. Another soul had slipped away.

I am fifty-seven. Having never been to Mexico, I find myself in Oaxaca, on a whim, vacationing. It is January, but the days are warm. I am in my Birkenstocks and loose, flowing rayon pants and shirt. I'm wandering, something I never do at home. At home I'm always "on task," finding some work to distract me from what's inside. Fear, that's what's inside. It's not *about* anything, usually. It's just a part of me.

But here, after a week or so, something shifts in me, and I am able to be aimless, to go nowhere, to do nothing. The fear begins to quiet. I hear voices coming from a church, young voices, and I follow the sound. I go inside San Juan de Dios, where a Folk Mass is taking place. From the outside, this seventeenth-century church seems like nothing special, but once inside, I am struck by the beauty of the ornate altar and by the paintings on the ceiling. I walk by the shrine to the Virgin. The church is almost full, and all ages are represented, but I'm surprised that so many of the worshipers are young. Indian families come in, trailing three and four little ones, some without shoes, plus babies in arms. The parents genuflect and then find a place to kneel, some on the stone of the floor. Some remain kneeling. In the chancel, two teenage boys are playing guitars, and a girl is singing. I do not understand Spanish, and for the four hundredth time during my trip, I'm telling myself I should learn the language of our neighboring country.

But in spite of the fact that I do not understand the words, I understand the meaning. The devotion, the passion, pour out through her voice. She is by turns angry, sad, powerful, sweet. She begins to weep. Is she weeping for her country? For the poor, many of whom fill the church? Is she weeping for a lost love? Or maybe she is, as I am, filled to the brim with beauty and a nameless longing, and so can't help but spill over.

I begin weeping. Feelings that had been under wraps for countless years come to the surface. I'm thinking of my mother, dead for twenty years now. I'm thinking how she would like to be here, how she would like to know that I am here. She who kept herself by cleaning and cooking for priests, she who went to Mass daily, she who never understood my defection from the Church: I want her with me now. She could understand this strange power, she would be dazzled by this beauty.

All during the service, people come and go. They speak to one another, nod their heads and smile. This is their place, it is obvious. For hundreds of years it has been their refuge. The priest begins to speak, and the congregation responds, sometimes with words, sometimes with song. It is a love affair between them. The priest delivers the homily with amazing passion, driving home his meaning with a hand slicing the air. I do not know the words, but I know he speaks of justice. I am not a visitor, I am a part of this, for my heart is here with these people, and my spirit is open to the movement of the Spirit. "Alleluia, Alleluia!" they sing, and I know why they sing. They sing because in the midst of terrible loss, of numbing pain, of fear, and of righteous anger – in the midst of all of this, they are called to life, they are called to live more abundantly.

The Church – with all its failings, with its human error, with its mistaking its voice for God's – with all this, yet the Church, the first and some say the only Church, suggests by its continued existence on this earth that justice is not just a foolish dream, that love is as real as the air we breathe, and ultimately, that death is not sovereign. The words keep coming back: "I will fear no evil. . . ."

And hell? I know what hell is now. It's letting fear separate me from the love of God, and from the love of others. Hell is simply that – separation, a rejection of the common humanity we share. It's being unable to believe that we're accountable to anything outside ourselves. I have come to believe that I am somehow held in the Everlasting Arms, no matter what – in spite of fear, which I still keep close at hand. Did I say I believe? Well, yes, I do. I have glimpses of the part that reveals the whole, if even just for a moment. Like in the cathedral that evening. I believe. How the circle does come round.

# Hell: A Memoir

I

SISTER GERTRUDE'S SHOE PEEKED OUT FROM UNDER HER LONG BLACK HABIT AND tapped the waxed tiles on the floor in the first grade room. Staring at that shiny shoe from my desk in the front row, I saw never-ending darkness. Sister moved to the blackboard and wrote in large block letters.

E-T-E-R-N-I-T-Y

All sixty of us stared at the word, hands folded on top of our desks. She chalked an impatient period and whirled around, pointing at Alan Baker.

"Alan, what does this word mean?"

Alan was on his feet immediately. He sounded it out: "E-TER-NI-TY. Umh, I'm sorry, Sister, I don't know."

"Well, can anyone else help us out here? Anyone? Anyone?"

Kathy Cole raised her hand. She was my best friend and I was in love with her. She had long honey-brown curls and was dressed in a white blouse with puffed sleeves, a lilac pleated skirt, and matching lilac anklets. Not one thing out of the Montgomery Ward's catalogue. Everything she wore came from Buttrey's store downtown. Her dad had a steady job with the Great Northern Railroad as a switchman.

"Yes, Kathy?"

Kathy stood, took a deep breath and in a clear voice said, "It means forever, Sister, forever, without end."

Sister parceled out a smile, then picked up her long rubber-tipped pointer.

"Eternity . . . forever, with no end." Her eyes narrowed. Her German accent grew thicker.

"But what does this really mean?" She tapped the board, popping the letters into air which suddenly seemed to have turned much warmer.

"Children, is Eternity longer than ten years?"

"Yes, Sister," we answered in unison.

"Longer than twenty-five years?"

"Yes, Sister."

"Longer than fifty years?"

"Yes, Sister."

"Longer than any of you have been alive?"

I didn't like the sound of this.

I looked around. Wasn't this going too far? But most of the other children were still following Kathy's confident nodding head and sure voice. "Yes, sister."

"One hundred years?"

"Yes, Sister." By this time, only half of us answered. Sister stopped, her blue eyes bright little points behind her eyeglasses. I felt the same way I had during my first ride on the Octopus at the country fair, a little dizzy during the ascent; sudden panic at our first plunge toward the ground.

Sister pressed on. "In a hundred years every single person in this room will be DEAD and in heaven or in hell."

The Octopus ride had unhooked from its base and blown off into utter darkness. Acid pushed up from my stomach to my throat. Gasping for air, I swallowed and trembled. When I opened my eyes, I was staring at Tommy Matter, who was sitting across from me. His blonde flattop seemed to glow a little. Next to me on the other side, big Tina English's blue skirt brushed above her thick ankles and her tiny feet began to tap real fast on the floor. I wondered if my own feet were still there. I couldn't feel them but when I looked down, there they were sitting side by side on the floor as though nothing had happened. I began to tap them fast, along with Tina. It helped. I began to calm down.

But Sister never missed a beat. "Yes, every single one of you will be gone — some to hell.

"And what's hell?" No one even tried to answer. I was spinning outward once again.

"It's eternal fire, eternal pain."

"Forever. Without end."

"Once you're there, even your parents can't get you out."

I lurched into a free fall, fighting a sudden desparate urge to pull my Casper the Friendly Ghost comic out and read it.

It was too risky. So, I sat, my mind tangled in Kathy's long hair, pretending each curl was a winding slide on the playground that I climbed up and went down over and over again.


II

From that day in first grade until I was fifteen, I was plagued by the idea of an eternal hell. A fire that tortured yet never transformed anyone into the relief of cold ashes . . . no release, just eternal flames and pain. I was growing up in an alcoholic family, so by the age of six, I already didn't expect much help from anyone. But I was stunned by the idea that EVEN my parents would not be able to get me out of hell if I ever got put there.

Over the years, I became very careful not to do anything that could put me into hell. This involved learning and obeying lots of rules ranging from not eating meat on Friday to not murdering anyone. There were elaborate rituals and concepts: seven sacraments, original, mortal and venial sin, holy days of obligation, Lenten sacrifices, Easter Duty, novenas, rosaries, Ash Wednesday,

Good Friday, the blessing of the throats and the entire Baltimore Catechism to memorize and recite back to Father Penna before First Holy Communion.

Really, though, it was much deeper than all that I am saying here. That day in Sister Gertrude's room, something in me began shaking. It was like living through an earthquake that knocks down your whole neighborhood but doesn't kill anyone. I never slept as soundly, played as wildly, or breathed as freely after that. There seemed to be no way to ease the constant shivery fear that started with that word on the chalkboard: ETERNITY.

III

I'm fifteen years old, sitting at the green wooden kitchen table with my dad, Frank. It's late morning. He doesn't have to be to his store clerk job until noon. Mom has already put on her white uniform and nylons and gone off to Greenacres, the rest home where she's a nurse's aide.

Dad and I are on our second cup of coffee. He puts in three heaping teaspoons of sugar and no milk. I use milk and no sugar. He's been in Alcoholics Anonymous for a while now and hasn't really drunk hard in about four years. I'm smoking my third Winston. He and Mom have decided it's better for me to smoke with him at home than to keep on sneaking around. I exhale and my question dances out into the blue smoke hanging over our heads. . . .

"Dad, do you believe in hell?"

"No, I don't, honey." The trembling slows for a moment.

"You don't?"

I almost wish he wouldn't say more, but he goes on, his voice slow and low. "Well, the way I figure is, I'm just a regular man . . . and I wouldn't want to make my worst enemy suffer like that for even one hour . . . much less for forever.

"And I think that God is probably better than me."

I peer closely at him through the smoky air. He exhales, taps the ash off his cigarette, and smiles at me.

Something deep in me shifts to a more steady place.

Stirring the sugar up from the bottom of his cup, his spoon makes a comforting scraping sound. I find a part of my lungs that I haven't breathed into for years and fill it with the tobacco-coffee-flavored air. The long out-of-control ride is slowing down. I'm coming in for a landing. Everything seems sharper, more solid: the hot strong coffee, the embers on the tips of our cigarettes, the worn wooden table, myself . . . and my dad.

# *from* Virgin Time

LEXINGTON, OXFORD, CHATSWORTH, CONTINUING DOWN GRAND AVENUE TO MILTON and Avon, as far as St. Albans — the streets of our neighborhood had an English, even an Anglican, ring to them. But we were Catholic. The parishes of the diocese, unmarked and ghostly as they were, posted borders more decisive than the street signs we passed on our way to St. Luke's grade school or, later, walking in the other direction to the girls-only convent high school.

We were like people with dual citizenship. I *lived* on Linwood Avenue, but I *belonged* to St. Luke's. That was the lingo. Mothers spoke of daughters who were going to the junior-senior prom with boys "from Nativity" or "from St. Mark's" as if from fiefdoms across the sea.

"Where you from?" a boy livid with acne asked when we startled each other lurking behind a pillar in the St. Thomas Academy gym at a Friday-night freshman mixer.

"Ladies' choice!" one of the mothers cried from a dim corner where a portable hi-fi was set up. She rasped the needle over the vinyl, and Fats Domino came on, insinuating a heavier pleasure than I yet knew: *I found my thrill* . . .

"I'm from Holy Spirit," the boy said, as if he'd been beamed in to stand by the tepid Cokes and tuna sandwiches and the bowls of sweating potato chips on the refreshments table. Parish members did not blush to describe themselves as being "from Immaculate

Conception." Somewhere north, near the city line, there was even a parish frankly named Maternity of Mary. But then, in those years, the 1950s and early 1960s, breeding was a low-grade fever pulsing among us unmentioned, like a buzz or hum you get used to and cease to hear. The white noise of matrimonial sex.

On Sundays the gray stone nave of St. Luke's Church, big as a warehouse, was packed with families of eight or ten sitting in the honey-colored pews. The fathers wore brown suits. In memory they appear spectrally thin, wraithlike and spent, like trees hollowed of their pulp. The wives were petite and cheerful, with helmet-like haircuts. Perkiness was their main trait. But what did they say, these small women, how did they talk? Mrs. Healy, mother of four-teen ("They can afford them," my mother said, as if to excuse her paltry two, "he's a doctor"), never uttered a word, as far as I re-member. Even pregnant, she was somehow wiry, as if poised for a tennis match. Maybe these women only wore a *look* of perkiness, and like their lean husbands, they were sapped of personal strength. Maybe they were simply tense.

Not everyone around us was Catholic. Mr. Kirby, a widower who was our next-door neighbor, was Methodist — whatever that was. The Nugents across the street, behind their cement retaining wall and double row of giant salvia, were Lutheran, more or less. The Williams family, who subscribed to *The New Yorker* and had a living room outfitted with spare Danish furniture, were Episcopalian. They referred to their minister as a priest — a plagiarism that em-barrassed me for them, because I liked them and their light, airy ways.

As for the Bertrams, our nearest neighbors to the west, it could only be said that Mrs. Bertram, dressed in a narrow suit with a pep-lum jacket and a hat made of the same heathery wool, went *some-where* via taxi on Sunday mornings. Mr. Bertram went nowhere

– on Sunday or on any other day. He was understood, during my entire girlhood, to be indoors, resting.

Weekdays, Mrs. Bertram took the bus to her job downtown. Mr. Bertram stayed home behind their birchwood Venetian blinds in an aquarium half-light, not an invalid (we never thought of him that way), but a man whose occupation it was to rest. Sometimes in the summer he ventured forth with a large wrenchlike gadget to root out the masses of dandelions that gave the Bertrams' lawn a temporary brilliance in June. I associated him with the Wizard of Oz. He was small and mild-looking, going bald. He gave the impression of extreme pallor except for small, very dark eyes.

It was a solid neighborhood rumor that Mr. Bertram had been a screenwriter in Hollywood. Yes, that pallor was a writer's pallor; those small dark eyes were writer eyes. They saw, they noted.

He allowed me to assist him in rooting out his dandelions. I wanted to ask him about Hollywood – had he met Audrey Hepburn? I couldn't bring myself to maneuver for information on such an elevated subject. But I did feel something serious was called for here. I introduced religion while he plunged the dandelion gadget deep into the lawn.

No, he said, he did not go to church. "But you do believe in God?" I asked, hardly daring to hope he did not. He paused for a moment and looked up at the sky, where big, spreading clouds streamed by. "God isn't the problem," he said.

Some ancient fissure split open, a fine crack in reality: so there *was* a problem. Just as I'd always felt. Beneath the family solidity, the claustrophobia of mother-father-brother-me, past the emphatic certainties of St. Luke's catechism class, there was a problem that would never go away. Mr. Bertram stood amid his dandelions, a resigned Buddha, looking up at the sky, which gave back nothing but drifting white shapes on the blue.

What alarmed me was my feeling of recognition. Of course there was a problem. It wasn't God. Life itself was a problem. Something was not right, would never be right. I'd sensed it all along, a kind of fishy, vestigial quiver in the spine, way past thought. Life, deep down, lacked the substantiality it *seemed* to display. The physical world, full of detail and interest, was a parched topsoil that could be blown away.

This lack, this blankness akin to chronic disappointment, was everywhere, under the perkiness, lurking even within my own happiness. "What are you going to do today?" my father said when he saw me digging in the back yard on his way to work at the greenhouse.

"I'm digging to China," I said.

"Well, I'll see you at lunch," he said, "if you're still here."

I wouldn't bite. I frowned and went back to work with the bent tablespoon my mother had given me. It wasn't a game. I wanted out. I was on a desperate journey that only looked like play.

The blank disappointment, masked as weariness, played on the faces of people on the St. Clair bus. They looked out the windows, coming home from downtown, unseeing: clearly nothing interested them. What were they thinking of? The passing scene was not beautiful enough – was that it? – to catch their eye. Like the empty clouds Mr. Bertram turned to, their blank looks gave back nothing. There was an unshivered shiver in each of us, a shudder we managed to hold back.

We got off the bus at Oxford Street, where, one spring, in the lime-green house behind the catalpa tree on the corner, Mr. Lenart (whom we didn't know well) had slung a pair of tire chains over a rafter in the basement and hanged himself. Such things happened. Only the tight clutch of family life ("The family that prays together stays together") could keep things rolling along. Step out of the tight, bright circle, and you might find yourself dragging your chains down to the basement.

The perverse insubstantiality of the material world was the problem: reality refused to be real enough. Nothing could keep you steadfastly happy. That was clear. Some people blamed God. But I sensed that Mr. Bertram was right, *God isn't the problem*. The clouds passing in the big sky kept dissipating, changing form. That was the problem – but so what? Such worries resolved nothing, and were best left unworried – the unshivered shiver.

There was no one to blame. You could only retire, like Mr. Bertram, stay indoors behind your birchwood blinds and contemplate the impossibility of things, allowing the Hollywood glitter of reality to fade away and become a vague local rumor.

There were other ways of coping. Mrs. Krueger, several houses down with a big garden rolling with hydrangea bushes, held as her faith a passionate belief in knowledge. She sold World Book Encyclopedias. After trying Christian Science and a stint with the Unitarians, she had settled down as an agnostic. There seemed to be a lot of reading involved with being an agnostic, pamphlets and books, long citations on cultural anthropology in the World Book. It was an abstruse religion, and Mrs. Krueger seemed to belong to some ladies' auxiliary of disbelief.

But it didn't really matter what Mrs. Krueger decided about "the deity idea," as she called God. No matter what they believed, our neighbors lived not just on Linwood Avenue; they were in St. Luke's parish, too, whether they knew it or not. We claimed the territory. And we claimed them – even as we dismissed them. They were all non-Catholics, the term that disposed nicely of spiritual otherness.

Let the Protestants go down their schismatic paths; the Lutherans could splice themselves into synods any which way. Believers, non-believers, even Jews (the Kroners on the corner), or a breed as rare as the Greek Orthodox, whose church was across the street from St. Luke's – they were all non-Catholics, just so much extraneous spiritual matter orbiting the nethersphere.

Or maybe it was more intimate than that, and we dismissed the rest of the world as we would our own serfs. We saw the Lutherans and Presbyterians, even those snobbish Episcopalians, as rude co-lonials, non-Catholics all, doing the best they could out there in the bush to imitate the ways of the homeland. *We* were the homeland.

The hierarchy we lived in, a great linked chain of religious being, seemed set to control every entrance and exit to and from the mind and heart. The sky-blue Baltimore Catechism, small and square, read like an owner's manual for a very complicated vehicle. There was something pleasant, lulling and rhythmic, like heavily rhymed poetry, about the singsong Q-and-A format. Who would not give over heart, if not mind, to the brisk assurance of the Baltimore prose:

*Who made you?*
*God made me.*
*Why did God make you?*
*God made me to know, love and serve Him in this world, in order to be happy with Him forever in the next.*

And how harmless our Jesuitical discussions about what, exactly, constituted a meatless spaghetti sauce on Friday. Strict construc-tionists said no meat of any kind should ever, at any time, have made its way into the tomato sauce; easy liberals held with the no-tion that meatballs could be lurking around in the sauce, as long as you didn't eat them. My brother lobbied valiantly for the meatball, present but *intactus*. My mother said nothing doing. They raged for years.

Father Flannery, who owned his own airplane and drove a sports car, had given Peter some ammunition when he'd been asked to rule on the meatball question in the confessional. My mother would hear none of it. "I don't want to know what goes on between you and your confessor," she said, taking the high road.

"A priest, Ma, a *priest*," my brother cried "This is an ordained priest saying right there in the sanctity of the confessional that meatballs are okay."

But we were going to heaven my mother's way.

Life was like that. Full of hair-splitting and odd rituals. We got our throats blessed on St. Blaise's day in February, the priest holding oversized beeswax candles in an X around our necks, to ward off death by choking on fishbones, a problem nobody thought of the rest of the year. There were smudged foreheads on Ash Wednesday, and home May altars with plaster statuettes of the Virgin festooned with lilacs. Advent wreaths and nightly family Rosary vigils during October (Rosary Month), all of us on our knees in the living room in front of the blank Magnavox.

The atmosphere swirled with the beatific visions and heroic martyrdoms of the long dead and the apocryphal. In grade school we were taken to daily Mass during Lent, and we read the bio notes of the saints that preceded the readings in the Daily Missal, learning that St. Agatha had had her breasts cut off by the Romans. We thrilled at the word *breast*, pointing to it and giggling, as if it were a neon lingerie ad flashing from the prayerbook.

Most of the women saints in the Missal had under their names the designation *Virgin and Martyr*, as if the two categories were somehow a matched set. Occasionally a great female figure canonized for her piety and charitable works received the label *Queen and Widow*. The men were usually *Confessor* or, sometimes, *Martyr*, but none of them was ever *Virgin*.

The lives of the saints were not only edifying stories but cautionary tales. Chief here was St. Maria Goretti, early-twentieth-century *Virgin and Martyr*, who had been stabbed to death by a sex-crazed farmworker. She preserved her honor to the end. Her murderer, "alive to this day," we were told, had gone to her canonization in St. Peter's Square on his knees.

More troubling still was the story of Thomas à Kempis, the great author of *The Imitation of Christ*, one of the treasures of medieval scholasticism. Why, asked someone in Sister Hilaria's fifth-grade class, was Thomas à Kempis not *St. Thomas?*

Ah, Sister Hilaria said, pausing, looking at us to see if we were ready for this truth. We were ready.

Naturally, Sister said, there had been a canonization effort. All the usual procedures had been followed. Thomas was coming down the homestretch of the investigation when "very disturbing evidence was discovered." She paused again.

"The body of Thomas à Kempis was exhumed, children, as all such persons must be," Sister said reasonably. We nodded, we followed the macabre corporate ladder of sainthood without dismay. "When they opened that casket, boys and girls, Thomas à Kempis was lost." For upon opening the moldy box, there he was, the would-be saint, a ghastly look of horror on his wormy face, his hand clawing upward toward the air, madly. "You see, children, he did not die in the peace of the Lord." They shut him up and put him back. "A good man still," Sister said, "and a good writer." But not, we understood, a saint.

There were, as well, snatches of stories about nuns who beat kids with rulers in the coatroom; the priest who had a twenty-year affair with a member of the Altar and Rosary Society; the other priest in love with an altar boy — they'd had to send him away. Not St. Luke's stories — oh no, certainly not — but stories, floating, as stories do, from inner ear to inner ear, respecting no parish boundaries. Part of the ether.

And with it all, a relentless xenophobia about other religions. "It's going to be a mixed marriage, I understand," one of my aunts murmured about a friend's daughter who was marrying an Episcopalian. So what if he called himself High Church? He was a non-Catholic.

And now, educated out of it all, well climbed into the professions, the Catholics find each other at cocktail parties and get going. The nun stories, the first confession traumas — and a tone of rage and dismay that seems to bewilder even the tellers of these tales.

Nobody says, when asked, "I'm Catholic." It's always, "Yes, I was brought up Catholic." Anything to put it at a distance, to diminish the presence of that heritage which is not racial but acts as if it were. "You never get over it, you know," a fortyish lawyer told me a while ago at a party where we found ourselves huddled by the chips and dip, as if at a St. Thomas mixer once again.

He seemed to feel he was speaking to someone with the same hopeless congenital condition. "It's different now, of course," he said. "But when we were growing up back there . . ." There it was again: the past isn't a time. It's a place. A permanent destination: *back there.*

"I'm divorced," he said. We both smiled: there's no going to hell anymore. "Do they still have mortal sin?" he asked wistfully.

The love-hate lurch of a Catholic upbringing, like having an extra set of parents to contend with. Or an added national allegiance — not to the Vatican, as we were warned that the Baptists thought during John Kennedy's campaign for President. To a different realm. It was the implacable loyalty of faith, that flawless relation between self and existence into which we were born. A strange country where people prayed and believed impossible things.

The nuns who taught us, rigged up in their bold black habits with the big round wimples stiff as Frisbees, walked along our parish streets, moving from convent to church in twos or threes, dipping in the side door of the huge church "for a little adoration," as they would say. The roly-poly Irish-born monsignor told us to stand straight and proud when he met us slouching toward class along Summit. Fashionable Father Flannery took a companionable walk with the old pastor every night. The two of them took out white handkerchiefs and waved them for safety as they crossed the busy avenue on the way home in the dark, swallowed in their black suits and cassocks, lost in the growing gloom.

But the one I would like most to summon up and to have pass me on Oxford as I head off to St. Luke's in the early-morning mist, one of those mid-May weekdays, the lilacs just starting to spill, the one I want most to materialize from "back there" — I don't know her name, where, exactly, she lived, or who she was. We never spoke. We just passed each other, she coming home from six o'clock daily Mass, I going early to school to practice the piano for an hour before class began.

She was a "parish lady," part of the anonymous population that thickened our world, people who were always there, who were solidly part of us, part of what we were, but who never emerged beyond the bounds of being parishioners to become full-fledged persons.

We met every morning, just past the Healys' low brick wall. She wore a librarian's cardigan sweater. She must have been about forty-five, and I sensed she was not married. Unlike Dr. and Mrs. Harrigan, who walked smartly along Summit holding hands, their bright Irish setter accompanying them as far as the church door, where he waited till Mass was over, his tail thumping like a metronome on the pavement, the lady in the dust-colored cardigan was always alone.

I saw her coming all the way from Grand, where she had to pause for the traffic. She never rushed across the street, zipping past a truck, but waited until the coast was completely clear, and passed across keeping her floating pace. A peaceful gait, no rush to it. When finally we were close enough to make eye contact, she looked up, straight into my face, and smiled. It was such a *complete* smile, so entire, it startled me every time, as if I'd heard my name called out on the street of a foreign city.

She was a homely woman, plain and pale, unnoticeable. Her face seemed made of the same vague stuff as her sweater. But I felt — how to put it — she shed light. The mornings were often frail with mist, the light uncertain and tender. The smile was a brief flood of light. She loved me, I was sure.

I knew what it was about. She was praying. Her hand, stuck in her cardigan pocket, held one of the crystal beads of her rosary. I knew this. I'd once seen her take it out of the left pocket and quickly replace it after she had found the handkerchief she needed.

If I had seen a nun mumbling the Rosary along Summit (and this happened), it would not have meant much to me. But here on Oxford, the side street we used as a sleepy corridor to St. Luke's, it was a different thing. The parish lady was not a nun. She was a person who prayed, who prayed alone, for no reason that I understood. But there was no question that she prayed without ceasing, as the strange scriptural line instructed.

She didn't look up to the blank clouds for a response, as Mr. Bertram did in his stoic way. Her head was bowed, quite unconsciously. When she raised it, keeping her hand in her pocket where the clear beads were, she looked straight into the eyes of the person passing by. It was not an invasive look, but it latched. She had me. Not an intrusive gaze, but one brimming with a secret which, if only she had the words, it was clear she'd want to tell.

# ACKNOWLEDGMENTS

I wish to acknowledge the support and encouragement for the creation of this book that I received from my editor at Beacon Press, Tisha Hooks. Tisha's enthusiasm was there from the time of our first conversation about the book and continued on through the process. Tisha suggested several of the writers from whom I collected essays, and she also made valuable suggestions about the organization of the pieces I chose.

Joanne Mulcahy, with her fine sensibility for both religion and literature, not only contributed an exceptional essay to this collection, but she also suggested to me several other writers whose work greatly enhanced the book. In addition, Joanne served as a reader for me, helping to guide my thinking as I went through the selection process. Two other friends, Dianne Stepp and Katie Raditz, also served as readers, lending their insights and suggestions.

Jan Larson, my secretary, made multiple copies of manuscripts for me throughout the process of creating this book, and in general supported me with her patience and ready aid with detail work.

I owe a great debt to Roberta Richards, my research assistant, who found high-quality writing for me to consider in creating this book. Roberta had a sure eye for excellence and was unfailingly dependable in her work with me. She also patiently went through the often frustrating task of finding out who owned the copyright for the published pieces and then secured the permissions for me. Because of my demanding life as a parish minister, this anthology would not have been possible without Roberta's help.

# CREDITS